Praise for *The Endowment Handbook*

"My working relationship with Laura spans two decades of witnessing the wisdom and counsel she has shared with thousands of nonprofit organizations across the United States and the world. This book is a challenge to seize this moment of the greatest wealth transfer in history. It is a compelling and pragmatic guidebook for the nonprofit professional, board member, and donor alike."

—**Steven S. Moore**, Chief of Staff,
The Columbus Foundation

"I have turned to Laura MacDonald on many occasions to make the complex simple in this essential world of charitable giving. In *The Endowment Handbook*, readers will see what all of us in the sector have come to expect: thoughtful consideration, practical application, and commitment to lasting impact for nonprofits. She has made endowments – thought to be reserved for elite institutions – accessible to all nonprofits looking to achieve long-term sustainability and impact in our communities."

—**Josh Birkholz**, CEO of BWF.
Author of *Fundraising Analytics and Benefactors*

"*The Endowment Handbook* is not just a book; it's a manifesto for building a community of passionate advocates who, together, can transform visions of positive change into permanent, tangible realities. It will take you on a journey through the essential elements of donor engagement and help you discover how to nurture relationships that withstand the test of time. It's a rewarding journey. Take it!"

—**Russell N. James III**, J.D., Ph.D., CFP®,
Professor & CH Foundation Chair in
Personal Financial Planning

"*The Endowment Handbook* is chock full of practical and useful information to help charities of all sizes and complexities to better serve their constituencies, grow their institutions, and secure their economic future. This comprehensive guide is state-of-the-art, insightful, and easy to read with many real-life examples and success stories. *The Endowment Handbook* is an excellent training guide and reference manual. It should be required reading for all nonprofit leaders – both board and staff members."

—**Diana S. Newman**, Author and retired
consultant to nonprofit organizations

"Laura MacDonald is one of the most insightful thinkers on philanthropy in the nonprofit world today. Our members have benefitted tremendously from her deep knowledge of fundraising trends and the philanthropic environment. But perhaps even more important is the way that she advocates for financial resilience and enduring relationships as fundamentals for organizations to deliver on their commitment to their communities. This book will be a vital guide for all of us in the years ahead."

—**Simon Woods**, President and CEO,
League of American Orchestras

"As CEO of National 4-H Council, I have witnessed firsthand the transformative power of strategic financial management in advancing our mission. Laura MacDonald's *The Endowment Handbook* is a timely and indispensable resource for nonprofit leaders navigating the complexities of financial resilience, particularly through endowment management. A standout feature of the book is MacDonald's nuanced exploration of strategic reserves, crucial for complementing traditional endowments, especially in times of crisis. *The Endowment Handbook* is a must-read for anyone committed to enhancing the financial resilience and impact of nonprofit organizations."

—**Jill Bramble**, CEO, National 4-H Council

"Laura MacDonald provides this generation of philanthropy professionals a comprehensive look at how endowments can create lasting impact while also motivating donors and potential donors to give at the highest levels possible. Her insights will help organizations establish thoughtful donor-centric methods for communicating the benefit and opportunity inherent in endowed funds. Critically, Laura addresses the newest endowment tools available for crafting donor impact. As a tool for good, this book creates momentum for organization executives, boards, and philanthropy leadership teams to address the opportunities endowments provide."

—**Ben Golding**, CEO, Advancement Resources

THE
Endowment
HANDBOOK

THE
Endowment
HANDBOOK

The Complete Guide to
Building a Resilient Cause

LAURA MacDONALD

WILEY

For general information on our other products and services or for technical support, please contact our Customer Care Department within the United States at (800) 762-2974, outside the United States at (317) 572-3993 or fax (317) 572-4002.

Wiley also publishes its books in a variety of electronic formats. Some content that appears in print may not be available in electronic formats. For more information about Wiley products, visit our web site at www.wiley.com.

Library of Congress Cataloging-in-Publication Data is Available:

ISBN 9781394252237 (Cloth)
ISBN 9781394252244 (ePub)
ISBN 9781394252251 (ePDF)

Cover Design: Wiley
Cover Image: © kursi_design/Adobe Stock

SKY10080500_072524

Dedicated to all those who inspire generosity through their devotion to the common good.

Contents

Foreword

In *The Endowment Handbook,* Laura MacDonald has revived muted conversations about endowments. Building on previous efforts, she moves the subject of endowments into this time and space, making it relevant for today. She argues that setting up an endowment is not just a random event. It must be intentional and backed by big considerations.

The book does three things at once: it provides a refreshed, quick, and brief history of endowments; it helps to define endowments; and it "workshops" those who are envisioning endowments. Laura's style of intentionally blending information and teaching makes the book a rich resource, and many will find the hidden treasure that they are seeking.

This is an excellent overview of the concept of endowment. It provides a succinct explanation of the different types of endowments and carefully draws the distinction between them from an organizational and donor perspective. Laura helpfully debunks several commonly held myths that hinder actions or create false excitement about endowments. She takes in the wider landscape and presents a condensed history of endowments and the potential pitfalls of establishing and maintaining one. She categorically states that this particular investment structure is not for everyone and, at the same time, argues for the important role that an endowment plays in the distribution of resources in communities, and invites us to do more to ensure the equitable distribution of funds through our nonprofit investment strategies.

Many institutions' archives preserve minutes where boards discussed setting up endowment, yet the idea was never implemented. I was privy to such historical manifestation at the very time that Laura asked me to review and provide feedback to the manuscript of her book. From my own position as board chair of an organization in conversations about endowment, I was curious and hungry for knowledge. From Laura's perspective, she relied on my extensive international experience to make judgements about the relevance of the book outside the United States and whether the language level of the book would be accessible to people for whom English is just one of their many languages.

My answer is "yes" to both questions. This is a difficult book to write and yet well written, with illustrating stories and statistics. It shows sound scholarship yet not mired in jargon. Clare Flynn, Director of Advancement at the United World Colleges, a federation of 18 schools in 18 countries, had this to say about the book:

"This book is an excellent practical resource, for those in governance, leadership, and operational roles, who find themselves considering an endowment for future sustainability. Laura offers the notion that 'big gifts stem from big ideas' for the many of us in the nonprofit sector involved in raising funds for the organizations and causes close to our hearts. Laura's book offers sound, practical advice and guidance for fundraisers and nonprofit marketers making the case for and demonstrating the impact of endowment support. She invites nonprofit leaders, staff, and supporters to come together to diligently craft their own compelling case for endowment as an opportunity to distill a shared vision for the future."

Laura and I have had more than 20 years of professional relationship that has addressed the needs of international organizations with a global reach. Indeed, a book like this has many audiences and can provide guidance anywhere in the world. There are those for whom this book describes their reality and others who want to learn from what has worked elsewhere. People will use this book in seminars and as a reference during research. For many like me, the book will be a resource to empower volunteer leadership on boards.

The book draws its knowledge and examples mainly from the United States, a country renowned for advanced philanthropy and where endowment – especially in institutions of learning like universities – is a praxis rather than a discussion. Many US endowments benefit the whole world. Rarely do people associate the grants they receive from foundations such as Ford, Rockefeller, Packard, Carnegie, and others as emanating from endowments. Indeed, millions of dollars from foundations to communities all over the world are evidence of the potential return on endowed investments.

One of the debunked myths is the popular but false belief that endowments are the end of fundraising. Schools such as Harvard or Stanford have endowments from which they serve needs while they continue to raise more funds. Because they have endowments, they are in a better position than those without when it comes to managing various financial risks.

Laura MacDonald's book is a great companion for volunteer leaders who serve on countless nonprofit organizations, schools, universities, city councils, libraries, museums, and so on. Volunteers at the helm of board leadership are entrusted with important decisions, but not always equipped with information and knowledge. In fact, leadership exposes management and boards to unimaginable complexities. Contrasts between scarcity and plenty, poverty and wealth, continue to create shameful gaps between those who have and the ones without. In the context in which I operate today, I am particularly convinced that endowment to support scholarships for students from vulnerable situations is a big idea inviting big endowment investments. Education is the leading proven equalizer to combat the inequalities in our societies.

With a wealth of examples and stories from real situations where endowments have worked and not worked, this book offers convincing proof that endowments are of immense value to organizations and institutions. It is a powerful book, with great stories and a message that is current and important. The ideas in this book can help boards and management address their fears and answer the genuine questions that must be dealt with before, during, and when an endowment is the option of choice. With such a dearth of new books on endowments, I believe that this book has the potential to ignite interest in new research and books on endowments. In sum, this book is both a call to action and a manual on how to do it.

—Musimbi Kanyoro
Nairobi, Kenya
April 1, 2024

Preface

In my work with nonprofit organizations across the country – and occasionally around the world – I encounter a wide range of attitudes. Some board members build up treasure as they worry about an organization's future despite an enviable balance sheet. Across town, a scrappy executive director may be prepared to throw every dollar they have to solve a wicked problem today without regard to next month's payroll. Some prominent institutions consist of a small group of community stakeholders while other powerful movements build a global corps of supporters and partners. Between these extremes are almost two million 501(c)(3) organizations in the United States alone – and thousands more non-governmental organizations (NGOs) around the world – all striving to do good work today and ensure their impact for the long haul. The most resilient are built upon a solid foundation of loyal donors and dependable funding – from endowments or their functional equivalents – that enable them to pursue their mission with confidence.

This is a particularly opportune moment to focus on endowments and the people who create them. In May 2023, a headline in *The New York Times* declared that "The Greatest Wealth Transfer in History is Here" (Smith, 2023). The article estimates that older Americans will pass down $84 trillion by 2045. While the majority will go to heirs, as much as $12 trillion may be bestowed upon nonprofit organizations according to the financial research firm Cerulli Associates. Imagine an additional $12 trillion fueling the causes that save lives, conserve the environment, and elevate the human experience. If that amount were endowed, it would create perpetual revenue equal to the *total* amount given to nonprofit organizations in the year 2020. But the funds will not magically appear. The organizations that receive a share of this bounty will be the ones that do the hard work to create systems and nurture relationships. Those that simply wait and hope are unlikely to benefit.

The Purpose of This Book

This book is intended to help nonprofit organizations create and nurture the systems and build the relationships that will fuel their cause and elevate their mission. It is focused on two key resources: money and people. While there are other important keys to resilience, such as brand, reputation, revenue diversity, disciplined budgeting and planning, relevance and impact, as well as an engaged board, even these factors are rooted in people, money, or both.

Who should care about the health and resilience of the nonprofit sector? Everyone. Whether someone gives to, works in, or is served by the nonprofit sector, the impact of charities is abundant. Nonprofit organizations employ approximately 12% of America's workforce and represent 5% of the total economy. The annual report *Philanthropy and the Global Economy*[1] produced by the research team at Citi estimates the global value of philanthropy at $2.3 trillion per year, or just under 3% of global GDP.

Many everyday citizens are unaware of all the ways their lives are impacted by nonprofit organizations. They are not aware that philanthropy supports the places where they learn, worship, and heal; the well-being of the environment that surrounds them; the experiences that bring them delight and wonder. A thriving nonprofit sector is essential to both our economy and our common good and can be achieved through the prudent management of these two critical ingredients: money and people.

More specifically, *The Endowment Handbook* is directed toward the current and future nonprofit leaders and development professionals who are responsible for nurturing relationships with donors, securing gifts, and managing endowed and reserve funds, especially those in mid-size and smaller nonprofits. Endowments are disproportionally held by larger, older, predominantly white institutions that have ample knowledge of how to build and manage endowments (although they, too, will find helpful guidance here). With this book, nonprofit organizations of any size and in every sector can develop the ability to begin an endowment and increase it over time by cultivating mutually rewarding relationships with their donors.

Overview of the Content

This is meant to be a practical guide, offering nonprofit professionals, board members, and donors with specific steps that can be taken to strengthen the organizations that serve the common good, organized in two parts.

Part 1

This is a discussion of financial resilience, most notably endowment: how it is defined, built up, and deployed in service to a cause as well as some of the criticisms and pitfalls to avoid. The first five chapters owe much of their content and inspiration to Diana S. Newman's book *Endowment Building*, which was published in 2005 by John Wiley & Sons as a part of the *Nonprofit Essentials* series. Here, the book is updated to reflect changes in the economy, donor behavior, and the regulatory environment. Diana is a friend and mentor who spent the final decade of her career as executive vice president of Benefactor Group, the firm I established in 2000. It was an honor to work with Diana, and an even greater tribute when she assigned her rights in the original publication to the firm.

Part 1 also discusses other means of financial resilience, such as strategic reserves, which may complement an endowment in strengthening an organization's resilience. Reserves have grown in importance and popularity as organizations – and especially their donors – confronted the constraints of endowed funds during the financial pressures of the COVID-19 pandemic. Much more than a "rainy day fund," modern approaches to financial reserves balance fiscal stability against the flexibility to invest in social ventures and other innovations. Reserves can provide the required startup capital when an idea shows promise to advance the mission and strengthen the bottom line, and may even fund the growth of the endowment, in a virtuous cycle. In recent years, entrepreneurial donors have shown a preference for the flexibility of reserves over the staid dependability of endowments. Chapter 6 also explores other, less common, ways to achieve reliable financial resources.

Endowment and Reserves Are Not the Same

While both endowments and reserves involve assets held for the long-term financial health of an organization, they are two very different concepts. One is meant to be held in perpetuity, releasing only a small portion of the invested funds to support programs and operations. The other is a revolving fund to manage temporary disruptions in operating cash or to provide one-time funding for episodic opportunities.

Comparing Endowment and Reserves

	Endowment	Reserves
Purpose	A permanent fund	Temporary funds
Primary types	True, quasi-, and term	Emergency (operating) and strategic
Policy and regulation	UPMIFA (true endowment only), GAAP	GAAP

	Endowment	**Reserves**
Accounting treatment (time)	Permanently restricted or temporarily restricted	Unrestricted
Accounting treatment (purpose)	May be restricted or unrestricted	
Goal	Perpetuity	Temporary financial needs or opportunities
Investment horizon	Perpetual	Short term

Part 2

This part shifts from financial matters to focus on the individuals whose hard work and generosity fuel causes, whether they are the donors who make gifts; the nonprofit professionals who secure and manage funds; or the broad corps of stakeholders who advocate, volunteer, and elevate the mission in myriad ways. Building resilience requires a coordinated and cooperative effort, rooted in enduring relationships. It cannot be delegated to any single individual. The keys to building enduring relationships are explored in these chapters.

Most nonprofit organizations, regardless of their fiscal heft, continue to call on donors to fuel their cause. The focus is on individual donors because they – rather than corporations or institutional foundations – provide as much as 85% of all charitable dollars given, according to *Giving USA*[2] (through direct giving, bequests, or closely held foundations), and are therefore the focus of these chapters. This part explores questions such as how and why people make charitable contributions – especially contributions to endowment – and how to earn and maintain their loyalty. Like any business model, the most stable system is one that relies on a significant proportion of its current "customers" (that is, donors) to provide recurring support. Because customer (donor) acquisition is both expensive and unpredictable, it is essential to retain these long-term relationships.

Finally, the concluding chapter (Chapter 9) provides various means to achieve and measure the success of relationship- and endowment-building strategies and ensure the desired benefits for the cause and those it serves.

The Resources appendix provides descriptions of various resources used in building and managing endowment and reserved funds, as well as links to templates and examples on various websites.

Disclaimer

Nothing in this book should be misconstrued as legal, accounting, or investment advice. While examples of methods for each are included in the text, they are just that: examples. Please consult with certified professionals, and – in the case of planned giving vehicles – encourage or *require* your donors to do the same. For one thing, I am simply a fundraising practitioner and unqualified to dispense formal guidance in these areas. In addition, this book reflects the legal and societal context of its time, which may well have evolved by the time a reader is applying its content.

Throughout this book, examples are drawn from the author's experience. For the most part, the organization is not named. In some cases, the examples are actually a composite of several organizations, donors, and/or situations. In all cases, they are rooted in one or more actual events.

A Few Notes About Language

The words "cause," "organization," "institution," "charity," and "nonprofit" tend to be used interchangeably throughout the text, although their meanings are not identical. While "nonprofit" has emerged as the dominant descriptor in North America, some have sought to replace this with the moniker "for impact," and most of the rest of the world uses "non-governmental organization" (NGO). A "cause" addresses a broad social issue such as racial justice or pediatric health or conservation of the environment. Many separate nonprofit organizations may work toward the same cause, each with its own programmatic approach, budget, and base of supporters. Trends point to donors' increasing loyalty toward a "cause" versus loyalty to any single nonprofit institution that serves the cause. For example, a donor may be committed to reducing food insecurity, but could express that loyalty through a gift to the foodbank one year and a gift to a nonprofit urban farm the next. The ability of any single organization to build financial resilience and enduring relationships depends, in part, on the resonance of its cause, its ability to differentiate from others serving the same cause, and its consistent cultivation of deep relationships that retain the donor's loyal support to their organization's pursuit of that cause.

Throughout the book, the words "donor" and "supporter" are frequently transposed, with a preference for the former. While "donor" implies someone who has given money, "supporter" is often understood as a more inclusive term that embraces those who have also given of their time, talent, ties, and testimony – traits that are also desirable and often lead to the giving of treasure.

"Major gifts" and "major donors" are frequently mentioned, reflecting the increasing reliance on big gifts to secure sufficient resources. Each organization has its own definition of "major donor," which is best determined using the Pareto principle: calculate 80% of contributed revenue and then, starting with the largest donor and in descending order, count the number of donors whose collective gifts provide that amount. Often it is just 5–10% of the total donor roll – the cut-off represents the organization's "major gift" threshold. However, use caution in applying the label because *any* donor could consider themselves "major," depending on the size of their gift in proportion to their capacity and/or their dedication of time and talent in addition to treasure. And for purposes of building endowment, it is often a donor's loyalty, rather than the magnitude of their gifts, that signals the likelihood of a legacy gift.

Is it "development" or "advancement"? It depends on whether the marketing team reports to the same leader or has a separate (sometimes siloed) structure. Throughout the book, I tend toward "development," because most of the references are to those with specific fundraising responsibilities whether their department is called "development," embedded within "advancement," placed in "external relations," or somewhere else. When there is a distinction, it is clearly identified. As explored in Chapter 7, it may be prudent to consider different titles altogether.

Part 2 describes the various traits of donors, including their generation. Here, the definitions developed by the Pew Research Center are used, with the terms "Millennial" and "Gen Y" treated as interchangeable.

Discussions of who gives to endowment, how they give, and why they give lean heavily on research into the traits, motivations, and behaviors of planned giving donors. Not all gifts to endowment are planned gifts, and not all planned gifts are directed to endowment. Nevertheless, there are few studies that look at endowment donors in isolation, while there is abundant research on planned giving donors, so the latter serves as a proxy.

Onward

Readers are drawn to this book because they are (or are preparing to be) involved in the enterprise of building endowment or reserves and nurturing relationships. The journey will require more than new skills and knowledge. Building resilience requires a shift in culture: from focusing on today to focusing on tomorrow; from funding operations to fueling dreams; from scarcity to abundance. Those who can navigate this journey will find great reward as the causes they are devoted to flourish.

—LMac

Notes

1. Andrew Pitt, Amy Thompson, and Karen Kardos, "Philanthropy and the Global Economy," *Citi Group* (Citi GPS: Global Perspectives and Solutions, November 2021), https://www.citigroup.com/global/insights/citigps/philanthropy.
2. Considering the sum of all gifts attributed to individual donors, bequests, and the half of foundation support that can be allocated to closely held family foundations and donor advised funds.

PART
1

Financial Resilience

resilience, n.

The quality or fact of being able to recover quickly or easily from, or resist being affected by, a misfortune, shock, illness, etc.; robustness...[1]

Introduction

In the familiar fable attributed to ancient Greek storyteller Aesop, the tortoise wins the race even though the hare has much more speed. The moral that "slow and steady wins the race" embodies many of the ingredients that can sustain a cause for the long haul: tenacity, humility, and determination. Like the tortoise, nonprofit leaders are adept at turning disadvantages into advantages, at understanding the need for consistent effort, and at facing adversity and insurmountable odds. All of those qualities can – and should – be applied when developing financial resilience.

Should nonprofit organizations focus on money when they're not about profit? Of course they should! "Nonprofit" is simply a tax designation, not a business model. As with any enterprise, financial resources are necessary to fuel operations. Employees and vendors must be compensated, debts repaid, and dreams funded. Even "overhead" must be supported. As Dan Pallotta, the provocative author of *Uncharitable,* declared in a March 2013 TED Talk, "the next time you're looking at a charity, don't ask about the rate of their overhead. Ask about the scale of their dreams."

For any cause to achieve and sustain the scale of their dreams, it must be more than a bootstrap operation, scrambling to shift money from one pocket to another like an exhausting and never-ending gerbil wheel. It is through endowment, reserves, and enduring relationships with loyal supporters that an organization can pursue its cause from a place of strength and stability.

In the YWCA (a global movement working in more than 100 countries to mobilize the power of millions of women, young women, and girls), there is a common saying that leaders "plant trees whose shade they will never enjoy." Leaders who accept the duty to create a resilient cause often do not enjoy the benefit of their labors. While they scramble to meet both the needs of today and the needs of the future, it is their hope that generations of successors will find their path less challenging and will be able to devote more energy to solving wicked problems or achieving brilliance, and less to the pursuit of funding.

Some may question whether it is appropriate to set money aside for the future through endowments or reserves, proclaiming it "hoarding" when there are pressing needs today. Others point to the necessity of generational equity, or not prioritizing the needs of today over the needs of tomorrow or vice versa. Perhaps the apt metaphor is a marathon: the training and discipline to get ready for that future race pays dividends today in better health and stamina (or a larger, more loyal donor corps) while it also provides a pathway to meet future goals. Just like someone running a marathon, a successful competitor sets a steady pace (like the tortoise) and understands that endurance is more important than speed. Too often, organizations are seduced by the idea that their efforts today will yield results tomorrow and set off at an unsustainable pace (like the rabbit), only to lose interest with the realization of the scale in time and effort without promise of immediate reward.

Yet, as with any journey, there are rewards along the way. Relationships are kindled and grow over time, to the betterment of both giver and receiver. Small victories are won. There may be intermediate destinations: a corps of X loyal donors, or endowment and reserves of Y dollars. Even as these goals are met, a leader will rarely say, "our cause has enough donors" or "enough money." Instead, they will inspire those around them to strive toward elevated targets as they seek to increase the impact and sustainability of the cause. Occasionally they will pause to look back at the progress that has been made and celebrate with all who contributed to the effort.

Before setting out on this journey toward resilience and sustained impact, it is essential to establish a clear destination, assemble the necessary team, equip them with the right resources, and plot a course, as the pages that follow describe. Safe travels!

Note

1. *Merriam-Webster's Collegiate Dictionary*, 11th ed. (2003), s.v. "resilience."

1 What Is Endowment?

T his chapter enables you to:

- Understand the role of endowment funds in nonprofit organizations and society.
- Explain the benefits and possible pitfalls of endowments for a cause, its donors, and its staff.
- Describe why some critics eschew endowments.
- Define three types of endowment and how they may be regulated.
- Review the history of endowments in various cultures.

Endowments, generally, are financial assets that are held permanently by a nonprofit organization and invested to create income and capital appreciation. A reasonable portion of the endowment's value is spent annually to support programs and operations, while the excess income and/or appreciation are accumulated in the fund, so it grows over time as a hedge against inflation. Endowments can be established to support the ongoing operating expenses of a nonprofit organization or for designated purposes such as scholarships, projects, programs, institutes, endowed positions, or any aspect of its charitable work.

5

This chapter presents the benefits and pitfalls of endowments for an organization, its supporters, and its fundraising team. It describes the three kinds of endowments, various accounting and reporting considerations, strategies for building endowments, and the historical context for endowments.

Endowment in Today's Context

Traditionally, endowment has been the gold standard for ensuring that a cause has financial resilience, especially in the United States. Colleges and universities have set this standard with endowments of eye-popping amounts that rival the total market value of large publicly traded companies like General Motors or General Mills. But this treasure has not been distributed equitably. The smallest endowment among the Ivy League schools is $8 billion, which provides Dartmouth College with nearly $350 million annually to fund programs and scholarships, but the typical Historically Black College or University (HBCU) endowment is well under $100 million. That's why they say that when PWIs (predominantly white institutions) catch a cold, HBCUs have pneumonia.[1] According to www. hbcumoney.com, the top 10 endowments among PWIs total more than $300 billion (about $920 per person in the United States), while the top 10 HBCU endowments are less than 1% of that amount, at $2.5 billion. No wonder Harvard University's leaders were called "tone deaf" when they launched a $100 million endowment campaign to fund its own study of its ties to slavery.

Academic research finds that only one American nonprofit in nine has endowed funds.[2] Most small and midsized nonprofit organizations – community colleges and local hospitals, social service agencies, arts and culture organizations, houses of worship, environmental advocates – have little or no endowment. These organizations have survived decreases in federal, state, and local governmental support for many core programs. They have experienced the changing interests of grantmaking foundations, receding support from local corporations taken over by out-of-town interests, the concentration of wealth and therefore greater reliance on donations from a diminishing percentage of households, economic headwinds, and the changing philanthropic values of new generations. In other settings, they may even face headwinds from charity regulators who may take a dim view of "tying up monies unnecessarily," as the Charity Commission in the United Kingdom had once stated. These are the organizations that can benefit most from this book.

> **Only one American nonprofit in nine has endowed funds.**

Although an endowment is not the panacea that many boards of directors hope for, it can provide a degree of certainty in projecting funding levels when the economy is uncertain and ensure a wellspring of resources for new programs and innovations in prosperous years.

Defining Endowment

The term "endowment" may be used informally to represent a variety of funds with several different specific definitions. Endowment and its various types must be understood to develop an effective charitable giving or financial management approach. Table 1-1 helps clarify what endowments are (and aren't).

Endowment is a broad term that is often used to describe the total of one or more endowed funds. An endowed fund is a charitable gift established in perpetuity in which the principal is invested for total return (both income and appreciation) and a small portion of the fund's total value (usually 4% to 6%) is paid out, generally on an annual basis (see more about total return in Chapter 5). The *beginning principal* is the value of the asset that was contributed by the donor; the *income* is the earnings produced by the principal;

TABLE 1-1   Endowments Explained

Endowments...	
. . . Are	**. . . Are Not**
Permanent assets, invested for growth and appreciation	A "rainy day fund"
A place to hold funds permanently	A temporary place to deposit a windfall
Invested for total return, distributing from both income and appreciation	Limited to distributions of interest earned
A source of reliable, stable support based on long-term investment growth	Volatile due to annual fluctuations in the market
Invested to produce an annual draw in support of the mission	Long-term savings, rarely deployed to support programs
Long-term assets that ensure future financial resilience	Short-term solutions to fix today's structural deficit

and *appreciation* (or *depreciation)* is the gain (or loss) in the value of the principal since it was contributed. An organization may have several endowed funds, established by one or more donors and for one or more purposes, in its endowment.

Merriam-Webster's Collegiate Dictionary (11th edition)[3] states that to endow is "to furnish with an income . . . providing for the continuing support or maintenance" of an organization. An endowment, then, is simply a pool of funds that is invested to provide ongoing financial resources to fuel the pursuit of a cause. Both state laws and generally accepted accounting principles (GAAP) apply to endowments in the United States. Governmental bodies in other jurisdictions may also regulate endowments and the fundraising efforts to achieve them.

Governing the Management of Endowment Funds

The Uniform Prudent Management of Institutional Funds Act (UPMIFA)[4] governs endowment spending by charitable corporations and some trusts in the United States. Almost every state and territory has enacted some form of the law since it was updated in 2006. An earlier version of the law, first enacted in 1972, lacked the word "prudent," which was added in 2006 to acknowledge the stresses placed on endowments during the Great Recession, when market forces meant that some endowments dipped below the value of the original gift and therefore could not provide *any* resources to help navigate very challenging economic circumstances.

UMIFA itself represented progress, which was revolutionary for the time since prevailing wisdom prior to 1972 limited investment opportunities – and therefore growth – of endowments. At that time, Janne G. Gallagher, senior counsel for the Council on Foundations, said:

> Before UMIFA, charity managers often believed that they could not rely on outside experts for investment advice and that investments had to be limited to the safest possible vehicles – cash, government bonds, and, perhaps, a few blue-chip stocks. UMIFA not only freed charity managers to delegate investment decisions to outside managers, but also allowed them to invest assets for long-term growth, not just current yields . . . Because UMIFA lets charity managers invest for growth, not just income, UMIFA also allows them to take that growth into account in making spending decisions for the endowed funds.[5]

UMIFA defined an endowment fund as "an institutional fund, or any part thereof, not wholly expendable on a current basis under the terms of the donor's gift agreement."[4]

The updated UPMIFA creates an even sounder and more uniform approach to charitable investments based on the "prudent-person rule." It permits a wider range of investment options and emphasizes the perpetuation of the original purchasing power of the fund (not just the original dollars). It also limits spending to 7% of the funds' total value unless the board can show that larger expenditures meet standards of prudence, and a formal vote to make a larger draw must be recorded in the board meeting minutes. See Chapter 5 for more information about setting a prudent endowment spending policy. The Financial Accounting Standards Board (FASB) also interprets UPMIFA to require that boards adopt specific disclosures to ensure the transparency of endowment management and expenditures.

From the Field: UPMIFA

UPMIFA has been enacted in 49 states (Pennsylvania being the only exception as of 2024). It provides guidance on the investment of endowment funds informed by modern portfolio theory. A charity is required to make decisions about each asset in the context of the entire portfolio of investments, as part of an overall investment strategy.

An organization determines prudent spending levels for its endowment (see Chapter 5) based on seven factors:

- The duration and preservation of the endowment fund
- The purposes of the institution and the endowment fund
- General economic conditions
- The possible effect of inflation or deflation
- The expected total return from income and the appreciation of investments
- Other resources of the institution, and
- The investment policy of the institution

The first of the seven factors looks at the duration of the endowment fund, which in most cases is perpetual. This requires the institution to consider generational equity: the institution must attempt to ensure that the purchasing power of the endowment fund, after inflation (factor 4), will be maintained for future generations served by the institution. But the spending must also fit within the expected total investment return (factor 5).

—Joe Bull, Philanthropy Advisory Counsel, LLC

Types of Endowments

FASB has identified three types of endowments.

- **True endowment** (also called permanent endowment). This is the type that is subject to UPMIFA in most states. True endowments are created when a donor has stated that their gift is to be held permanently as an endowment, either for general purposes or for specific uses as identified in a written gift agreement. Therefore, true endowments are always "restricted as to time" (that is, *permanently*), and sometimes "restricted as to use" (that is, intended for a specific purpose such as funding a medical clinic, art acquisition, or scholarships). True endowments are documented in a legally enforceable written agreement between the donor and the recipient organization, signed by representatives of both parties. FASB requires that the original value of the gift(s) that created a permanent endowment must be maintained, not used up, expended, or otherwise exhausted, which means that no draw can be taken if a fund's investments perform poorly, and it dips below the value of the original contribution. On the balance sheet, true endowment is classified as *permanently restricted net assets*.

  To complement the restriction as to time (that is, permanent), some donors also restrict the use of the funds drawn from the endowment, Common restrictions on the purpose of an endowment include scholarships, programmatic funds, funds endowing a position (such as curator or professor), or funds to maintain facilities (especially if the facility was named in honor of the donor).

- **Quasi-endowment** is sometimes called "board designated endowment," although the latter can cause confusion when board members misinterpret it to mean that the proceeds can be spent at the board's whim. Year-to-year, the board may elect to place excess revenue, windfalls, or unrestricted gifts into the quasi-endowment. Because a future board could vote to remove all or a part of the quasi-endowment's principal, it is not true endowment. A board-designated endowment is classified as *unrestricted net assets*, and its principal may be spent under FASB guidelines, although to do so creates peril for any organization, as described in the sidebar.

In Practice: Don't Eat Your Seed Corn

While boards can technically invade the principal of quasi-endowments, such a decision risks undermining the confidence of future donors. Endowed funds are publicly reported on Schedule D of an organization's informational tax return, IRS 990. Experienced donors often turn to an organization's 990 when they are considering a significant contribution, especially a gift to the endowment. The IRS 990 may appear to be a dry recitation of institutional financials; it actually portrays the story of the organization's prudent – or imprudent – allocation of resources in pursuit of its mission.

Consider the following Schedule D of a foster care and youth services agency in Kentucky, and the hesitancy a donor might feel when asked to add to that agency's endowment:[6]

Part V **Endowment Funds.**
Complete if the organization answered "Yes" on Form 990, Part IV, line 10.

	(a) Current year	(b) Prior year	(c) Two years back	(d) Three years back	(e) Four years back
1a Beginning of year balance	20,647,158	19,875,700	22,357,190	21,062,612	19,812,313
b Contributions . . .	1,575,574	6,975	44,000	358,049	161,676
c Net investment earnings, gains, and losses	6,747,683	796,483	2,138,193	1,635,039	2,392,668
d Grants or scholarships . . .					
e Other expenditures for facilities and programs . . .	1,598,036	32,000	4,663,683	698,510	1,304,045
f Administrative expenses					
g End of year balance	27,372,379	20,647,158	19,875,700	22,357,190	21,062,612

2 Provide the estimated percentage of the current year end balance (line 1g, column (a)) held as:
a Board designated or quasiendowment ► 89.080 %
b Permanent endowment ► 10.920 %
c Term endowment ►
The percentages on lines 2a, 2b, and 2c should equal 100%.

Although the board was permitted to take the extraordinary draw of $4.6 million illustrated in Row E, Column C – amounting to almost 21% of the funds' balance at

---

the beginning of the year – the prudent donor may be concerned about board discipline regarding future draws from the endowment. Or, as we say in the heartland, it appears that the organization is "eating their seed corn," even though they might actually be spending wisely on growth initiatives. An IRS 990 does not tell the full story, so donors may jump to their own conclusions.

If there is a likelihood that today's excess funds might be spent for special initiatives in the future, an organization is wiser to place them in strategic reserves (see Chapter 6) and avoid clouding the picture of an otherwise well-managed endowment.

- **Term endowment** is less common. A term endowment is created for a set period of years or until a future event, at which time the principal can be expended. For example, a ballet company created a term endowment, attracted several donors to support the initiative, and expended the funds for the creation of new works over 10 years leading to a milestone anniversary celebration. In another instance, a donor created an endowment for a reproductive rights organization and required that spending limits be lifted if the funds were ever needed to mount a legal challenge to the termination of *Roe v. Wade* (as has since occurred). Once the term runs out or the event occurs, the principal may be expended. The portion of term endowment that must be maintained for the specific term is classified by FASB as *temporarily restricted net assets*.

The various endowed funds in an organization's endowment must be labeled as one of these three types for accounting and reporting purposes, although they can be combined for investment purposes (see Chapter 5). Each of these types might be drawn for general uses or designated to fund specific purposes as defined by the donors such as scholarships, education programs, professorships and other staff positions, research, facility maintenance, art acquisition, and so on. It is incumbent upon the organization to ensure that a donor's designated purpose for the use of the endowment will advance the cause and remain "evergreen," and that investment practices balance growth and income with the liquidity required for annual distributions.

The Benefits of Endowment

Endowments can offer benefits to the organization and those it serves, to supporters, and to the development professional. If an organization has the wherewithal to create an endowment, it conveys permanence and credibility. Endowment provides fundraising staff the opportunity to present options to donors and demonstrates that the organization is prepared for and worthy of long-term investment in service to its mission.

For the Organization

Education, health, economic opportunity, justice, arts and culture – virtually any cause can be emboldened when its nonprofit champions have financial stability provided by ample endowment. For organizations and the communities they serve, the benefits of an endowment that amplifies the mission can include:

- **Expanded sources of income.** Because a permanent endowment is an invested pool of funds that provide a reliable source of income in perpetuity, the organization can count on annual distributions for its charitable work. With appropriate investment and spending policies (see Chapter 5), an endowment's purchasing power is preserved, even in the face of market fluctuations or inflation. An endowment of $1 million that provides $45,000 each year to fuel an early learning program can be designed to provide sufficient inflation-adjusted funding for that same program in 20 or 40 years. At the end of approximately 22 years, the endowment draws will have returned 100% of the original philanthropic investment, yet the proceeds will continue forever.

- **Stability and credibility.** A well-managed endowment sends a message of planned and prudent long-term fiscal responsibility, enhancing the reputation of the organization. The fear that a large endowment will deter giving is a myth: organizations with healthy endowments are attractive to donors for all the reasons explored in Chapters 7 and 8.

- **A complement to annual fundraising.** Far from a deterrent, organizations with healthy endowments are more likely to win favor with donors, especially those who view themselves as philanthropic investors. Donors are reassured when an organization can draw funds from an endowment to add to today's donations, ensuring that programs and activities are fully funded.

- **Ability to attract talent.** When endowment funds are used to endow a chair or position, for example, a portion of the funding might increase the compensation, provide research stipends, or enhance professional development enabling the organization to attract the strongest talent. Endowed positions often confer distinction. A portion of the funding might also supplant the ongoing costs for the position, enhancing budget resources across the organization.

- **Independence.** Endowments designated for specific purposes can provide a measure of independence from economic, governmental, and social forces. For example, an art museum was in danger of losing its photography curator when the board resolved to streamline the curatorial roles and emphasize education programs instead. The curatorial position survived when a concerned donor established an endowment that was sufficient to cover the program, which continues to delight patrons with inspiring exhibitions and elevate the museum's national stature.

- **Flexibility for management.** Endowments offer options to meet new challenges by providing greater financial flexibility and self-sustaining income streams. Endowments can augment uncertain income sources and provide a more balanced revenue mix; they can strengthen income statements and balance sheets, creating leverage for bond-rating capacity and borrowing.

- **Expanded strategies for campaigns.** A church-related organization was planning a statewide campaign for $8 million. Nearly everyone expected a certain individual to lead the campaign and provide a $1 million gift; but he explained that he lacked the liquidity for such a gift and felt he must decline the leadership role. Yet, because the campaign goal included $3 million to build endowment, he was able to make a $250,000 pledge for the capital project and an irrevocable deferred gift of $750,000 for endowment (see more about gift vehicles in Chapter 8). With the $1 million commitment in place, he ably led a successful campaign.

For the Donor

Donors are motivated to give to endowment for many reasons, whether they are creating a new fund or adding to an existing one. An organization must be prepared to articulate these benefits to prospective donors and their financial and legal advisors.

- **Perpetuates the donor's values and priorities.** An endowment gift is a powerful reflection of the donor's values and can perpetuate them in the wake of changing circumstances, providing assurance that programs that are important to the donor will survive. A small group of donors created an endowed fund to sustain programs in the humanities when their tuition-reliant *alma mater* faced significant financial headwinds.

  However, designated endowments must also allow sufficient flexibility to adapt to change. For example, when the polio vaccine eradicated the disease throughout the industrialized world, many hospitals sought to redefine endowed funds that were created in the early 1960s to provide lifetime care to people with polio.

- **Creates an enduring legacy.** Because an endowment gift will be invested permanently, it can serve as a permanent tribute to the donor, extend their values, and inspire future generations of donors. It can offer the donor an opportunity to be linked perpetually to a cause that was important to them during their lifetime.

- **Elevates the ability to give.** Many donors can make a larger gift through planned giving vehicles and designate it for endowment than they dreamed possible. An endowment gift is often a donor's final and largest gift to a cause they valued, because it is fulfilled after the donor's lifetime. For donors, the ability to devote the assets they accumulated over their lifetime in a final act of everlasting generosity can be extremely gratifying. A couple in San Diego worried they might not have sufficient resources to enshrine a treasured family member's memory, until they learned that they could combine a current pledge with a promise of a portion of their estate to "name" a room at the local Ronald McDonald House.

- **Ensures ongoing support.** An endowment gift gives an opportunity for donors to perpetuate their annual support. For example, the donor who consistently gives $250 to a cause can sustain those annual gifts by adding $5,500 to the organization's endowment fund. This can provide great comfort and peace of mind.

- **Allows incremental funding.** Many donors fear depleting their assets during their lifetimes, yet they want to see the impact that an enduring gift can create. They may establish an endowment gift through their estate, and then make annual gifts that represent the amount that would be distributed if the fund had already been established. This arrangement is sometimes called a "living endowment" or "virtual endowment." In this way, donors experience both the joy of giving and the reassurance that their eventual endowment will achieve the impact they desire.

- **Provides a lifetime income.** Some kinds of deferred gifts, such as charitable gift annuities, pay income to the donor for life with the remainder going into the organization's endowment after the donor's passing. See Chapter 8 for an explanation of these gifts, the opportunity to provide stable income during a donor's lifetime, and the risks that must be managed by the organization.

- **Alleviates burdens.** Some donors, particularly as they age, are uneasy with managing their assets and making investment decisions. A split-interest gift (see Chapter 8) enables the donor to receive regular income for life without the burden or cost of managing investments.

- **Permits additions at a later time.** An endowment fund can be established with an initial gift and the principal increased over time through investment growth and additional gifts from the donor or their friends and family. This can be a handy vehicle for people, especially family members, who wish to make meaningful gifts to someone who seemingly already has everything they could need or want. It can also allow a donor to "grow into" an endowed fund: such as the young alumni couple who made an initial gift to endow a program in the College of Arts and Sciences at the University of Tennessee (including matching gifts from each of their employers), enabling them to establish the fund at an early age, add to it over several years, and eventually fully fund the Justin and Amber Cutler Endowed Faculty Award.

In Practice: Endowing a Cause versus an Organization

In recent data, donors have shown more loyalty to a cause such as pediatric health or conservation than to a single organization. For them, selecting a single organization to receive their endowment gift(s) may be like choosing a favorite child, while dividing assets among a number of organizations may dilute the impact of an eventual endowment payout.

There may be alternatives. A local community foundation may have affinity funds. For example, the Columbus (OH) Foundation offers donors Focus Funds including a collection of Green Funds, and a Legacy Fund supporting LGBTQ+-serving organizations. Some national/global regranting organizations with a specific focus also offer the opportunity to build endowments focused on specific causes. An endowed fund at the Global Fund for Women distributes its draws in grants to women-led and woman/girl-serving organizations around the world; the National Christian Foundation focuses primarily on supporting Christian causes; while the National Jewish Endowment does the same for that faith tradition.

For Fundraisers and Their Colleagues

Endowments are built by people: the donors who give and the staff and volunteers who work to engage and inspire them. Typically, a fundraising professional coordinates the effort to establish and increase endowment, working closely with financial administrators, board members and other volunteers, everyone on the fundraising team, and, ultimately, the entire staff of the organization. All these team members are more likely to contribute to success if they understand the advantages of an endowment from their point of view.

> Endowments are built by people: the donors who give and the staff and volunteers who work to engage and inspire them.

- **Offers options to attract, retain, and inspire donors.** The fundraising team will want a full array of giving opportunities to discuss with donors. Increasingly, sophisticated donors expect endowment to be one of those options for two reasons: because it allows them to focus on the future and because they can make gifts out of assets rather than current earnings. As a result, conversations with donors can be a much richer, mutually rewarding experience.

- **Helps to realize growing expectations.** Organizational budgets increase over time for many reasons: to meet growing needs, to achieve higher aspirations, to allow for inflation, and to retain and reward valuable employees. Not all growth can be accommodated with continual increases in annual fundraising or earned revenue. An endowment can absorb some of the ever-increasing revenue goals, especially since a well-managed endowment fund keeps pace with inflation.

- **Builds a pipeline of current and future gifts.** Donors who support endowment – through current or deferred gifts – are more likely to support an organization's current needs, whether the annual operating fund, special projects, or a capital campaign. It's only logical that someone who has a stake in the organization's future is motivated to ensure that it has a robust present. In addition, some donors may be inspired to establish a deferred gift to endow a program in the future, and pledge current, ongoing support so that they can see the impact of the program now (a "living" or "virtual" endowment as described earlier).

- **Creates a donor-centered discipline.** Too often, the fundraising team is asked to focus on the "needs" of the organization. Every organization covets unrestricted gifts to fund current operations, but donors usually prefer to target their giving where they can witness its direct benefits for the community – now, and into the future. Endowment fundraising helps leadership and fundraising staff develop a donor-centered discipline with an understanding of donors' intellectual, psychological, emotional, and financial needs. The organization must be willing to be as visionary as the donor, perhaps taking risks in programmatic and financial areas. The donor determines the timing, size, and form of the gift. Donors' dreams and donors' money drive giving, inspired by the vision of the organizations and the needs they see in the community.

Endowment Criticisms and Pitfalls

The benefits of endowment for a cause, the community it serves, and its donors and staff may be attractive, but there can also be problems and critiques. The criticism is not new: in an essay for *The Atlantic* in May 1929, Julius Rosenwald (founder of Sears, Roebuck, and Co.) brought "attention to the underlying question of whether perpetual endowments are desirable." New voices – such as Justice Funders and proponents of Community Centric Fundraising – question the underlying premise of endowments, pointing out that they are often created by donors whose wealth can be traced to extractive industries or exploitational practices, and the paradox of large assets set aside for the future rather than deployed to do good today. Criticisms fall into several general categories:

- **Endowments can become obsolete**, like those that were established at hospitals to ensure perpetual care for polio patients. When polio was effectively eradicated in the industrialized world, hospital administrators were required to march to each state's equivalent of "Widows and Orphans Court" to change the terms of the funds if the donors or their heirs could not be consulted.
- **Because endowments are perpetual, they often reflect the legal and social mores of the period when they were established.** This can be problematic when the law and society change. For example, many endowed scholarships at universities across the country were established to ensure that students who face barriers because of race can have access to a higher education, yet a Supreme Court ruling in 2023 limits when and how colleges can consider race as a factor in the admissions process. Endowments may also be devoted to activities that the organization no

longer wishes to be a part of, especially if those activities benefit people with privilege at the expense of others. Consider a fund that requires history to be taught in a limited way, or a partial scholarship that still requires the student's family to contribute a considerable amount of tuition. For these reasons, organizations with large endowments can become the target of critics.

- **Endowed funds can become insufficient to fulfill donors'** *wishes* if growth does not keep pace with rising costs. That's what led to controversy at The Ohio State University. Michael Moritz established an endowment in 2001 with a gift of $30.3 million, but by 2017 the fund balance was just $21.9 million.[7] A variety of reasons were cited: investment losses, the imposition of a 1% management fee, another larger fee to fuel other fundraising activities, and the fact that the donor's requirements to fund multiple faculty positions, scholarships, and other activities placed a greater funding burden than the endowment could reasonably meet. The donor's heirs sued the university, resulting in unflattering attention from the media and probes by lawmakers.

- **Donors may be attracted to establish endowment for only fashionable activities** – like acquiring new works for an art museum – while neglecting everyday needs such as staff salaries and utility costs, creating an imbalance in funding. And donors may have unrealistic expectations for the amount of control they will maintain over the use of the endowment draw, which can create problems with the organization, its accrediting body, and the IRS.

- **Endowments add a layer of complexity and expense** to an organization's financial management. Even if management is delegated to a third party, such as the local community foundation, an organization still has to deal with accounting standards and legal requirements in how they invest, classify, report, and spend endowed funds.

- While endowments generally do not "crowd out" everyday donors' ongoing support for an organization, **some institutions' endowments have grown so large that donors begin to question** the impact of their gifts. They may be uncomfortable with the inequity of continued support of institutions that are seen as "wealthy" while other worthwhile causes remain under-funded. Critics denounce them for "hoarding." With endowments exceeding $25 billion, universities such as Harvard, Yale, Stanford, and Princeton have had to justify continued fundraising efforts. In a few cases, this has led to innovative risk-taking, such as the abolition of tuition payments for students who fall below a relatively generous income threshold.

- **Some cultures and/or religions eschew endowment.** For example, when an evangelical couple was asked to support a fund to endow missions, the couple referenced their conviction that the need would be negated by the "second coming," which they considered imminent.
- **There is growing recognition that some endowments were created by bad actors whose business practices created wealth at the expense of the common good,** whether historic slave holders and "robber barons" or more recent pharmaceutical heirs.
- Beyond problematic donors, there is **a movement that questions the very premise of endowments.** Justice Funders' "Resonance Framework for Philanthropic Transformation" is rooted in the "equitable redistribution of resources and power," observing that: "Many might say that, by definition, philanthropy is about redistributing resources. Yet to truly embody this principle, philanthropy must move far beyond the 5 percent payout requirements for grants and distribute ALL of its power and resources. This includes spending down one's endowment . . ."[8] Regardless of the merit (or lack thereof) of this criticism, it faces hurdles due to state laws restricting the amount that can be drawn from an endowed fund, generally accepted accounting principles, and the legal enforceability of written agreements between donors to an endowed fund and the organization that holds it.

These challenges point to the inflexibility of endowment, especially if a donor places onerous restrictions or an organization does not invest wisely. For these reasons, some younger donors – especially those who created their own wealth from entrepreneurial activities – reject endowments altogether or favor the nimbleness of strategic reserves (see Chapter 6).

A (Very) Brief History of Endowments

Endowments and their functional equivalents are cited in literature from ancient Greece and Rome. The Roman Emperor Marcus Aurelius created four endowed chairs in AD 176, one for each of the major schools of philosophy.[9] There is a similar concept in Islamic law called *waqf* describing a donation of a building, land, or other assets with no intention of reclaiming them. References from the ninth and tenth centuries tell of a pond and orchard in Egypt designated for the feeding of the poor. Today, the largest waqf is in Saudi Arabia and holds $11 billion. Many other cultures have a concept equivalent to endowment in their ancient traditions, ranging from the Tang Dynasty in China (618-907 CE) that endowed Buddhist monasteries, to West African empires that provided land grants for cultural endeavors.

In Support of Education

Like today, many early endowments supported education. In eighth century Turkey, wealthy princes endowed academic chairs and established funds for residential students. In the ninth century, rajas endowed schools to promote learning leading to the rise of Indian sciences, mathematics, and astronomy. At the same time in the Muslim world, rulers and princes provided funds to build and maintain libraries.[10]

Among the many advancements during the Renaissance Age in Europe, endowments emerged to support the modern university system. Lady Margaret Beaufort, Countess of Richmond and grandmother to Henry VIII, endowed chairs in divinity at the universities of Oxford and Cambridge, still in effect today.[11] Henry Lucas, a mathematics professor, created the Lucasian Chair at Oxford in 1663 with a gift of his library. One of the first to be appointed to the position was Isaac Newton; one of the most recent was Stephen Hawking.[12]

At about that same time, a young minister named John Harvard died of tuberculosis (or "consumption" as it was then called). Harvard was the last surviving member of a prosperous family from Surrey, England.[13] He left his entire library and half of his estate to a new institution designed to educate clergy in New England. His bequest not only immortalized his name: it also laid the foundation for the largest university endowment in the world.

Early endowments such as Harvard's grew quietly and slowly over succeeding decades through lotteries, subscription programs, and the episodic solicitation of wealthy individuals. Endowment growth accelerated with the advent of more organized fundraising campaigns. As Professor Bruce Kimball posted on histphil.org in June 2017:

The first comprehensive, multi-year, mass fundraising drive, … was . . . conducted by Harvard University between 1915 and 1925. Considered path-breaking at the time, the Harvard Endowment Fund (HEF) drive established many new fundraising policies and practices that are now taken for granted, but were contested, negotiated, and finally adopted, to become the accepted customs of conducting such campaigns.[13]

By the early 1920s, at least 75 other colleges and universities were following the Harvard example, which subsequently was adopted widely across the nonprofit sector to conduct campaigns for capital, endowment, and programmatic support.

Endowment became more widely achievable when the original "Leave a Legacy®" program was created at Diana Newman's kitchen table in the early 1990s. Then the vice president of The Columbus Foundation, she worked alongside Steve Rish, who was then head of corporate philanthropy at the insurance company, Nationwide. The public awareness campaign they created spread across America as a program of the National Association of Charitable Gift Planners. It continues to provide resources that any nonprofit organization can use to encourage donors to include charitable bequests to benefit the causes they care about.

In 2008, the place of endowment was further codified when the IRS updated Form 990 (the informational tax return required of most nonprofits) and added Schedule D to supplement the information on their tax return with five years of data on endowment assets, fees, new contributions, and grants paid. The resulting transparency has allowed a more thorough analysis of endowments.

Endowments have extended far beyond their original roots in religion and learning. The Metropolitan Museum of Art, for example, began its General Endowment Fund by a motion of the board in May 1905 and held assets of $302,115.29 by the end of that year. Despite growing to almost $3 billion by the end of FY 2022, the Met's repeated deficit budgets have been widely reported. Shriners Hospitals for Children started an endowment shortly after being established in the early 1920s; its endowment was valued at $8.8 billion on its 2021 IRS 990, Schedule D. Sizeable endowments are still held by churches (Trinity Church, Wall Street at $9.9 billion), now joined by conservation organizations (The Nature Conservancy at $7.9 billion), and even the Hong Kong Jockey Club (at $8.6 billion), which announced a partnership with the Rockefeller Foundation to "bolster public health across the globe and protect some of the most vulnerable people from the impacts of climate change" according to a December 2023 press release. The largest endowment is thought to be held at Ensign Peak Advisors, which manages the assets of The Church of Jesus Christ of the Latter-Day Saints and holds $124 billion.[14]

Endowments Today

Today, endowments around the world hold more than a trillion dollars ($US) in assets. Yet, as with other philanthropic and economic models, endowment resources are inequitably distributed. Unlike Harvard or Yale, the typical HBCU has less than $50 million in its endowment, which produces a humble annual draw of just $2.25 million (although a 2024 grant from the Lilly Endowment will provide an additional $5 million to each HBCU's endowment with the requirement that they match it with $5 million in gifts from others). Beyond higher education, only one nonprofit organization in nine in America benefits from endowed funds.

The concentration of endowment holdings in the United States among a few large universities may be one reason that higher education endowments were singled out in the 2018 Tax Cuts and Jobs Act, which placed an excise tax on net investment income of any university's endowment that exceeded $500,000 per student. It is thought that fewer than 50 institutions were affected, with tax liabilities ranging from less than $250,000 to more than $50 million. And there have been more recent proposals to increase the tax and expand the institutions that would be affected.

How much endowment is "enough" for any given cause? For many, the answer aligns with the thoughts of American actress and comedian Amy Poehler: "It doesn't matter how much you get, you are always left wanting more." An endowment must grow extremely large before it begins to attract negative attention, trigger a tax liability, or diminish the zeal of current donors, so "too much" is rarely a concern.

There are a number of ways to determine "enough," such as benchmarking against others in the same sector or identifying specific vulnerable activities that could be stabilized through endowment funding: for example, a senior living community's residents created an endowed fund of $750,000 spinning off annual draws of $32,000 to ensure that there would always be a part-time chaplain. Often, endowment milestones are adopted as part of a strategic planning process or integrated into the overall goal of a combined annual-capital campaign.

Endowments Are Not for Every Cause

A fledgling water conservation organization gained cachet when a respected funder provided a sizeable start-up grant. Their 20-year plan to transform the region's waterways was compelling. A small leadership team assembled and developed a list of all the capacities that needed to be established, including fundraising. As they engaged donors, they had a singular focus: "help us build an endowment so that we never have to ask you for money again." They failed, and within six months the organization fell out of favor. Why did the organization's appeal for endowment funding fail to connect? Consider:

Donors to endowment are usually long-time supporters of a cause; they trust the nonprofit organization deeply because it has shown a consistent ability to deliver impact and nurture relationships. The water conservation group had not yet celebrated its first anniversary.

Board members were still being recruited and many had yet to make their first gift to the organization. The gifts that had been received were devoted to current operations. Many endowment gifts come from an organization's board members; outside donors expect to see the board demonstrating their commitment and confidence as they consider their own gift.

To warrant an endowment, an organization needs to exhibit its ability to manage finances. This organization had never balanced a budget or produced an audited financial statement.

The energy devoted to building endowment distracted the organization from pursuit of annual or multi-year support that could have allowed them to launch their work, establish a track record of success, and expand their capacity, eventually becoming endowment-ready.

> *The promise to "never ask donors for money again" struck many as both disingenuous and wrong-headed.* After all, the annual engagement of supporters is one mechanism for maintaining an organization's connection to and accountability with the community.
>
> *Endowments are intended to be perpetual, yet this group did not have a clear vision for the role it would play once the 20-year plan was implemented.* Although this was an extreme case, it demonstrates many of the reasons that it is not prudent for every nonprofit to pursue endowment. Success in building endowment requires several factors, including a demonstration of long-term impact, established policies, stable financial management, and board commitment (as discussed in the upcoming chapters). For some organizations, endowments can even be antithetical to the cause, especially those that have a short-term mission or serve only immediate needs.

Summary and Next Steps

A sizeable endowment is not for every organization, nor does it guarantee the resilience of a cause (as evidenced by the perennial financial struggles of several organizations with sizeable endowments). It is just one ingredient to be complemented with other strengths: a relevant mission, impactful programs, prudent financial management such as reserves and – most importantly – a community of people who are steadfast in their fidelity to that cause. With a foundational understanding of endowments, an organization must evaluate whether to devote its resources to endowment building. The upcoming chapter explores the ingredients necessary for building endowment, provides resources and knowledge to assess readiness, and helps in determining the endowment-building strategy that best serves an organization and its donors.

Notes

1. "2022 Top 10 HBCU Endowments," *HBCU Money*, February 21, 2023, https://hbcumoney.com/2023/02/21/hbcu-moneys-2022-top-10-hbcu-endowments.

2. Andrew Lo, Egor Matveyev, and Stefan Zeume, "The Risk, Reward, and Asset Allocation of Nonprofit Endowment Funds," in *The Summer Institute of Finance* (Shangai, China, 2021), https://papers.ssrn.com/sol3/papers.cfm?abstract_id=3560240.

3. "Endow," in *Merriam-Webster's Collegiate Dictionary, 11th Ed.* (Springfield, MA: Merriam-Webster, Inc., 2020).

4. Uniform Laws Commission, "Prudent Management of Institutional Funds Act - Uniform Law Commission," www.uniformlaws.org, 2006, https://www.uniformlaws.org/committees/community-home?CommunityKey=043b9067-bc2c-46b7-8436-07c9054064a3.

5. Janne Gallagher, "Legal Briefs," *Foundation News and Commentary* 44, no. 2 (March 2003).

6. www.guidestar.org (Candid), accessed October 7, 2023, https://www.guidestar.org/profile/61-0445834.

7. Tom Lawrence, "Ohio State Benefactor's Family Seeing Red over Mishandling of $30.3 Million Endowment," *Legal Newsline*, August 19, 2020, https://legalnewsline.com/stories/548961543-ohio-state-benefactor-s-family-seeing-red-over-mishandling-of-30-3-million-endowment.

8. "Guiding Values & Principles," Justice Funders, accessed March 5, 2024, https://justicefunders.org/resonance/guiding-values-principles/.

9. Dorothea Frede, "Alexander of Aphrodisias," *Stanford Encyclopedia of Philosophy*, October 13, 2003.

10. "Lady Margaret's 500 Year Legacy" (Wayback Machine: University of Cambridge, May 16, 2007).

11. R Robert Bruen, "A Brief History of the Lucasian Professorship of Mathematics" (Cambridge University, May 1995), http://www.lucasianchair.org.

12. Conrad Edwick Wright, "John Harvard," *Harvard Magazine*, January 1, 2000, https://www.harvardmagazine.com/2000/01/john-harvard-html.

13. Bruce Kimball, "The Uneasy Convergence of Elite and Mass Fundraising in Higher Ed: The Harvard Endowment Fund Drive, 1915-1925," July 27, 2018, https://histphil.org/2018/07/27/the-uneasy-convergence-of-elite-and-mass-fundraising-in-higher-ed-the-harvard-endowment-fund-drive-1915-1925/.

14. Aran Ali and Joyce Ma, "Ranked: The World's Top 50 Endowment Funds," Visual Capitalist, May 16, 2023, https://www.visualcapitalist.com.

2

Are You Ready to Build Endowment?

This chapter enables you to:

- Understand the prerequisites to building endowment.
- Take stock of an organization's status and determine whether the time is right to initiate an endowment-building effort.
- Engage key staff, donors, and other stakeholders whose support of endowment-building will be essential.
- Identify and "de-bunk" some of the myths that stand in the way of progress when building endowment.

Building an endowment requires specific fundraising techniques and fiscal discipline. It is essential for some causes while unsuitable for others. This chapter discusses the signs of an organization's readiness to launch a new endowment or build upon a nascent one. Some organizations conduct a formal assessment to determine if their development office is ready and the donors are receptive. The role of volunteers must be determined: will there be an endowment committee or an informal group of endowment champions? Based on an evaluation of several factors, every organization must identify how to build internal capacity and when to start the endowment-building process.

33

Prerequisites for Endowment Building

No rule book dictates which organizations are ready to build an endowment and which are not, but there are several factors to take into consideration. Any organization that decides to prioritize endowment should assess strengths in the following areas and shore up weaknesses before devoting substantial resources to the effort. The factors, listed in order of importance, are:

- **The board of directors and leadership team are committed to building endowment.** The board of directors should resolve that endowment is a priority for the organization through a formal motion documented in the minutes (see the Resources section in the back of the book for sample motion language). Board members and staff leaders must understand that endowment building is a long-term process and demonstrate patience to match their understanding, even as others may be impatient to build buildings or fund programs with immediate gifts. Board members can demonstrate their commitment to meeting the future financial needs of the organization by making an individual gift of their time, treasure, and ties; managing the budget; devoting organizational resources; and establishing ambitious yet realistic measures of success.

From the Field: Board Buy-in

"I often assess the buy-in from my board by determining if they are willing to invite their friends and peers to the table. If they are not willing to have that conversation on behalf of the organization, it may be because the case has not been made effectively or clearly enough. Alternatively, it may be that they hold misconceptions themselves that the organization needs to address."

—Katy Trombitas, Vice President of Advancement,
Columbus State Community College

- **The organization is strong, has a clear mission, and earns donors' trust through the impact of its programs.** There should be a history of strong and growing programs over the last 5 to 10 years. The organization should have a written strategic plan that defines the vision, mission, goals, objectives, specific projects, and resource allocation that illustrates the role of the endowment. There must be a capacity to commit current resources (people and money) with the understanding that the return on investment may be many years in the future (and many multiples of the investment!).
- **Current finances are stable, and sufficient reserves are in place.** As discussed in Chapter 6, reserves and endowments serve two distinct purposes. While an endowment ensures long-term relevance and viability, reserve funds help to weather sudden storms or seize immediate opportunities. Because of the temptation to reallocate quasi-endowed funds for these immediate needs, it is important to have reserves in place before building an endowment.
- **Leaders (staff and volunteers) are stable, knowledgeable, and available.** Committed leaders are prepared to devote time to the various tasks required to implement endowment-building strategies. Discipline is required to focus on the importance of the future amid the urgent needs of today. Potential endowment champions and creative leaders are actively involved with the organization's fundraising program. A well-trained staff is available to plan endowment programs and rally volunteers. Professional development is expected and provided. Expectations for contributing to the endowment-building effort are built into job descriptions throughout the organization (not just front-line fundraisers'.) and the work is measured by more than the amount of cash that is raised each year (see Chapter 9).
- **There is a compelling case for the future.** A vision for the future paints a picture of impactful programs, successful revenue generation, and sound investment management. The organization's mission is evergreen. All this is described in a case for support that illustrates how future draws from the endowment

will advance the cause (see Chapter 4). It is an inspirational call to action that resonates with donors because it aligns with their desire to help people rather than focusing on the organization's needs. To paraphrase management guru Peter Drucker, "Organizations don't have needs, people do."

- **An effective fundraising program is in place.** The organization receives broad support from everyday donors through a growing annual fund with high donor retention, has an effective major gifts program, and has identified donors who are ready to make planned gifts (see Part 2). Supporters are recognized for contributions of time, talent, treasure, testimony, and ties. They are engaged through email and social media; letters and literature; intimate and large-scale events; and personal visits from development officers, other team members, or board members. The entire relationship with the donor is maintained in a robust constituent relationship management system (CRM) that tracks detailed information about individuals and provides meaningful analytical reports on demand.

- **Early gifts build the confidence of other donors.** The power of "social norming" in charitable giving and the influence of the "follow the leader" effect have been widely documented. (see Chapter 7). To leverage these influences and secure commitments from a large number of supporters, an organization should have a track record of attracting major support for current programs and capital purposes and/or a corps of loyal supporters who have made modest gifts over a span of many years, as well as a proven process to continually identify and engage new supporters. There must be a robust list of donors who have accumulated considerable assets during their lifetimes – typically those who are over the age of 50. The organization should have already received commitments (current or deferred) from "insiders" such as board members to establish the endowment fund and reassure future donors that they are in good company.

- **A constituency-wide plan for marketing, communications, and stewardship is in place.** The organization's outreach is rooted in good strategy and analyses to engage various audiences. Messages resonate and include data and stories: there are "no stories without data and no data without stories," as attributed to Jacob Harold, a social change strategist and cofounder of Candid. Every constituent is provided opportunities to interact rather than relying on a steady stream of one-way messages. All donors receive a prompt and personalized "thank you" when they give and receive follow-up messages that describe the impact of their giving. (See Chapter 4 for more about donor messaging.)

- **Written endowment policies have been adopted.** The organization has documented and approved policies for gift acceptance, investment and spending, selection of investment managers and other advisors, and requirements for gift and fund documentation. Policies provide clear guidance for staff and boundaries for donors. Procedures are documented for such tasks as the administration of gifts and the authority to negotiate gifts and fund agreements, as well as when to involve a donor's advisors or family. Guidelines are in place for named endowments, allowable restrictions on the use of funds, recognition and stewardship protocols, and donor designations (see Chapter 5).

Few, if any, organizations will rate highly in all areas, but each area should be carefully assessed with a plan in place to strengthen areas of weaknesses, and a commitment to reassess all the factors on a periodic basis. Organizations with significant gaps may need to step back and focus their efforts on preparedness before leaping in to pursue endowment gifts. You can use the Endowment Readiness Test in the Resources section at the end of this book to evaluate an organization's endowment readiness.

Assessing Readiness

Once an organization has decided to begin or accelerate an endowment building effort, it should next assess both internal readiness and donors' sentiments. Since endowment efforts should be integrated into the engagement of all donors, not just major donors, the assessment will inform more than endowment building; it will provide a good indication of the overall health of the fundraising program. It will strengthen the organization's relationship with all donors who agree to take part, engaging them in an exciting vision for the future and envisioning their role in bringing it to reality.

A well-implemented assessment must be designed to answer the following questions:

- How can the assessment connect people to our cause and our endowment?
- Will endowment-building efforts fit into our comprehensive fundraising plan?
- How important is an endowment to our organization?
- How appealing is an endowment to our current and potential supporters?
- What internal capabilities need to be addressed? Do we have the right people, processes, technology, and culture upon which to build a program?
- Do our current donors have the financial resources – especially assets – to help us achieve our endowment goal?
- What aspects of an endowment might be most appealing to our donors, such as endowed scholarships, faculty or staff positions, signature programs, facility maintenance, care for collections, or something else?
- Do our stakeholders regard us as a trustworthy organization that can manage an endowment effectively?
- How can we measure and convey the beneficial impact of an endowment?

If endowment is one component of a comprehensive campaign alongside capital and programmatic fundraising goals, the assessment can shed light on the feasibility of the larger vision. The Endowment Readiness Test in the Resources section at the end of the book provides a means to evaluate these factors.

Who Conducts the Assessment?

One option is to assign the assessment to staff. When an assessment is done internally, it has several advantages. Staff members already know the organization and its constituents. Their conversations in the community will strengthen bonds between the organization and its stakeholders. Assessment expenses will be minimal, although the process will be labor intensive and the staff members who are involved may need to redirect their attention from their current assignments.

An outside consultant can bring objectivity to the process. Internal and external audiences may be more candid with a third party. An outside expert or firm has probably seen many organizations' fundraising and endowment programs. Their recommendations may be more credible in the eyes of board members and the community. However, the consulting team will need to learn about the organization so that they can convey information accurately and reflect the organization's values. Their services are generally provided for a fixed fee.

The decision does not have to be either/or – there may be a hybrid solution. For example, an outside expert could assess the internal readiness factors given the awkwardness of a staff member evaluating the work of colleagues. External discovery work such as interviews, surveys, and group discussions might be facilitated by staff members with guidance from the advisors who will also participate in the analysis. If the assessment includes a screening of current donor data to gain an appreciation of donors' philanthropic affinity and capacity – and it should – that will almost certainly be outsourced.

In Practice: Engaging Outside Experts

The decision to focus on endowment building can feel like a "big bet." It will require the investment of resources where the return might not be seen for many years. For many organizations, the guidance of outside experts provides confidence that the organization's strategies are prudent and investment is warranted. Then the question arises, "How do we identify the best consulting partner(s)?" Consider these steps:

1. **Assign a leader.** Determine who will make the final decision, and who will have input. A surprising number of organizations set out to hire a vendor/partner without identifying who the decision-makers and influencers will be. This is especially painful when a senior staffer or board member wanders in halfway through the process and wants to weigh in.

2. **Agree on what you need.** Clearly define the scope of the consultant's work, the criteria you'll use to evaluate the candidates, and score each criterion. What kinds of clients and experience should the firm have? Are you looking for comprehensive strategy, or local knowledge? How much are you able to spend?

3. **Identify candidates.** This is pure information gathering. Start with listings from credible sources such as the Giving Institute and AFP. Evaluate each candidate's website. Augment that information with experiences of similar organizations. Ask peers, board members, and coworkers – what is the reputation of the candidate firms? Are there others they recommend? Then have an informal chat with each firm. This may take time, but it will provide a feel for what a working relationship might be like.

4. **Request and review proposals.** Using the criteria defined in Step 2 as a guide, ask each firm to describe their process, deliverables, team members, timeline, and cost. The more structured the request, the easier it will be to compare the proposals. Be specific about the due date for proposals, client references, the delivery method, and who should be contacted with questions. Each firm deserves to have their proposal reviewed carefully, so limit the number of candidates considered at this point.

5. **Select and interview finalists.** There may be two or three (no more than three) firms that fit the defined criteria. Ask that they prepare a presentation. The fairest and most efficient process keeps the presentation schedule tight all firms on one day, or one each on consecutive days. Use the same approach for each candidate – in-person, on video, or hybrid. Everyone who has a say in the final decision must sit through *all* presentations. Then make the decision quickly while the impression left by each firm is still fresh. Use the objective scoring method that was created in Step 2.

6. **Do not initiate the process if it is inauthentic.** If there is a suspicion that the final selection is *a fait accompli* – based on previous relationships, office politics, or other factors – then pull the plug. Save everyone the time and money.

Discovery Methods

A thorough assessment will use several methods to gather information about the sentiments of the organization's supporters and its internal readiness.

- **Personal interviews** are the most reliable method to gain insights from influential supporters, including board members, long-time donors, major donors, and community leaders. These typically last 30 to 60 minutes and should be conducted by the most personal means possible: in person, via videoconference, or on the phone. Each participant should receive a brief description of the organization's envisioned future and the role the endowment will play, sometimes called a "preliminary case for support" (see Chapter 4). If a giving decision is likely to be made by both spouses or partners (and it usually is), try to engage both in the discussion. This should be a conversation (not an interrogation) that explores their perceptions of the organization's strengths and weaknesses, experiences as a donor, commitment to the organization's goals and resonance of its case, and the likelihood that they will support an endowment effort with their time, talent, and/or treasure. They may also be asked to identify others whose support could be crucial to the effort's success.

- **Group discussions** with small gatherings of 6 to 12 people can elicit much of the same information as personal interviews. These can be especially effective with interconnected groups such as alumni, volunteers, docents, or retired employees of the organization. Group discussions surface common attitudes, values, and motivations, which shape the future endowment-building case. Generally, participants hesitate to "name names" or discuss money (theirs or other peoples') in a group setting, so a follow-up survey to collect this information is prudent. For community-based organizations, group discussions can be held in person at a supporter's home, a restaurant, or in the organization's facilities where the mission is evident. Organizations with widespread supporters can utilize all the tools available through videoconferencing services, as most people became comfortable with the technology during the COVID-19 pandemic.

These platforms have the advantage of multiple communication channels, including discussions, "chat" features, instant polling, and even the ways to manage an overzealous participant who talks over the views of others.

- **Online surveys** can reach an even wider audience. While they are less effective in strengthening the relationship between the participant and the organization, a well-crafted survey can be a powerful tool. First, ensure that you have clearly defined learning objectives before creating the survey so that each question is tied to a specific objective. Make it as short as possible. Use clear and concise language, respecting recipients' attention span and minimizing survey fatigue. Offer a variety of response options. A mix of closed-ended (that is, multiple-choice, Likert scale) and open-ended questions allows respondents to express their opinions in different ways while providing quantifiable data. (See more about surveys in Chapter 7.)
- **Internal readiness** includes four primary components: people, processes, systems, and culture. Within each category, consider what to assess. For example, in the "people" category, identify topics such as organizational structure, values alignment, and employee engagement. For systems, consider data integrity, system useability, and reporting and analytics. Use a combination of interviews, discussion groups, and surveys with staff and board. This will help to identify internal attitudes toward endowment. Reviewing documents such as job descriptions, fundraising plans and policies, and sample solicitation materials will reveal areas of strength and those that need attention. This should also include a thorough historical giving analysis to gain insights into giving trends and donor inclinations. This, along with the wealth and affinity screening mentioned earlier, will help identify current supporters who appear to be good candidates for endowment gifts.

In Practice: Screening Data to Find Endowment Donors

A search for donor data screening vendors will return dozens of possibilities. Selecting the right one can accelerate the growth of your endowment while the wrong one can send you chasing dead ends.

Like any search, first, determine your requirements and create a scorecard. In the end, "screening" must assess more than wealth. Wealth alone does not indicate a propensity for charitable giving. Some of the indicators that purport to identify wealth might instead pinpoint spending: an expensive home might mean the donor is wealthy, or it might mean that the donor is struggling to pay a jumbo mortgage. The type of wealth matters. Donors are much more likely to support an endowment through accumulated assets rather than current household income.

In addition to wealth and charitable giving indicators, an effective screening tool finds patterns in a database: which donors or prospects show the giving patterns that align with endowment support? If some donors have already given to endowment, some screening tools can identify the traits they have in common and then identify others with similar traits, aka "look-alikes." A strong indicator of endowment potential is loyalty: donors who may not appear to be wealthy but have given consistently over many years (a screening tool is not required to find these folks). Because many donors support endowment through planned gifts, modest loyal donors may make some of the most generous gifts to your endowment when they bequeath a home or make your organization a beneficiary of their retirement assets.

The best screenings go a step further and compare your donor data to massive databases of charitable giving, consumer habits, psychographic traits, and more to provide a robust understanding of each donor's capacity and affinity.

Screening can help segment a large pool of donors into manageable cohorts, each requiring customized strategies. But before a donor is approached, the results from the screening need to be verified. Screening data is imperfect (sometimes spectacularly so). An independent girl's school was surprised to hear that a young alumna had considerable wealth – until they determined that the presumed wealth was misconstrued because of her home address: she was living *gratis* in a carriage house on her very wealthy aunt's estate. Also, if the donor's name is "Mary Smith," the results may inadvertently include the wealth and giving from a billionaire while your Mary Smith is a retired schoolteacher.

- **Benchmarking and case studies** can build an understanding of the role endowment plays at comparable organizations. Many sectors provide benchmarking reports such as the *Voluntary Support of Education* report prepared by CASE or the Association of Art Museum Directors' *By the Numbers* report. Additional data can be gleaned from IRS Form 990, which summarizes organizations' endowment holdings in Schedule D and can provide insights about fundraising expenses, revenue, and other helpful metrics. Forms 990 are publicly available and easily accessible at sites such as Candid's guidestar.org and ProPublica's non-profit explorer (see the links in the Resources section). Based on these sources, the assessor can select a few comparable organizations for in-depth interviews or surveys. This process can help to establish realistic expectations for the organization and examples of strategies that have worked (or not) for peers.

But beware, the goal of benchmarking is not to copy other organizations (some have labeled benchmarking as a "path to mediocrity"), any more than deciding what size pants to wear based on the pants a neighbor is wearing. Benchmarking is one of *many* inputs to help you determine direction.

> Modest loyal donors may make some of the most generous gifts to your endowment when they bequeath a home or their retirement assets.

The Assessment Report

A report of findings and recommendations can help an organization determine if, when, and how to build endowment as well as individual prospects who might be the best candidates for giving to or volunteering in the effort. It will also test the case for endowment and determine which messages resonate and which types of funds appeal most to the donors.

Make it a formal process. A notable museum retained a consultant to assist with endowment building. When the consultant suggested starting with an assessment, the museum's director replied "Oh, we've already done that." The consultant asked to see the report, only to learn that the assessment had been rather informal, and the results were all in the director's head. The lesson learned: it's not an assessment unless the findings and recommendations are in writing!

The internal assessment will inform decisions about systems and technology:

- Do we have the right CRM (customer relationship management) tool and is it configured to track information about endowment prospects and donors?
- What policies must be reviewed and updated?
- Are there enough gift officers with the right skills to manage prospect and donor relationships?

If the answer to the last question is "no," that does not necessarily mean that you must hire a planned giving specialist, many of whom command a high salary in a competitive niche. For many organizations, all development staff – from annual gift managers to leadership gift officers – can and should be trained to spot donors who are well positioned to support the endowment and how to initiate a conversation about it. Bequests are the most common type of planned gift and are not complicated. However, if the prospect wants to explore sophisticated gift-planning scenarios (such as gift annuities or trusts), seek the input of experts.

The external assessment will help to answer critical questions that the board should ask prior to devoting resources to endowment building, such as:

- Is this the right time to launch an endowment-building effort, and how much should we expect to raise in a reasonable amount of time?
- What is the right strategy for engaging our donors and securing gifts?
- What is the role of volunteers and who are some of the candidates to take on this responsibility?
- Are there early donors who are ready to make a gift that will raise the sights and bolster the confidence of others?
- Which aspects of endowment are most appealing to donors, and what messages are most likely to resonate?

When the assessment is complete, it is a best practice to present the results to the board. Devote ample time to distill the analysis so that it is clear to a group of people who may have limited knowledge of endowments and prepare to answer a lot of questions. If the board decides to proceed, a formal motion and vote are recorded in the official minutes. This provides gravitas and authorizes management to allocate resources – both time and money. See the Resources section for a sample board motion to build endowment.

Recruiting Endowment Champions

Once an organization has committed to building an endowment, it must look to its leaders to provide more than competent management; it needs excited and engaged *champions* in the C-suite, on the board, and throughout its community. Champions set an example through their own contributions to the endowment, a willingness to talk about their commitment, and through partnership with the development team members who are responsible for identifying and engaging potential donors.

The composition and roles of a corps of endowment champions will differ based on the endowment-building method(s) an organization plans to adopt (as described in Chapter 3). Whether they sit on a campaign cabinet, serve on an ad hoc endowment task force, comprise a legacy society committee, or are informally gathered as a "kitchen cabinet," these champions set the pace for a successful effort. Their efforts are nurtured by senior leaders and their contributions of time, talent, and ties are recognized as much as their gifts of treasure. They are generally found among current and past board members, long-time donors, and in key volunteer corps like an agency's hands-on helpers, a college's alumni association, or the museum's docents.

Champions must understand that their responsibility is to the organization, and not to exploit their role for professional or financial gain. On rare occasions, financial advisors or estate attorneys may see their involvement as a way to gain clients or insurance brokers might hope to weave one of their products into the mix of giving options. Neither is appropriate. Skilled service in support of a worthwhile organization can burnish someone's reputation in intangible ways, which is sufficient reward for the committed volunteer.

Endowment Myths

Before focusing on endowment, an organization should identify and debunk the myths that might be harboring in the minds of their donors, staff, and even board members, and perhaps revealed during the assessment process. This is one of the champions' most important roles: to pinpoint and debunk the myths that might stand in the way of endowment building. Champions educate themselves, the board, and potential donors so that these "urban legends" can be politely dismissed while legitimate concerns are acknowledged and addressed. Some of the most common myths include the following.

"Endowments are a sign of too many riches"

Some misperceive endowments as hoarding of resources for an unknown future rather than using the resources to address needs today. Or that if organizations choose to set aside some of their revenue for the endowment or spend resources attracting endowment gifts, then they must have more money than they need to achieve their mission.

Yet fluctuations in revenue, economic headwinds, and rising demands for services call on the prudent organization to seek the dependability of endowment funding. In an article in the 27 May 2004 issue of the *Chronicle of Philanthropy*, Dennis R. Hammond states:

> Prudence demands, and common law encourages, institutions to set aside some of each year's unspent earnings, together with gifts given in perpetuity, to help maintain operation in future years when the revenues, earnings, and gifts to the annual fund are inadequate . . . There will be inevitable periods of conflict between short-term operational needs and the long-term need for growth and maintenance. Board members must evaluate their institutions' idiosyncratic needs during market or operational shocks. But in that ambiguous art of balancing present and future demands, one fact remains unambiguous: Endowments are not a luxury but a necessity.[1]

"If donors give to the endowment, they'll give less to the annual fund"

This old fear has proven baseless. It is rooted in scarcity ("there's not enough . . .") rather than vision and abundance. Endowment donors, with few exceptions, are long-time contributors to current operations who decide to also provide lasting endowment gifts – the former through current earnings and the latter through assets. Once their endowment gifts are completed or pledged, they are usually even more committed to fund ongoing operations. They envision the future through their support for the endowment and build a bridge through their commitments to today's impact.

Research from Professor Russell James, the American Council on Gift Annuities, and the Indiana University Lilly Family School of Philanthropy all show that once donors have made a planned gift, their annual gifts to that organization *increase* by a substantial amount.

"We can't raise endowment because we don't have a planned giving specialist"

It is true that some gifts in support of endowment come in the form of complex deferred gifts that are realized after the donor's estate is settled, but that does not mean that every organization must have a dedicated (and often highly compensated) planned giving officer. That model can be the best approach for large, sophisticated organizations. However, most endowment gifts are not overly complex, and a planned giving effort will largely mirror proven traditional fundraising strategies – a focus on nurturing relationships and asking thought-provoking questions. It is only when the donor is ready to consider specific gift vehicles that expertise is required, which is often provided by the donor's own advisors. If necessary, an organization can contract with a specialist, partner with the local community foundation, or nurture its own corps of professional advisors. And, since 80% of planned gifts still come in the form of a simple bequest, the need to rely on these professionals may be less than expected.

"Endowments are complex; only experts on staff can engage donors"

While managing an endowment requires a sophisticated understanding of finance, those same skills are not required to solicit endowment gifts. The job of the fundraiser is to help donors express their convictions about the importance of a cause and its capacity to advance the common good today and in the future. This does not require an in-depth understanding of the difference between a CRUT, a CRAT, and a lead trust. Once the prospect's interest is piqued, endowment building requires in-depth knowledge about the organization, cultivation of long-term relationships, broad understanding of planned giving options, exceptional stewardship of the donor and the gift, and the capacity to craft a gift agreement.

Often, it involves partnerships among endowment champions, staff members, and professional advisors. The champion may know the prospective donor personally and be able to share experiences from their history with the organization. At the same time, a staff member can explain the nuances of various gift planning techniques, the institution's plans and policies, and determine when it is appropriate to call upon professional advisors (including the potential donor's advisors, outside counsel, or the staff of the local community foundation). Once the prospective donor is comfortable exploring an endowment gift, the volunteer's role lessens, freeing them to engage additional prospects.

Endowment building requires consistent face-to-face visits with current and prospective donors over time. This disciplined effort falls to gift officers who manage these relationships in portfolios and document all interactions in the CRM. Many donors do not feel comfortable discussing their personal finances with a peer; they are more likely to do so with a trained staff member who has earned their trust over time.

"It takes too long to see results"

Remember the tortoise and the hare – it is slow and steady effort that wins the race. Frequently, endowment gifts can take 12 to 24 months (often even longer) from cultivation through gift completion. When the late Linda Bowers created the office of leadership gifts at The Ohio State University, she was assigned responsibility for managing the relationship with a prominent family. While the family made numerous contributions over the years, it was the week of Linda's retirement 30 years later when the family finally committed an eight-figure endowment gift. If donors utilize a deferred giving vehicle like a bequest or trust, an organization may not receive the revenue for many additional years. However, as illustrated in this story, the amount of the gift is often substantial: 10 to 1,000 times the donor's average annual gift. The return on each dollar invested in planned giving is typically the highest of all fundraising techniques when measured over the course of years.

Endowment initiatives do not produce quick results. Some volunteers and staff may find more fulfillment in tackling immediate tasks while others take a longer view. The latter will experience the pleasure of witnessing the joy endowment donors feel as they can give larger amounts that have a more transformational impact than they dreamed they could ever achieve.

"We must spend resources today for gifts that might not materialize for years"

That is correct, but it need not be an impediment. How many nonprofit leaders and board members wish that their predecessors had planted the seeds for endowment growth a decade or two ago? "The best time to plant an acorn was 20 years ago," according to the old adage, and "the second-best time is today." The commitment of resources to cultivate and secure gifts, prepare and review paperwork, establish policies and procedures, screen potential gifts, administer the endowment, oversee its investment, and thank and steward donors must be considered at the beginning of the process.

Endowment building requires investing today's resources to deliver on the promise of a pipeline of assets that will be received by the organization's future leaders. It is a tree whose shade may not be enjoyed by today's leaders, but will earn the gratitude of future beneficiaries.

"If we invest our endowment, it could lose value"

Investment losses can occur in any given year but should be considered over the long arc of time. The growth of the endowment needs to allow for withdrawals to fund programs *and* appreciation to keep pace with inflation. There are few (if any) vehicles that will provide the necessary amount of growth to maintain an endowment's "buying power" other than exposure to equity markets, which generally go up but can also go down. A safe investment in a money market fund with low yields may seem low risk, although the risk that the endowment will languish in comparison to other investments is almost certain. When an organization follows the endowment investment policies discussed in Chapter 5, investment volatility is less of a concern than maintaining perpetuity.

Summary and Next Steps

Endowment building does not happen on a whim. It demands careful thought and detailed planning, informed by a thorough assessment of the organization's readiness to proceed. An organization's commitment to endowment building should be validated through board action and backed up with the allocation of resources: staff, systems, and volunteers. It will face objections rooted in endowment myths and require some patience.

With the necessary ingredients in place, an organization can move forward to intentionally build its endowment. The next chapter explores a variety of strategies and provides specific resources to ensure that any strategy put into practice is able to adapt to changing circumstances.

Note

1. Dennis R. Hammond, "Endowments Are Not a Luxury," *The Chronicle of Philanthropy*, May 27-28, 2004, p. B26.

3

A Summary of Endowment-Building Methods

This chapter enables you to:

- Explore various strategies for creating or adding to endowments.
- Determine the strategy/ies that might be most appropriate for an organization or cause.
- Understand the roles of board members, leaders, fundraising staff, and others in implementing an endowment-building strategy.
- Learn about the role of emerging technologies, such as artificial intelligence, in engaging endowment donors.

With an organizational commitment to build or reinvigorate endowment, the next phase of work begins. There are several strategies that might be adopted. An organization on the cusp of a capital campaign might consider adding funding for an endowment to the goal. Another with a large corps of mature long-time donors might launch campaign-style fundraising focused solely on endowment. Some engage a passive "slow drip method," with messages about leaving a legacy placed subtly on every communication with donors. Many embrace an *Endowment Action Plan*, which clearly defines the case for support, measurable goals, tactics to reach the goals, the time frame, and staff and budget requirements.

Other aspects of an endowment-building initiative, such as working with potential donors (Chapters 7 and 8), management and investment methods (Chapter 5), donor and volunteer stewardship and recognition (Chapter 9), and marketing and evaluation (Chapter 4) are discussed in length in subsequent chapters.

> An Endowment Action Plan clearly defines the case for support, measurable goals, tactics to reach the goals, the time frame, and staff and budget requirements.

The Pros and Cons of Endowment-Building Methods

Any organization may adopt several approaches to endowment building over time. A new strategic plan may elevate the imperative of endowment building, while a transition in fundraising leadership could signal waning interest. As any organization commits to building up its endowment, it needs to consider the pros and cons of each approach to determine which one(s) will best meet its needs at any given time. In almost all cases, endowment building takes place alongside – and must complement – annual fundraising activities. The following sections summarize several methods, with supplemental information about measuring success in Chapter 9.

Integrating Endowment into a Capital Campaign

As an organization prepares to launch a campaign to create new facilities or programmatic initiatives, consider including an amount for endowment. This can be particularly effective when some of the endowment is earmarked for the maintenance of envisioned buildings or to sustain the programs that will be accommodated there.

Before adopting this strategy, an organization should assess donors' interests by conducting a campaign planning study and ensure that the rationale for endowment is a vital part of the campaign case for support (see Chapter 4).

Pros of this approach include:

- Endowment building leverages the resources already devoted to the fundraising campaign.
- Campaign volunteers can serve as endowment champions.
- Endowment may appeal to donors who don't wish to support capital.
- Donors can make more significant gifts by blending a current pledge for the capital objectives with a deferred gift devoted to endowment.
- Gifts that lead to permanent recognition (that is, "naming") of a building or its features can require that a portion of the gift be devoted to a maintenance endowment because, after all, the donor will want the new/renewed buildings to preserve their good name.

Cons include:

- Blending capital goals with endowment goals can weaken the focus each objective warrants.
- Cost overruns can entice leaders to shift undesignated gifts from endowment to capital, shortchanging the endowment goal.
- Volunteers and staff may find it challenging to convey multiple messages and discuss various giving vehicles.
- Pledge forms and gift agreements are more complicated.

An Endowment-Only Campaign

All of the trappings of a typical capital campaign can be applied to a singular focus on endowment, including a dedicated corps of high-level volunteers, a strong case for support translated into print and digital marketing tools, a giving pyramid to illustrate the number and magnitude of gifts needed to achieve a goal, and early ("quiet") and public phases. Again, it is essential to evaluate the feasibility of an endowment-only campaign through a campaign planning assessment.

Pros of this approach include:

- Elevates endowment as a clear organizational priority.
- Establishes clear goals to measure progress and assign accountability.
- Empowers staff to invest resources.
- Bolsters confidence in the organization's sustainability.
- Provides a clear structure to transform long-time donors' annual gifts into perpetual, endowed support.

Cons include:

- Resource-intensive with a long-delayed return on investment.
- Does not appeal to all donors.
- Potential for unmet expectations when success is announced but the impact is not immediately apparent to staff and stakeholders.

In Practice: Alternatives to Endowment-Only Campaigns

A museum in America's upper Midwest had developed a *pro forma* demonstrating that an endowment of $50 million, producing an annual draw of $2.2 million, would underwrite their exhibitions and collections care and balance reliance on annual fundraising. They envisioned a straightforward campaign attracting five-year pledges so that the endowment would be in place for their 50th anniversary. Staff crafted a compelling rationale for donors' support and retained a consulting partner to conduct campaign planning assessment.

To their dismay, museum leaders learned that their simple model was not so easy or even practical. Corporate and foundation funders pointed to internal policies that prohibited them from giving to endowment (after all, they viewed their accumulated assets as something of an endowment). Similarly, some of their loyal individual donors expressed a preference for making a gift where they could see the impact immediately, including members of the board who helped to craft the plan. Others were enthused, but asked if they might provide some of their support through a bequest that was already written into their estate plans but might not be realized for decades. Oh my.

In the end, the museum developed a plan to accomplish its goals through an inventive mix of current unrestricted, current restricted, and permanently restricted gifts. The corporations and foundations could support the museum's capacity building (that is, campaign expenses) while sustaining annual operating support; some individual donors could underwrite exhibitions and collections care for the next five years, leaving endowed gifts from others to mature. Other donors made "blended gifts," providing $20,000 per year so that they could see the benefits of their support during their lifetime and designating the museum as a beneficiary of $500,000 from their retirement assets to ensure that the programs could be sustained. And a few gave outright gifts to the endowment through a transfer of assets. Rather than celebrating $50 million at their milestone anniversary, they crafted a creative campaign celebrating one work from the collection each week for the 50 weeks leading up to the milestone.

The "Slow Drip" Method

The "slow drip" method entails subtle – even subliminal – messages over a long period of time about "leaving a legacy" to the organization. Email signatures might have a link to the "ways to give" information on the website; print and digital gift forms might always include a check box to indicate interest in deferred giving; and the newsletter might occasionally feature the story of a donor who supported endowment.

Pros of this method include:

- Can be implemented at little or no cost.
- Focuses on bequests, which constitute 80% of planned gifts (see Chapter 7).
- Can rely on simple and low-cost (or free) planning tools.
- Entirely staff driven.

Cons include:

- Lack of goals or accountability measures.
- No expectation of cash infusions into the endowment today.
- Difficult to track donor engagement or bequest expectancies.
- Easily relegated to a low priority.
- Entirely staff driven.

The Endowment Action Plan

When a campaign isn't in the offing, but the "slow drip" method won't produce sufficient results quickly (and it almost never does), an Endowment Action Plan can be woven into an organization's ongoing fundraising and friend-raising efforts. This method can be especially appealing because it relies primarily on existing fundraising staff and resources applied in a thoughtful, consistent manner. It can flex to complement a capital campaign or other initiatives.

Pros of this method include:

- Elevates endowment to a fundraising priority.
- Provides a structured process with clear accountability measures.
- Defines clear roles for staff and volunteers.
- Integrates easily into the overall fundraising program.
- Strengthens overall fundraising capacity.

Cons include:

- Requires consistent leadership and support.
- Challenging to maintain focus when annual fundraising goals are aggressive.
- May lead to endowed funds that don't focus on organizational priorities.
- May strain organizational capacity.

An Endowment Action Plan is often the preferred method when an organization is committed to building endowment but does not have a campaign on the horizon. It can integrate all of the marketing strategies (see Chapter 4) and fundraising techniques devoted to the annual fundraising program.

An Endowment Action Plan is more intentional than the "slow drip" method, but can easily get overshadowed by the myriad priorities of day-to-day fundraising in pursuit of annual operating support. That's where the RACI method comes into play. Success requires focused effort, which can be elevated through the clear identification of those who are responsible (usually a senior member of the development team – or even the CEO), accountable (distributed across the development team), consulted (usually a dedicated corps of endowment-building champions appointed by the board), and informed (the full board and C-suite). Applying this RACI method can help ensure that the endowment-building plan is implemented consistently and refreshed annually based on the progress made and the lessons learned. See "Bringing It All Together" later in this chapter for a deeper description of an endowment action plan, and Chapter 9 for the performance metrics that sustain steady progress.

Variations of Endowment-Building Tactics

There are myriad other ways that endowment building can be encouraged. Some are stand-alone tactics, while most can be woven into one or more of the strategies described previously.

Campaign Variations

There are many variations on campaigns. Some organizations adopt "special gifts campaigns" or "mini-campaigns" to focus a subset of their donors on a special-purpose endowment. This is common in higher education, where members of a graduation class may create endowment funds tied to a landmark reunion. Museums might rally an affinity group to create an endowment to acquire, care for, and interpret a specific artform, such as contemporary art or photography. The retirement of a beloved leader can provide a platform to create an endowed fund in their name.

A campaign may not be the best strategy for an organization that is taking the first steps of its endowment journey with very modest goals. "Sometimes groups just want 'something to take the edge off' – the stiff drink approach to endowments," Kim Klein writes in Fundraising for Social Change. "They want a pot of money that generates between $5,000 and $10,000 a year, so they only need between $100,000 and $250,000. An endowment campaign is not the best vehicle to raise this small amount of money: For any need of less than $25,000, an organization should consider increasing its annual fundraising goal, perhaps by diversifying to a new strategy or being more aggressive with current donors, or just opening a savings account. Generally it is not worth the effort of starting an actual endowment campaign if your goal is to raise less than $500,000 (p. 330)."[1] Instead, this scenario may call for an Endowment Action Plan.

Matching and Challenge Gifts

Matching and challenge gifts have demonstrated effectiveness and can be applied to endowment building. An equine therapy program sought to build endowment for the care of its horses. Since the care for each animal was estimated to be $10,000 to $12,000 per year, a donor could endow the care for a single horse with a gift of $250,000. To create initial momentum for the effort, a board member pledged to match the first eight commitments, so that a donation of $125,000 would establish one "horse care fund" when combined with the board member's match. Similar strategies could be used for funds of any size.

Giving Circles

Collective giving vehicles such as giving circles can provide donors of any means the opportunity to join with others to create endowed funds larger than any single member could achieve. Together, they can build sufficient resources to provide meaningful support.

Members of a giving circle pool their money and sometimes their time or other assets and decide collectively how to allocate the resources. Sometimes, a nonprofit organization stimulates the creation and ongoing work of a giving circle, and sometimes, the circles emerge organically. Circles can be as informal as a year-end collection at a book club, or highly structured like the Women's Giving Alliance in northeast Florida. WGA members give $1,500, with a portion allocated to current grants and a small allocation for the endowment. Over 20 years, these small allocations grew to an endowment of more than $5 million. Members of WGA gather and vote to allocate the proceeds of both the current and endowed funds. According to Philanthropy Together,[2] an organization that encourages collective giving, there are more than 2,500 giving circles in the United States with 150,000 participants. See more about giving circles in Chapter 4.

Legacy Societies

Legacy societies are created by many organizations to encourage donors to arrange planned gifts (described in Chapter 8) and disclose their intentions by offering membership in a special donor recognition group. Legacy society membership and recognition may also be extended to those who make a current gift to endowment (after all, such donations should be rewarded, not unintentionally discouraged). Legacy society members are recognized in listings and may receive special invitations, such as an annual leadership briefing. The legacy society name may celebrate the organization's heritage, such as the year of the organization's founding or the name of an early patron – further demonstrating the role of generosity in sustaining the cause. Legacy societies provide a comfortable way to approach donors: "I hope you will join with others as a member of the 1890 Society," may be a softer appeal for both the donor and fundraiser than "Please make a $20,000 gift to our endowment," and can even drive gift amounts: "Please consider a gift of $189,000 for our endowment."

Providing Recognition and Naming Opportunities

For many donors, permanent recognition and naming opportunities beyond legacy society membership are appealing. The ability to establish a "named fund" that honors the legacy of an individual or family can be appealing to many donors because it gives the donor the opportunity to enshrine the honoree in perpetuity. Named chairs in higher education are a common example. The recognition may range from listings in print or digital media, a plaque installed in a prominent location, inclusion in program materials, or even the "naming" of a classroom or an entire building, depending on the size of the gift. Recognition does not need to be public to be meaningful: some donors prefer a commemorative item that can be displayed in their home or office. However, naming policies and gift levels require meticulous planning and clear policies to ensure that the gift is sufficient to make a difference (see Chapter 5) and aligns with the organization's vision and values.

Annual Fundraising Events

A group that ensures healthy food for all the children in its region hosts an annual fundraising event with a celebrity speaker and a large host committee. Once the event expenses are paid, the net proceeds are deposited into an endowed fund at the local community foundation. Because the fundraising and marketing materials specify that the proceeds will benefit the endowment, it is classified as permanently restricted true endowment. The event has the added benefit of introducing a large number of new donors to the cause.

Peer-to-Peer Fundraising

Peer-to-peer fundraising initiatives that employ purpose-built technology have gained popularity and can be especially effective in engaging younger donors. A group of volunteers invites others to support the cause, generally through social media, and often deploying tools such as posts and email messages provided by the organization. They may ask their peers to donate on a specific "giving day," or to give in response to the volunteer taking on an endurance challenge such as walking or running a prescribed distance or dancing for an extended number of hours. Short videos can be employed to allow volunteers to tell their story. Peer-to-peer efforts are typically short bursts of fundraising activity and often focused on a specific outcome such as endowing a scholarship or other concrete and attainable goal.

Endowment as Public Policy

In a more recent development, voters in the state of Texas showed strong support for Proposition 5, a statewide constitutional amendment that will create a $3.9 billion endowment fund from budget surpluses to fuel research at "emerging" universities, with a goal of making them more impactful and competitive. Other states have incentivized gifts to endowment with special enticements such as tax credits in Iowa, Kentucky, Maryland, Montana, and North Dakota. Such state initiatives are especially important to counter the negative impact of the 2018 "Tax Cuts and Jobs Act," which significantly diminished federal tax incentives for charitable giving.

Proactive Policies

Any organization can (should) adopt a board policy to allocate the major share of any undesignated bequest to the endowment, as described in Chapter 5. After all, the assets that a donor accumulated over a lifetime shouldn't be expended in a single year to pay the electric bill or deferred maintenance costs. And because bequests cannot be predicted, no organization should count on these monies to balance their annual budget. Instead, a small amount of each bequest received – perhaps the first $25,000 – might be allocated to this year's budget, with the remainder devoted to the endowment. Because this is a decision made by the board and not the donor, the funds will be considered quasi-endowment.

In Practice: The Emerging Role of Artificial Intelligence[3]

Even as this book is written, the use of AI in fundraising and philanthropy is rapidly evolving. There are six distinct AI technologies, several of which have applications in building endowment, first described by the author in a post for Forbes.Com:

- **Large language models** are the most ubiquitous use of AI, sometimes called "generative AI." ChatGPT and Bard are among the best-known early examples. Maybe they can write a case for endowment or a "thank you" letter to an endowment donor, but will it sound warm and authentic? It may be a place to start but the output will need a human touch before sending to a donor. And the warnings on these tools also confirm that they can be wrong yet persuasive. For example, ChatGPT recently stated that "professional fundraising counsel may involve … a percentage-based compensation structure tied to funds raised …" a big ethical no-no.
- **Machine learning** (or deep learning) can be applied to large datasets to predict outcomes. One such use is analyzing a large donor dataset to identify the best prospects for current or planned gifts to support the endowment. Careless use of tools like these can expose an organization to concerns about data security and donor privacy.
- **AI automation** can make support functions like stewardship more efficient. Imagine a website widget that can answer a donor's most basic questions and identify the right development officer for follow-up. But, as an eating-disorder helpline discovered when their chatbot dispensed potentially deadly advice, chatbots may not be ready to replace humans in all cases.
- **Blockchain** creates an "immutable ledger" to track financial transactions. Imagine tracking all expenditures related to a designated endowment, providing effortless accountability and reporting. We're not there yet, but it's coming.
- **AI/IoT**, or AI applied to the "internet of things," can provide constant monitoring, measurement, and

(continued)

management. AI/IoT already surrounds us through "smart" technologies like thermostats and security systems, which could decrease operating costs – all implemented through the draw on an endowment dedicated to maintaining facilities.

- **Artificial and/or virtual reality** will become a powerful storytelling tool, helping trigger a donor's empathy. It might be expensive or even impossible to take donors to an untouched wilderness, but a visit through a virtual reality headset could convince them of the need to endow its preservation.

AI holds great promise, and where could that potential do more long-term good than by fueling endowments? Yet the risks are also significant. Nonprofits enjoy a greater level of trust than every other sector, which can be undermined when a donor receives an artificial-sounding letter or learns that sensitive personal data was shared with a third-party vendor. AI may be heralded as unbiased, but it actually reflects the biases of its human creators. Caution – and good policies – will be needed here. A good resource for any organization considering the use of AI is the "Framework for Responsible Use of AI," which can be found at www.fundraising.ai.

Hoarding Funds

One tactic that *won't* work is hoarding. Too often, a cautious board treats the endowment like a "rainy day fund" in a climate of constant sunshine. They leave the funds in the endowment to grow, thinking that their fiscal discipline will impress donors, but it has exactly the opposite effect. What donor wants to shift funds from their investment accounts only to have them sit idly on the books of a nonprofit organization whose investment strategies may not be as effective? Most donors want to experience the fruits of their generosity.

Even if the annual draw isn't "needed" to fund programs, it should be released into the operating budget and devoted to good works. As a result, the organization's mission will be advanced, donors will experience the joy of giving, and there will be a new story of philanthropic impact to add to the content library. Because money is fungible, the board can then elect to deposit an amount equal to the draw into the quasi-endowment, which will provide even greater financial strength and flexibility in the future.

> Most donors want to experience the fruits of their generosity.

Roles: Who Helps to Build Endowment?

Regardless of the strategies employed, everyone involved with an organization or institution can participate in the endowment-building program – success depends on it! The work of endowment building cannot be delegated to one staff member or volunteer; it is a team effort. Even in a "small shop" with limited staff, board members and advisors can contribute to the effort. In a larger organization, effective endowment building accentuates the traits of a strong culture of philanthropy, where everyone is aware of the merits of endowment, engages with supporters and nurtures their interests, and ensures that the organization is worthy of perpetual support because it is well managed in pursuit of its mission. Consider the following roles:

- The **board of directors** provides essential leadership and direction. By creating and refreshing the organization's strategic plan, they define the role of endowment. By adopting (and periodically reaffirming) a motion to build the endowment, they demonstrate commitment. They develop and approve appropriate gift acceptance and investment policies, invest resources – budget and staff time – in endowment, monitor endowment progress and performance, and ensure that endowment draws align with the donor's intent and benefit the community. They demonstrate patience and persistence of vision. Each individual on the board also has responsibilities: to support the endowment as their own financial resources permit, to serve as an enthusiastic advocate, and to demonstrate their commitment by showing up at endowment-related events, introducing their own peers and professional advisors to the organization and its endowment, and supporting the development office as they call on prospective donors.

- The **president, CEO, or executive director** is responsible for monitoring the creation and implementation of an endowment-building strategy. The persistent vision and support of this leader ensures that endowment is an ongoing topic for board attention and a priority for staff members who receive the necessary support and resources.
- The **chief financial officer** manages the stewardship of funds and works with the development office and board committees to draft policies and agreements for the board's approval. Members of the finance staff prepare investment performance updates for the board, and prepare accurate content for the donor stewardship reports, the annual report, audited financial statements, and tax filings. Occasionally, the CFO may meet with donors and their advisors to explain investment vehicles and spending policies and may also draft gift agreements.
- The **chief fundraising officer** ensures that specific, measurable endowment-building tactics are defined and that each party participating in the effort has the requisite understanding and resources to fulfill their role. This leader also creates a culture of cooperation so the entire team works collaboratively to engage donors and secure gifts. They spread credit liberally.
- Other "frontline" **gift officers** understand the endowment and are adept at identifying the alignment between a donor's interests and the potential alignment with a specific endowment gift.

They are assigned responsibilities to work with specific donors, meet with them on a regular basis, present giving opportunities including endowment, and consistently record their actions in the CRM. In a large organization, there may be a dedicated **planned giving officer** who supports their colleagues and manages a small cohort of unique donors. The optimal traits for these fundraising professionals are explored in Chapter 8.

- The **development operations** (or advancement services) team helps to identify, qualify, and research potential endowment donors; record and track gifts, pledges, and deferred intentions; and support stewardship efforts.
- **Marketing and communications professionals** must support the effort through consistent and compelling messages about endowment compiled in a *case for support* (see Chapter 4). It is essential to educate the giving community about the basics of endowment: what it is, how it is accumulated and deployed, and the benefits for those who are served. This marketing must precede any endowment-building effort, especially a campaign. It may take the form of focused messages on each of the non-profit's channels, of endowment stories woven into talking points and remarks at special events, or intimate "leadership briefings" leading up to the effort. The messages are rooted in stories about donors and the constituents who benefit from endowment gifts and draws (see more about fundraising stories in Chapters 7 and 8). These stories are woven regularly into day-to-day communication platforms including social media, earned media, paid media, the organization's print publications, and even onsite displays. Imagine the power of an inspired donor who creates a fund to furnish supplies in an early learning classroom – with the story told through the eyes of donors, educators, and parents.
- Even **program staff** have a role to play. After all, they are in daily contact with clients, patients, students, visitors, or patrons and can see the opportunities where endowment could make a difference. Program directors, teachers, deans and academic

leaders, clinicians, and others are willing to interact with potential donors and educate them about their work and its impact, knowing that an endowed fund created by an inspired donor could elevate and perpetuate that impact.

• The teamwork extends even further. **Professional advisors** can play an important role in substantiating the merits of the organization's endowment management (see Chapter 8). Often, **auxiliary groups**, like the hands-on volunteers at a foodbank, docent corps of a museum, or the alumni association of a small college, can become informed ambassadors (and are a promising source of potential donors). And finally, the **donors** themselves may be among the most enthusiastic influencers, creating a "follow the leader" effect that can assure others that the cause is worthwhile.

> The work of endowment building cannot be delegated to one staff member or volunteer; it is a team effort.

Bringing It All Together with an Endowment Action Plan

Given all the strategies to choose from and the involvement of so many people, any serious commitment to building endowment must be clearly planned and documented, not left to chance. In the case of endowment as a part of a campaign, the discipline should already be in place. Whenever endowment building happens outside of a campaign, an Endowment Action Plan is essential.

An Endowment Action Plan must be a written document that is refreshed annually and integrated into the overall annual fundraising plan. It should reflect the strengths and weaknesses identified in the assessment described in Chapter 2. It establishes a long-term goal (perhaps 5 to 10 years) with an estimate of the number of gifts, average gift amounts, and the number of potential donors who must be engaged on an annual – or even quarterly – basis.

The Endowment Action Plan should include the following information:

- The rationale for building endowment articulated in a case for support (Chapter 4)
- Gift options available to donors (Chapter 8)
- Staff responsibilities
- Volunteer roles and structure (Chapter 9)
- The process for identifying and qualifying potential endowment donors (Chapter 7)
- Tactics to engage potential donors (Chapter 9)
- Extending the invitation to give and documentation (Chapters 8 and 9)
- Recognition and stewardship of endowment donors (Chapter 5)
- Marketing the endowment (Chapter 4)
- Budget (Chapter 9)
- Evaluation of the Endowment Action Plan (Chapter 9)

The written plan doesn't need to be a long, detailed narrative. It can be as simple as a chart (see the simple example called Endowment Action Plan Example in the Resources section). By revisiting the plan each year, reflecting on past results, and anticipating the payoff for consistent effort, the plan will become more refined and accurate. A summary of the plan should be a part of the board's budget rationale so their buy-in ensures that the endowment gains sufficient resources and attention, and the board understands that they bear some responsibility for its success, just as they do for all fundraising tactics. The measurable activities should be integrated into the CRM so that progress can be measured easily and reported regularly.

Summary and Next Steps

All this planning and documentation may sound daunting, and there is a strong temptation to take shortcuts and just seize opportunities along the way. Don't do it! As Thomas Edison said, "Good fortune is what happens when opportunity meets with planning." Others may complain that the final tally at the end of the year always differs from the model described at the outset. They should be reminded that "plans are nothing, planning is everything" (Dwight Eisenhower).

Taking the steps necessary to plan the path to a robust endowment is an essential prerequisite for developing the case for giving, which is discussed in the next chapter. Then, with a solid plan and compelling case, an organization is in an excellent position to identify and engage potential donors and help them consider the best ways to structure a gift (Chapter 8), and to ensure good stewardship of endowed resources by adopting effective policies for gift acceptance and endowment management (Chapter 5).

Notes

1. Kim Klein, *Fundraising for Social Change* (Hoboken, New Jersey: Wiley, 2016).
2. "About» Philanthropy Together," Philanthropy Together, June 29, 2023, https://philanthropytogether.org/about/.
3. Much of this content originally appears as Laura MacDonald, "AI and Nonprofits: Not If or How But When," *Forbes.com Nonprofit Council* (blog), September 17, 2023, https://www.forbes.com/sites/forbesnonprofitcouncil/2023/09/27/ai-and-nonprofits-not-if-or-when-but-how/?sh=ee5e7eb2bf6a.

4

Making the Case for Support and Marketing Endowment

This chapter enables you to:

- Articulate the role of a case for support in building endowment.
- Understand the process of writing a case for support and the roles of various contributors.
- Determine whether a case has the content to substantiate and differentiate a cause and resonate with donors.
- Translate the case for support into a variety of marketing messages and materials.
- Identify the audience(s) for endowment marketing and address their interests.

Why should a donor give to endowment? After all, every cause strives to meet immediate needs and fund important initiatives today. How can an organization ask for future support without undermining urgency and securing current support? If a donor decides to give to endowment, how will their funds be managed and deployed to make a difference? And why should one particular organization be entrusted with the endowment, when there are so many others devoted to the same cause? A strong case for support (a "case") will answer all these questions and more, and then become the bedrock for all endowment marketing.

Start with a Compelling Vision

Big gifts stem from big ideas. Most gifts to endowment are "big," although the definition of "big" may vary depending on the cause and the donor. So the best rationale for endowment is rooted in a big, visionary idea captured in the case. For a land conservancy in Appalachia, it was the urgency of ensuring perpetual protection for acres of untouched wilderness that would be deeded to the organization only if there were assurances that it could be stewarded forever. For a pediatric health center in California, it was the vision of a new state-of-the-art care site that could be financed through bonds, but only with the financial guarantee of an operating and maintenance endowment in place. For an art museum in the Midwest, it was a donor's desire to ensure that the curators could seize sudden opportunities to acquire new works from diverse living artists.

> Big gifts stem from big ideas.

The absence of a clear, compelling vision articulated in a case can thwart the most meticulous planning and diligent effort. Consider the dilemma of a community's united appeal for the arts that raised most of their annual funding through workplace-giving campaigns. Proceeds were allocated annually to maintain a vibrant arts scene that was one of the city's hallmarks. Leaders observed that donors were nearing retirement, and their ranks weren't being replaced by an influx of younger employee-donors. In response, they asked existing donors to "annuitize" their support by giving a gift to the endowment so that the draw would replace their annual gift. It fell flat. An art-loving middle-manager consistently gave $1,200 per year through payroll deduction – her single largest charitable gift most years. She was unmoved when asked to make a pledge of $25,000: it was beyond her means to give that much, especially as she neared retirement and was anxious about resources. It seemed to diminish the significance of her current giving, and the request was rooted in a financial equation with no context for the importance of perpetual support for the cause. She felt she was being treated like an ATM, not a valued donor. It lacked vision.

To be effective, a strong case for support must answer four key questions.

- **What is the big idea?** As illustrated in the previous story, an organization must present a vision worthy of major investment. Donors are interested in more than a transaction. They aspire to achieve transformation.
- **Why this cause?** Donors – especially those considering significant investments – wish to give where they see the greatest potential to achieve impact: the hospital best positioned to cure a disease, for example, or the human rights organization with the strongest track record of supporting women. To answer, "why this cause," a case must *substantiate* (prove the organization is trustworthy and can deliver on its promises) and *differentiate* (demonstrate that the organization is in the *best* position to fulfill its mission and realize supporters' dreams).
- **Why now?** Momentum, urgency, growing need or opportunity – a case should credibly define the reasons a donor ought to consider a gift or commitment at *this* particular moment in time. Urgency might be embedded in a strategy, such as a time-limited matching gift. It should also be conveyed through impact: funding research to save lives today and in the future or endowing the community organizer role to protect hard-won gains.
- **Why should donors care?** Most importantly, the case for support must *resonate* or provide content that can evoke an emotional response to the cause.

Each of these ingredients is discussed in greater detail in the coming pages.

What Is a "Case for Support"?

A case for support is a written document that describes how donations will be used to advance the cause. It can be called by other names (see the sidebar In Practice: "What's In a Name?"). The length of the document varies widely by cause, organization, mission, and purpose. It is usually too long to hold the attention of a typical donor, but that's not the primary audience, as discussed next. The case is an *internal* resource document that ensures a consistent message. It is a *policy* document that defines the fundraising objectives and, therefore, the gifts that will be counted toward the stated goal. It is a *resource* document that can be used by everyone from the stewardship office to the external marketing partner, making their efforts more efficient and consistent.

In Practice: What's in a Name?

Case for support. Case statement. Case for giving. Case. Statement of need. People use a variety of monikers, sometimes interchangeably and sometimes with different meanings.

According to the *AFP Global Fundraising Dictionary*,[1] a case explains "the reasons why an organization both needs and merits philanthropic support, usually by outlining the organization's programs, current needs, and plans." A case for support is a fundamental resource for any organization implementing a capital, endowment, or comprehensive campaign. It is a best practice to develop a case for all fundraising initiatives, including annual fundraising and endowment-building programs.

Usually, the formal case for support is a comprehensive resource document. It ensures that everyone involved in the fundraising effort understands the rationale for giving and the use of contributions. It is also a policy document that should

---

be approved by the board. Sometimes it is described as a "philanthropic investment prospectus." Because it carries the burden of so much due diligence, it is not primarily a donor-facing document. Rather, it is a tool for gift officers and the consistent resource to be used whenever creating messages for supporters in a variety of media.

Some practitioners use the term "case statement" to refer to an external marketing document that is a summary of the case for support, supplemented with simple illustrations and graphic elements – sort of like a magazine article. Others might refer to this condensed version of the case as a "donor prospectus." This document is more comprehensive than most marketing materials, used with sophisticated donors who perform extensive research before making a major gift. Others may use "case for support" and "case statement" interchangeably.

"Case for giving," "fundraising case," "donor prospectus" and similar terms are almost always synonyms for "case for support." The term "statement of need" has fallen out of favor because most practitioners understand that "need" isn't a strong rationale for giving.

Whatever an organization chooses to call its fundraising rationale, it is important to define terms and audiences before setting out to create and utilize documents.

Who Is It For?

Before any writing can commence, define the audience for the case for support. It is not intended for general distribution. Its primary audience is internal: staff members and key volunteers who are responsible for crafting fundraising messages and engaging one-on-one with donors. It should be shared with the entire board and – ideally – adopted by the governing body as a policy document in order to codify the fundraising objectives. For example, an independent school that is focused on endowing scholarships and other student access initiatives wouldn't want to count a gift to endow the athletic facilities as a part of their endowment campaign goal (although they may still accept the gift and recognize the donor). On occasion, a sophisticated donor or a donor's advisors may request the document so that they can ensure an organize has done its due diligence. Largely, the case is in the background, constantly mined for talking points, grant applications, and marketing materials, and periodically updated to reflect the most current information.

> The primary audience for the case is internal: staff members and key volunteers who craft fundraising messages and engage one-on-one with donors.

What Is Its Purpose?

A case for endowment support can be a challenge to write. Endowment donors who give to the future of the organization must be confident of the long-term value and viability of an organization and its mission. An organization must be able to articulate a complex message, boiled down into simple and strong concepts that can be easily conveyed to donor audiences through platforms ranging from social media to weighty coffee-table tomes. It must meet the following criteria:

- The case positions gifts to the endowment as investments that are consistent with the values and interests of the donor and the larger community served by the cause.
- The case is based on strengths, not organizational "needs." Successful organizations identify issues in the community and then demonstrate how their – and their donors' – response forever meets the needs of those they serve, such as clients, students, or audiences.

- The case must see the organization through the eyes of its supporters, rather than its own introspective point of view. The voice positions supporters as the agents of change, either individually or collectively. For example, rather than saying "our cause can endure and change the world with your support," reframe the acknowledgment for change by stating that "donors can change the world by endowing our cause."
- The case positions the organization – its impact and longevity – in a broad context of community and society. It sets a tone of abundance, rather than need. For example, the organization has abundant vision to elevate the cause and donors will sustain the work with their support.
- For an endowment, the case bolsters confidence that the cause is evergreen, and the organization is trustworthy and will sustain its efforts indefinitely.
- Both emotional and rational, the case includes stories that appeal to the heart, as well as statistical data that demonstrate the broad impact of the work.
- The case must make an impact, which is best accomplished if it is succinct, organized, and meaningful. It also conveys a sense of urgency to encourage immediate action by the donor.
- The case must be accurate and, in order to be of ongoing value, it should be refreshed periodically to keep the information current.

What's Included in an Endowment Case for Support?

There may be a temptation to take a "kitchen sink" approach to the case for support. Even though it is a detailed "philanthropic investment prospectus," it should not become a *magnum opus* with every tiny detail of the organization's existence and vision. The narrative should be punctuated with both data and stories following the mandate of philanthropy expert Jacob Harold, "no stories without data, no data without stories." The outline of a strong case for endowment support might look like this:

- **Introduction:** A strong case begins with something larger than the institution. It places the organization in the context of the cause it addresses. A case for an art museum may begin with a brief treatise on the transformational role of creativity in society. An organization that focuses on a specific disease might begin by illustrating the worldwide benefits of eradicating the disease. Sometimes this narrative is conveyed through a powerful story (see more about fundraising stories in Chapter 7). The introduction goes on to summarize the organization's vision and concludes by presenting the fundraising objective. All of this is contained in a brief yet powerful three or four paragraph statement that can sometimes stand alone as a fundraising "manifesto."

Then comes the expansive content of the document, organized to convey a rational and compelling story with the following ingredients:

- **Background:** This section provides enough background to demonstrate that the organization has a relevant mission, pursues it through effective activities, enjoys solid management, and is guided by trusted leaders on the board. This section may be punctuated with stories that illustrate the beneficial outcomes for those served by the cause. The objective is to demonstrate the organization's trustworthiness.
- **The vision – or big idea:** This lofty goal will be fulfilled by building sustainable financial resources. The rationale might be supported with credible research illustrating the challenge to be addressed, stories about the constituents to be served, and linked to a current, effective strategic plan.
- **A call to action:** This describes the role of endowment in solving wicked problems or realizing evergreen goals. In this section, various endowment fund giving opportunities might be described, such as endowed scholarships or leadership positions; funds that align with specific expressions of the mission (animal care at the zoo, land acquisition for a conservancy, or research for a cause focused on climate change).

- **A rousing conclusion:** This brings it all together in something of a mirror of the opening. It restates the vision and the role that endowment will play in realizing the vision and then sustaining the good work.

The purpose isn't to describe everything under the sun, but to provide enough information to:

- **Substantiate** the organization's capacity to deliver effective and impactful activities in pursuit of a relevant mission, its fidelity to the vision, and reliability in managing resources. Often, this is achieved through data that illustrate the impact of programs.
- **Differentiate**, or demonstrate why a particular organization is best suited to deliver on the promise. While this can be a place for self-laudatory accolades and awards, differentiation can also be demonstrated through the endorsement of trusted experts, or testimony from grateful members of the community.
- Finally, a case must **resonate**. Put simply, it must contain nuggets of content that make people care. The best way to evoke this emotional response is through stories of impact. See Chapter 7 for the distinction between anecdotes and stories, and the elements of an effective fundraising story.

The failure to address any one of these ingredients will doom the effectiveness of the case for support. Table 4-1 illustrates the result of having missing ingredients.

TABLE 4-1 Missing Case Ingredients

Missing Case Ingredient			Resulting Donor Response
~~Substantiate~~	**Differentiate**	**Resonate**	"I don't believe you can deliver on your promises."
Substantiate	~~Differentiate~~	**Resonate**	"Someone else can do it better."
Substantiate	**Differentiate**	~~Resonate~~	"I don't care."

Developing an Endowment Case for Support

Writing tends to be a solitary task, but the writer can't simply go off to the woods to spend hours in isolated concentration. The objective of the case writing process is two-fold: to develop a document that will serve as a useful resource for all endowment-building activities and to extend ownership of the cause by engaging a variety of stakeholders in the process.

> The objective of the case-writing process is two-fold: to develop a document that will serve as a useful resource and to extend ownership of the cause by engaging a variety of stakeholders.

Form a Task Force

Sometimes, a Case for Support Task Force is assembled, which engages key supporters and staff leaders to help guide the process and vet the document at various stages of its development. A task force is typically comprised of representatives of the internal stakeholders necessary to affirm the organization's vision and shape its messaging: leaders from executive, fundraising, and marketing and other subject matter experts. External stakeholders, such as select board members or donors, can also be invited to serve on the task force or join designated meetings to provide insight and counsel – and to deepen their engagement with the organization.

To avoid the dangers of "writing by committee," task force members should be given clear assignments. For example, they may be asked to identify potential interviewees, gather an inventory of stories, or secure the endorsement of respected experts. When they are asked to weigh in on the content of the document, their input can remain at an appropriately high level (that is, no "my favorite word!") by asking them to respond to four simple questions – What is the "big idea"? Does the case substantiate? Does it differentiate? Does it resonate?

The process of developing the case for endowment support is more than a creative writing exercise; it is also a consensus-building exercise. Surprisingly, the development of a case for support might be the first time that fundraising objectives and proposed uses for the endowment – programmatic, financial, and other – are defined in writing. It builds consensus, since the written document may introduce various stakeholders to the rationale for endowment and its proposed uses, stated definitively. A board member may have thought "we need to endow the president's salary," while the CFO covets unrestricted endowment, and a young alum recognizes the need for endowed scholarships. The process of writing and reviewing the case for support will help to bring about a common vision for the use(s) of endowed funds. One of the first responsibilities of the Case Task Force, therefore, is to come to agreement and help to bring about a common vision for the use of endowed funds. What activities are being prioritized for endowment support, how much do they aim to secure, and what opportunities will donors have to designate their gifts and be recognized? Hopefully, some preliminary work has already taken place to define endowment and recognition policies (see Chapter 5).

Much content for the case can be gleaned from existing documents like the strategic plan or an encyclopedic grant application. To add interest, the writing team might interview front-line staff and beneficiaries of the organization to integrate their stories. When possible, potential endowment donors and advocates should be consulted: their involvement brings credibility and may increase the strength of their support or the magnitude of their gifts.

Consider a Case Brief

Writing a case for support can be a daunting assignment. The writer devotes many hours and much energy to the task. To ensure that the case is headed in the right direction consider a preliminary step: the creation of a case brief. The brief is not an outline or a summary of the proposed document; rather, it serves as the recipe. A succinct three- to five-page document lays out the direction the writer plans to take by defining the audience, voice, key messages, and proposed goal. It postulates answers to questions such as: why build endowment, why now, and what is our desired impact? How will investments in endowment align with the values and interests of donors? If endowment building is integrated into a campaign (stand-alone or comprehensive), the case brief is a good time to introduce a campaign theme.

Gaining consensus at this stage increases the likelihood that a substantial amount of work will be rewarded with a useful resource. Because the next step is the hard work of writing.

Engage Key Supporters

The writing process may also be leveraged to engage potential endowment supporters. Key supporters can be asked to review the case brief or an early draft, either individually and informally or as members of a task force created for the purpose. If the endowment-building effort will have a campaign theme, social media can be employed to determine which turns-of-phrase elicit the greatest positive response.

In an age of 280-character social media posts and ubiquitous videos, a lengthy written document may seem anachronistic. Yet, organizations that shortchange this crucial step find that their endowment-building efforts languish due to the lack of a shared vision or clear purpose for the fund(s). Or they find that small, endowed funds proliferate based solely on the interests and capacities of donors: it's not uncommon to find a small college or independent schools with a plethora of tiny scholarship or academic funds that place a burden on management, provide scant benefits to the recipients, and may go unused for years. By marrying the case for endowment support with appropriate policies (see Chapter 6), the cause will be well served for generations to come.

With these principles in mind, the writing can commence.

From the Field: Using the Case for Support Process as a Donor Cultivation Tool

The case for support can also be a powerful tool to engage donors. By inviting supporters to help shape the case for support, organizations demonstrate how highly they value donors' insights, stories, and experiences.

A careful balance must be struck between authentically seeking and using feedback, and ensuring the organization remains "in the driver's seat" and maintains control over the ultimate vision.

Organizations have utilized strategies such as the following to cultivate donors in meaningful ways while gathering information that is useful and useable.

- **Donors can be interviewed when a writer is gathering information for the case for support.** Specific and appreciative questions are preferred: when have you seen the organization at its best? Why should others trust this organization with their philanthropic investments? In your view, when this vision is fulfilled, what will be different and better?
- **Supporters can be invited to share their personal stories and testimonials.** This can include their experiences as recipients of the organization's services, and/or the factors that motivated their past generosity.
- **Key donors can be asked to review the case brief or an early draft of the case for support**, either individually and informally or as members of a task force created for the purpose. When involving donors at this

(continued)

stage in the process, organizations should be sure to employ guardrails to guide the feedback desired and mitigate "line editing."

• **If the endowment-building effort will have a "theme," social media can be employed** to determine which turns-of-phrase elicit the greatest positive response.

—Contributed by Megan Simmons,
Senior Writer, Benefactor Group

To complement the case for support, a proactive organization will also maintain a content library of stories, refreshing it from time to time. These can be written narratives or audio or video recordings, showing the impact of endowment for the beneficiaries, the cause, and the donor. Stories should be aligned with the endowment-building objectives described in the case and approved by the board.

How the Case for Support Is Employed in Endowment Building

This all seems like a lot of effort for a document that is utilized by just a handful of staff members, creative vendors, and donors. Yet, it is a crucial step that should not be skipped or minimized. Both the *process* of gaining consensus and engaging stakeholders and the work *product* ensure that endowment building is widely understood and embraced.

It is a best practice to ask all board members to read the full case for support and to affirm it through a formal action documented in the board minutes. That way, fundraising objectives are less likely to drift when a donor wants to create a new endowment that doesn't advance the organization's mission.

The case for support now becomes an essential resource. When a creative design firm is retained to develop public-facing materials, their work is streamlined (and costs are reduced) because all content can be drawn from the case. A grant writer doesn't need to start from scratch for each proposal; they can pluck paragraphs *verbatim* from the document. Whether the board chair needs talking points, or the social media team needs short quips, the case for support is the source. By relying on a singular document for all of these messages, the initiative is more likely to gain a following because all stakeholders are hearing powerful stories and a consistent rationale.

> It is a best practice to ask all board members to read the full case for support and to affirm it through a formal action.

Marketing the Endowment

With the completion of a compelling case that has been affirmed by stakeholders, it is time to create the messages and collateral that will engage and inspire donors. "Digital and print collateral isn't what persuades donors to give," according to fundraising brand strategist Chad Paris. "These mediums elevate the organization's campaign as a reflection of its brand. They bolster the confidence of the best ambassadors – staff and volunteers – by giving those ambassadors tools to communicate about the vision." People give because of relationships, and the role of marketing is to deepen the connections between people and the causes they care about.

Marketing is most effective when it is woven into the entire fundraising process and engages all groups within an organization. A successful strategy for marketing the endowment starts with consistent messaging (drawn from the case for support) and integrates with all other assets from the organization's brand (or a distinct campaign brand if endowment building is integrated into a campaign effort). Some organizations achieve this synergy by combining their fundraising and marketing functions in a single department, which is often called an "advancement" or "external affairs" model. This holistic model can be further strengthened with the addition of other outward-facing functions such as alumni affairs, volunteer management, or government relations. It ensures that all efforts are coordinated to achieve shared goals. In an organization where fundraising (or "development") is separate from other functions, relationships with coworkers in marketing – or outside vendors – must be carefully tended so that they understand the purpose and importance of endowment building.

Identifying the Audience

Several different audiences can influence success in building endowment. These audiences must be clearly identified so that marketing strategies will appeal to them.

- **Individuals and families.** More than 90% of gifts to an endowment come from people – either through lifetime gifts or through their estates. Part II of this book is devoted to the traits and behaviors of individuals who make generous charitable gifts, especially enduring gifts to endowment. While a deep understanding of these donors will help to guide personal engagement, a general understanding can help to shape marketing materials and strategies. Some of the most common traits include:
    - Close ties to the organization through voluntarism and participation
    - A long record of giving, regardless of gift amount
    - Service on a leadership body such as the board of trustees, foundation board, or alumni association board
    - Age 50 or older
    - Few direct heirs, or successful direct heirs

- Evidence of endowment gifts to other organizations

The identification of these potential endowment supporters may be as simple as scrutinizing the donor rolls or as sophisticated as a philanthropic screening of the database (see Chapter 7).

- **Foundations and corporations.** Foundations and corporations are less likely to make gifts to endowments. Why? In the case of the former, they view themselves as an endowed cause with annual grantmaking as the primary expression of their values (see Chapter 7). Corporations seek the accountability and connectedness that comes from annual giving. Yet both of these sources may support endowment efforts by funding marketing materials, staffing, technology, or other capacity building. Some corporations and foundations contribute challenge or matching gifts that provide incentives for individuals to give. Or they might help to launch or sustain a program with current gifts for a few years as an endowment is created to fund the program permanently. This last tactic can be especially effective because institutional funders tend to avoid gifts and grants that lead to a long-term dependency.

Even if they don't give directly to endowed funds, keep the representatives of corporations and foundations informed about endowment plans and progress. Their confidence will be bolstered when they see an organization taking steps toward resilience.

There are a few exceptions. The Ohio Society of CPAs found that accounting firms throughout the state were willing to fund scholarship endowments, knowing that the result would be a source of diverse candidates entering the field of accounting. The owners of private businesses who have a long-term association with a cause may be personally interested in supporting an endowment – either in their own name or via the business. Be sure that these audiences are kept up-to-date on endowment building efforts, too.

- **Allied professionals.** A women's fund in Canada reported that nearly 60% of its endowment gifts came through referrals from professional advisors. These counselors can dramatically accelerate endowment building efforts – or hamper them if they aren't convinced that their clients' money will be well managed or relationships well tended. Marketing directly to wealth advisors, trust and estate attorneys, tax accountants who serve individuals and families, "family office" consortia, and even insurance brokers can ensure that they are prepared to encourage their clients' charitable giving. It is unlikely – though not unheard of – that these professional advisors will advocate for gifts to any specific organization or cause. Rather, marketing efforts provide them with information that makes it easy to facilitate their clients' existing philanthropic priorities.

  Develop a corps of well-informed professional advisors. Ask donors who they work with; see if the local community foundation maintains a committee of advisors; or seek input from associations of wealth planners, tax accountants, and trust and estate counsel. Engage this group through general and endowment-focused marketing efforts. Consider hosting occasional professional development for them (ensuring that it will meet their industry's requirements for continuing education). But be careful that they do not overstep boundaries and begin to view your pool of donors as a ripe opportunity for business development.

- **The in-house team.** The hard work of endowment building relies on every employee to serve as an informed advocate. Front-line team members such as caregivers in healthcare, early learning teachers, or faculty of a college can provide the stories that fuel the case for support. Volunteers who interact with the public can propel a donor's interest. Those in the finance office can respond to questions about endowment management. A stray comment by anyone from the board chair to the gallery guard can bolster or undermine efforts to build endowment. Each of these people should understand:

- How the endowment will provide for the long-term health of the entire organization
- How their efforts relate to – and benefit from – the growth of the endowment
- How the endowment works
- How prospective donors to the endowment will be identified, cultivated, and asked for gifts

Always be prepared to respond to inquiries from professional advisors, potential donors, and other members of the community. Many organizations include a "ways to give" section on their website that provides opportunities to support broadly defined programs through gifts to the endowment, legal and tax identification information, and even the specific wording for making a charitable bequest that can be added to a will (see an example in the Resources section).

Marketing Strategies and Tools

Marketing plans define what will be done to promote gifts to the endowment, as well as how, where, and by whom. The likelihood of meeting fundraising goals and exceeding expectations increases with thorough planning and effective implementation, documented in a brief written road map. Marketing strategies should be measurable so that an organization can track metrics and determine which strategies provided the greatest ROI.

The primary goal of all endowment marketing is simply this: to encourage prospective donors to raise their hand and indicate their interest in learning more. That's it. Once a prospective donor has indicated interest, a representative of the organization can engage them in further discussions about potential ways to fund endowment through a current or planned gift (see Chapters 7 and 8), programs or activities that can benefit from an endowed fund, opportunities to create a legacy through donor recognition, and more. But none of those conversations can take place until endowment giving has piqued the donor's interest. Some of the ways to encourage a donor to self-identify include these tactics, which are described in greater detail in the pages that follow:

- Ask "Have you included ABC cause in your will?" in every form of print and digital communication and add it (with a link) to the email signatures of appropriate staff members who communicate frequently with donors through email. See sample language for bequests in the Resources section.
- Include check boxes in every reply device and online giving portal. Allow respondents to choose from ☑ "I have included ABC cause in my estate plans" or ☑ "I am interested in learning more about supporting XYZ charity through my estate plan."
- Encourage donors to make contributions to endowed funds that align with a loved one's interests and will create a lasting legacy in their honor or memory.
- Provide interactive tools on the website that will allow donors to create their own illustrations of planned gifts and endowment growth – and then encourage them to request more information.
- Invite appropriate prospects to attend workshops and seminars – perhaps in partnership with the local community foundation or professional advisors – to learn more about financial techniques that can allow generous support for endowment while meeting their personal financial goals in retirement.
- Tell stories about the joy that a donor realized in supporting an endowed fund, and the impact of endowed programs on those you serve.

Repetition of similar messages through multiple media channels is necessary, because most donors need to hear or read the same phrases several times before taking action.

Direct Response

Outbound mailing and email campaigns can reach the largest number of people for the lowest cost and effort. But it can be a challenge to send a compelling message in an effective format to people with an affinity for both endowments and the cause. Recipients can be segmented in the database based on the criteria identified earlier in this chapter, as well as in Chapter 7. It is unlikely that purchased lists will be worth the expense since most endowment donors are already engaged with the organization.

> It is unlikely that purchased lists will be worth the expense since most endowment donors are already engaged with the organization.

Keep in mind the best practices for the medium that is employed. For example, donors are most likely to respond to a mailing that is a simple two- to three-page letter, with multiple calls to action throughout the letter and in the postscript, and signed by a peer rather than a development officer or even the president or CEO. Avoid the expense of supplemental leaflets and disregard the misperception that shorter letters are better. Emails must start with a compelling subject line, can include photos and links that provide more information on the website, and should be optimized for mobile devices. A particular advantage of email is that it allows almost immediate feedback through A/B testing to see what subject lines are most likely to result in a high open and click-through rate. If the mailing or email campaign produces results, consider resending the message about six weeks later to all who didn't reply the first time around: the response rate should be about half of whatever the first outreach produced. Either medium should include at least one story about a donor or beneficiary.

Newsletters, E-news, Alumni Magazines, and More

The longer format of these methods can provide opportunities to tell longer stories, with rotating focus on diverse donors and beneficiaries; impact on various programs; and highlights of social workers, faculty, researchers, curators, and other staff whose work benefits from endowed funds. Because the primary goal of marketing is to encourage prospective donors to indicate their interest (not necessarily to propel a gift), anything related to endowment should provide a way to connect, such as a QR code or old-fashioned reply card in a print publication or a contact form linked to a digital article.

Website Content

Images that relate to endowed programs and donors can be included in the rotating "hero images" or prominent photographs on the main landing page. Pages with more detailed content about endowment funds should be easy to navigate. See the "Endowment and Planned Giving Marketing Partners" sidebar for thoughts about various marketing firms that provide content that can seamlessly complement a website design and offer vetted information about giving to endowment.

In Practice: Endowment and Planned Giving Marketing Partners

Several reputable vendors provide services to help nonprofit organizations market the endowment in print or digital platforms. These tend to focus on planned giving strategies. Their content can be integrated seamlessly into an organization's website or newsletter. They might also provide services such as direct response (mail or email), outbound call centers, and widgets such as gift calculators that can attract visitors to the website. Their content has been vetted by legal and financial advisors to ensure that it conforms to current requirements. They can be found in the directories of various fundraising associations, such as local chapters of AFP, AHP, CASE, CGP, Giving Institute, and others.

Free resources are available through the Leave A Legacy® program via the website of the National Association of Charitable Gift Planners, introduced in Chapter 1. Many community foundations and the national foundations of some causes also provide simple materials that can be adapted by the organizations they support.

A few enterprises will provide your supporters with the opportunity to create a will through a web tool at little or no cost. While these can sound enticing, they need to be assessed carefully to ensure that they serve the best interests of the cause and its stakeholders, including donors, their heirs, and the corps of professional advisors. The percentage of users who complete the process and then maintain a charitable bequest is low compared to more traditional estate planning. An organization using one of these tools must be especially attentive to stewardship.

Social Media

Brief anecdotes about endowment donors and the beneficiaries of endowed funds should be integrated into a regular rotation of social media posts. Either type of story can be especially gratifying for the advocate, who can easily "like" or "share" with their own connections on the platform.

Speaking Engagements

Many community groups such as social, fraternal, and civic associations are constantly seeking content for their monthly meetings. A brief presentation about the cause, the role of endowment, and perhaps a live or video testimonial from a donor or beneficiary can reach audiences that are receptive to charitable giving.

Briefings

Small groups can be gathered based on a common affiliation or interest, such as graduating class or academic major, neighborhoods, affinity groups, professions, and so on. The content might be delivered by a key staff member, volunteer, or board member supplemented with a slide deck, video, and possibly hand-outs. Staff or a group of volunteers should establish guidelines for the briefings, including purpose and goals, content, timing, responsibilities of hosts, assignments for follow-up, and criteria for evaluation. Then hosts from various backgrounds, geographic locations, and demographic traits can be recruited to host a briefing and gather participants.

Giving Circles

Giving circles can be considered both a marketing method and a fundraising strategy (as described in Chapters 3 and 8). They are a form of collective philanthropy, where donors with similar interests gather to pool their resources, learn about a cause, and select recipient(s) of their shared gifts. They can be especially effective in motivating "everyday philanthropists" who may erroneously think that only the wealthy contribute to endowments. According to a study by the Lilly Family School of Philanthropy at Indiana University, giving circles are exploding in popularity because they allow members to engage more deeply in a cause or issue.[2] Some circles are independent and select from a variety of recipients, while others are devoted to a single cause and support a variety of activities within that organization. Each circle may have predetermined expectations for the amount each participant will contribute, and a process for learning about the endowment options that support various aspects of the cause and related nonprofit organizations. Periodically (once or twice a year), they will vote on which of the giving opportunities will receive their collective gift. Circles are often supported by an organization's staff, although decision making is rather autonomous. One challenge for the staff is to ensure that each member of the giving circle is included in the donor database.

Recognition

Charitable giving is a social behavior that is often influenced by the knowledge that others support a cause. Donor recognition can be one of the most effective ways to generate this "social norming." All donor recognition programs should be designed with a dual purpose: to strengthen the bond with the donor and to attract others to follow the donor's example. A good recognition program will also provide a comfortable way to talk with a potential donor about a gift of a specific amount. For example, "it sounds as though you attribute much of your success to Professor Smith—would you like to explore endowing a chair in her discipline?"

As discussed in Chapter 3, recognition can range from listings in print materials such as the annual report or a program booklet or online, to "named" funds that commemorate the donor in association with a specific program or staff position, such as a "named" faculty chair, curatorial role, and so on. It may acknowledge gifts that have already been received (either a single gift or cumulative giving) or may acknowledge donors who have made arrangements through their estate plan. Some recognition may be featured on site, such as an installation in the lobby of a prominent building.

Unlike commemorative recognition in capital campaigns, named endowments and programs do require a careful consideration of cost. For example, a gift to endow and "name" an academic chair, curator, community health worker, or any position needs to produce enough annual revenue to make a meaningful impact on budgeted expenses. At a 4.5% draw, an endowed gift of $2.5 million will produce $112,500 annually. While this may substantially subsidize the compensation for the role, few donors are inspired to make a gift that simply replaces annual operating expenses. A named endowment or program should include some marginal increase – such as funding for research or professional development – in addition to relieving the budget from the basic costs of personnel or other expenses that are already budgeted.

For donors who lack the capacity – or interest – to create a singular endowment for a position or program, many organizations establish *field-of-interest funds* focusing on general activities. For example, a zoo may have an endowment for animal nutrition; a settlement house may have an endowment for outreach; or a museum may have a fund for collections care. A donor can make a gift of any amount, which is then pooled with donations from others to create a fund that is large enough to have an impact, and all of the fund's donors can be recognized annually.

A formal recognition policy should be developed and aligned with the policy for recognizing all types of gifts (see Chapter 5) and should take into consideration the following:

* What type(s) of gift will be recognized: current gifts and pledges? Irrevocable deferred gifts such as certain trusts? Revocable deferred gifts such as a simple bequest?
* Who can be recognized: only individuals? What about families, foundations, or even corporations (and will the latter be able to incorporate their own brand into recognition)?
* How long will the recognition last? Given that endowed funds are intended to last forever, will the recognition be perpetual as well?
* Will recognition be "above the name" (i.e., the "Jane Smith Curator of Photography") or "below the name" (i.e., "The Leadership Lecture Series made possible through the generous endowed gift of Curtis Jones")?

Personal Outreach

The most effective marketing strategy involves staff members or volunteers reaching out to engage potential donors personally. Often these contacts are prompted by the potential donor's indication of interest. These visits are not interviews, meetings, or solicitations. They are opportunities to explore a donor's motivations and interest, leading to the establishment (or elevation) of trust and confidence in the organization.

Selecting the Right Marketing Methods

Marketing methods, as evidenced by the preceding subject matter, are almost limitless. The marketing team may be tempted to indulge in creative experimentation, which is useful only if consistent messages are rooted in the case for support and the results of each "experiment" can be measured to inform future decisions. Few organizations have the resources to implement every possible tactic, so it is important to focus on doing a few consistently and well rather than scattered efforts that do not yield results. Table 4-2 clarifies the purpose of typical endowment marketing tactics.

The staff and vendors involved in making decisions for marketing the endowment must understand the donor's needs and wants and then tailor marketing efforts to the characteristics of different audiences. Take into consideration the variables discussed in the following sections, which are also explored more fully in Chapter 7.

TABLE 4-2 The Purpose of Typical Endowment Marketing Tactics

	Make Case	Build Case	Generate Leads	Qualify Leads	Close Gifts	Steward Donors	Repeat Gifts
Direct response	x	x	x				
Owned media	x	x	x			x	
Paid media	x	x				x	
Public speaking	x	x	x				
Briefings	x	x	x				
Giving circles	x	x	x			x	x
Legacy societies	x	x	x			x	x
Donor recognition	x	x	x			x	x
Personal visits		x	x	x	x	x	x

Sufficient Staff

The goal of endowment marketing is to generate inquiries from potential donors. There must be sufficient staff to follow up on these inquiries promptly. Even if follow-up is assigned to volunteers, staff are still needed to prepare materials, track the relationship in the database, and process gifts. And once a donor has made their gift or deferred commitment, staff members must continually monitor their interests through effective stewardship practices. (See staffing and budget recommendations in Chapter 9.)

The Traits of Endowment Donors

Because giving to endowment is often through planned gifts, the ability to make a significant gift is measured by accumulated assets rather than by current earnings. Some people may earn large salaries but spend everything they earn on lifestyle choices and obligations to others. People who indulge in a luxury lifestyle may not be good potential endowment donors. Those who have accumulated assets – in the form of cash, investments, real estate, tangible property, retirement plans, and so on – have developed a habit of giving and are better able and more likely to consider investing in endowment. The likelihood that they will make a planned gift to support endowment is indicated by their consistent, year-after-year support for an organization regardless of the gift amount.

According to the *Bank of America Study of Philanthropy*[3] conducted every two to three years by Indiana University, high net worth (HNW) households – those that earn $200,000 or more each year and have $1 million in accumulated assets in addition to the primary residence – participate in philanthropy at very high levels. This definition represents about 3% of the American population. The 2023 study cited that more than 85% of these households make charitable gifts each year (a decline from nearly 90% in 2017), giving an average of \$34,917 (p. 16). By comparison, participation in charitable giving more broadly has declined. Less than 50% of *all* American households made contributions to 501(c)3 organizations by the 2020s. But that doesn't necessarily mean the latter group is less generous. There is emerging evidence that they practice generosity in ways that are less likely to be formally recognized (such as a "round up" donation when buying groceries), and that nonprofit organizations have failed to engage them as effectively as they do wealthier donors.

A donor's wealth and their attitudes toward money may not be readily apparent (see the sidebar In Practice: "Philanthropy, Endowments, and Bias"). Individuals and families from all sorts of backgrounds have the means and desire to invest in the future of their communities. Many live modestly and as a result have saved and accumulated assets that are not obvious. Consider Sylvia Bloom, who grew up in Brooklyn during the Great Depression, put herself through college, and worked as a legal secretary. She lived modestly and invested quietly, to the extent that she was able to bequeath more than \$6 million to the Henry Street Settlement in New York City. Or be inspired by Oseola McCarty, a washerwoman from Hattiesburg, Mississippi, whose hard work and thriftiness enabled her to endow a scholarship at the University of Southern Mississippi. Endowment marketing should include donors at all income and (assumed) asset levels.

In Practice: Philanthropy, Endowments, and Bias

Too often, philanthropy – and especially sophisticated giving such as support for endowment – is associated with a stereotypical image: an older, successful, white, male. Historically, systemic inequalities and social structures have favored this demographic group. As a result, there are a preponderance of endowed funds named for this type of

(continued)

donor with fewer recognizing the generosity of women and people of color. When women and people of color do make generous gifts, they are unlikely to claim the mantle of "philanthropist" according to a study by Indiana University's Lilly Family School of Philanthropy[4] – which, ironically, was endowed through a gift from the pharmaceutical pioneer's foundation (a white male).

How can endowment-building efforts redress this historic bias? Consider some of the following actions:

- Ensure that the organization respects and represents the diversity it wishes to attract to the corps of donors. A BIPOC (Black, Indigenous, People of Color) donor is unlikely to endow an institution that has few – or no – people of color in leadership positions.
- Expand efforts to identify and engage donors. Too often, bias is rooted in donor databases, and efforts to identify "look alike" donors will simply reinforce the bias. Tailor outreach efforts to appeal to a wider demographic, engage this broader audience through volunteering, invite them to provide financial support only after a relationship has been established, and work toward earning their ultimate trust resulting in a gift to the endowment. This is a long-term effort because it needs to address deeply rooted historic inequities, so patience and persistent investment will be required.
- Look beyond the obvious indications of wealth. While a philanthropic screening may be useful in ferreting out traditional indications of wealth such as publicly held securities or multiple homes, it may miss some of the factors that produce generational wealth among new Americans, such as small businesses and landholdings in the "home" country.

- Examine donor recognition assumptions. Consider the example set by the Maroon Arts Group, a fledgling organization celebrating Black creativity in Ohio whose donor recognition policy states "MAG is deeply grateful for the generosity of all its donors, and in that spirit will recognize them equally, rather than by the magnitude of their gift."
- Does an existing legacy society honor someone whose early wealth was gained through practices that are now viewed as exploitational? A new name may need to be considered before nonwhite donors will be interested in aligning their estate plans with the organization.

Age

The donors who are most likely to give to endowment are mature. By the time they have reached their 50s and 60s, they have established a habit of giving (and, if they aren't regular donors by then they are unlikely to start donating to anything, let alone endowment, regardless of their wealth). These people are more likely to have accumulated assets, have reached their peak earning years, their children are transitioning to adulthood, and obligations such as mortgages are generally fulfilled. If the family enjoys intergenerational wealth, they may have received an inheritance. Conversely, if the donor is in the first generation to accumulate assets, they may have considerable responsibilities to extended family that they prioritize over philanthropy.

According to an analysis in The New York Times,[5] Baby Boomers (those born 1945–1965) have amassed the greatest amount of wealth in history, while Millennials (those born 1981–1996) have surpassed Baby Boomers in terms of sheer population numbers. This suggests that Baby Boomers may have the greatest potential to make current gifts to endowment funds in the 2020s and 2030s, while Millennials will succeed them by the 2040s as they earn and inherit assets. An organization should not wait until a donor is older to begin talking about plans to give through their estate. Research published by Giving USA®6 found that planned giving prospects and donors write a first will at age 44 and nearly half of them include charitable provisions. They tend to update their will at least two times as they experience major milestones such as the youngest child graduating from college, death of a loved one, retirement, or the sale of a business. Organizations that receive significant bequests in support of their endowment establish relationships with donors before they turn 50, engage the donor in a meaningful way over a span of decades, and ensure that donors' advisors have access to the information they need to document donors' plans to support the cause.

> Planned giving prospects and donors write a first will at age 44 and nearly half of them include charitable provisions.

Location

Some causes are national or even global in scope, while others focus on a particular community or region. A database of publicly recognized gifts of $1 million or more at The Lilly Family School of Philanthropy shows that donors are most likely to make a major gift within 100 miles of their residence. The primary exception: their *alma mater* if it is outside of this radius. A complicating factor may be donors with a secondary residence. These "snow birds" tend to continue most of their philanthropy in the community that has the strongest attachment. So the focus of marketing for the endowment may be widespread as a result of social and digital platforms, while personal visits are most likely to occur closer to "home."

Maturity of the Organization

Donors view endowment as an investment. A sound organization that has an established track record of impact and prudent fiscal management can more easily substantiate their case for longevity. A younger organization may need to devote more effort in making the case for its mission and long-term viability.

An Expansive Volunteer Corps

Long-term volunteers are among the best prospects for gifts to the endowment. Docents, alumni association directors, ushers, neighborhood watch members, and similar volunteer corps are often filled with individuals who match the profile for likely planned givers. But their loyalty cannot be taken for granted. Members of the volunteer corps deserve careful engagement and best practices – like the involvement of peers. Once these ambassadors are convinced of the merits of an endowment, they can become powerful advocates for the cause.

Summary and Next Steps

Endowments are generally created by donors who dedicate their generous gifts for the perpetual benefit of the cause. To engage donors, an organization must have a compelling rationale for giving, articulated in a written document called a case for support. The case for support then becomes a resource document that drives messaging strategies through a variety of marketing platforms.

An organization also must establish practices and policies for managing and deploying endowments. While these can seem tedious, they are absolutely essential. Savvy donors will inquire about endowment policies before making a gift, and the beneficiaries of endowed funds deserve the safeguards that ensure that these financial resources will achieve the desired impact, as explored in the next chapter.

Notes

1. Barbara Levy, ed., "Case for Support," in *AFP Fundraising Dictionary*, 2017, https://afpglobal.org/fundraising-dictionary.
2. Jessica Bearman and Jason Franklin, "Dynamics of Hosting: Giving Circles and Collective Giving Groups," 2018: https://philanthropy.iupui.edu/research/topics/index.html.
3. Lilly Family School of Philanthropy, Indiana University, "The 2023 Bank of America Study of Philanthropy: Charitable Giving by Affluent Households," *IUPUI Scholarworks*, October 2023, https://scholarworks.iupui.edu/items/31aafdfd-a6a6-486e-978c-35c705409f2c.
4. Una Osili, PhD, et al., "What Americans Think about Philanthropy and Nonprofits," *IUPUI Scholarworks*, April 2023, chrome-extension://efaidnbmnnnibpcajpcglclefindmkaj/https://scholarworks.iupui.edu/server/api/core/bitstreams/b5904a8a-5081-42cd-bd44-56740b98fb67/content.
5. Talmon Joseph Smith and Karl Russell, "The Greatest Wealth Transfer in History Is Here, with Familiar (Rich) Winners," *The New York Times*, May 14, 2023, sec. Business, https://www.nytimes.com/2023/05/14/business/economy/wealth-generations.html.
6. Elizabeth Dale, "Leaving a Legacy: A New Look at Today's Planned Giving Donors," *Giving USA* (Giving USA Special Report, 2018), https://store.givingusa.org/collections/special-reports-spotlights/products/leaving-a-legacy-a-new-look-at-planned-giving-donors-digital-edition?variant=39331664658511.

5

Policies and Practices for Managing Endowment

This chapter enables you to:

- Understand the importance of sound policies to provide guidance and protect the reputation of organizations building endowment.
- Adapt policies to maximize both the growth of endowed funds and the impact of distributions.
- Know the different kinds of policies and their application.
- Determine how to develop, adopt, implement, and update policies regularly.
- Select and monitor advisors to manage funds and investments.

An endowment is a treasure that demands careful and transparent *stewardship*, which is defined in *Merriam-Webster's Collegiate Dictionary* (11th ed.) as "the careful and responsible management of something entrusted to one's care."[1] This important responsibility is ultimately assigned to the board of directors. When an organization receives its tax-exempt status under state and federal laws, the board of directors – and its individual members – assumes a "duty of care," "duty of loyalty," and "duty to manage accounts" on behalf of the public the organization serves and to avoid any self-dealing or conflicts of interest.

> An endowment is a treasure that demands careful and transparent stewardship.

This chapter explores all three factors in managing endowment growth: gift acceptance, investment, and spending policies. It provides resources for staff and volunteers who work with donors, and the board of directors and administrators who will carry out financial stewardship of the assets entrusted to their care. It also explores policy issues that need to be discussed and adopted.

Endowment Governance

How does an organization and its board members ensure proper stewardship of endowment funds? Through policies. Policies are dull – that is, until they are missing, poorly done, or ignored. Then policies can become very exciting, and not in a good way (see the sidebar In Practice: "The Perils of Missing or Ignored Policies"). Board members do not manage. They govern through policies. It is the board's duty to ensure that an organization has sufficient policies to protect all of its assets: its reputation and brand, staff and clients, and its endowment. It is then the job of management to follow those policies as they pursue the mission.

As discussed in Chapter 1, true endowments are established when donors designate their gifts for endowment; quasi-endowments are established when the board of directors designates organizational assets; and term endowments are established by either donors or the

---

In Practice: The Perils of Missing or Ignored Policies

A conservation organization in the Midwest hired outside counsel to conduct a comprehensive (and expensive) review of its governing policies. Why? Because their policies were outdated and – even worse – often ignored. Despite repeated warnings from auditors, the "C-suite" assured the board that they were just following the standard practices of every other organization, and a few gray areas were necessary to compete for audience and contributions. Then a local media outlet investigated and found that those C-suite leaders were actually exploiting the outdated policies and the absence of board oversight for personal gain: using the organization's funds to support a lavish lifestyle for themselves and their extended families. Needless to say, the fallout resulted in significant harm to the organization's reputation, loss of accreditation, declining contributions, felony convictions for three officers, and a board under the magnifying glass. All of which could have been avoided if their policies were thorough, up to date, and followed rigorously.

---

board for a set period of time. For all three types of endowments, their growth in the future is governed by three factors:

- **Additional gifts.** New gifts to the endowment increase the size of the capital assets which, in turn, generate even greater returns. Usually, donors who contribute gifts to endowment have been cultivated over a period of time to develop their trust in the organization, deep understanding of the cause, and excitement about the future. Staff, board members, and other endowment champions are responsible for designing and implementing strategies that inspire donors to make new gifts to the endowment, as discussed in Chapter 3. For quasi-endowments, the board may regularly or periodically transfer funds to the endowment. They must also conform to gift acceptance policies that protect the organization's reputation and reduce risk.

* **Return on investment.** Endowment assets also increase with good investment results. A long-term investment objective for most endowment funds is to provide a stable and consistent level of program support, in perpetuity. To accomplish this objective, endowments seek to maximize the purchasing power of the assets so they will keep pace with inflation over time and provide continuing revenue to the organization. This requires an investment policy that spells out the endowment's goals and diversified investment strategies.

* **Spending policies.** The third factor in increasing the purchasing power of the endowment is the annual amount distributed to programs by the endowment. This amount is often called *net assets released*. Because the endowment's primary purpose is to support the cause, board members are sometimes tempted to distribute (spend) all of the endowment's growth and earnings. This practice can cause dramatic fluctuations in program support and fail to protect against future inflation. The standard practice is to develop a spending policy that balances growth of the *corpus* (that is, the amount originally given) with distributions for future programs.

On the other hand, an especially risk-averse board may be tempted to hoard the funds in the endowment and not distribute anything for fear that a "rainy day" may come. This practice discourages donors who, after all, give their gifts with the expectation that the funds will be used to make a difference, not merely to be shifted from one savings account into another. Further, preparation for "rainy days" should come in the form of reserves (see Chapter 6).

Each of these factors is explored more fully throughout this chapter, while links to resources that may provide templates or examples of various policies can be found in the Resources section.

Endowment Growth via New Gifts

An organization serving women and girls in Florida received a call from a faithful donor: would they accept a gift of property? The donor wanted the organization to hold the property for two years, and then use the proceeds of a sale to bolster their small endowment. With excitement, they began to explore the opportunity, only to learn that the "gift" consisted of a defunct gas station in a troubled part of the city surrounded by chain link and razor wire. The board chair and executive director sought advice, which consistently warned against proceeding due to potential contamination, doubts about a viable buyer, and the potential liabilities in holding the property. Had sound gift acceptance policies been in place, they would not have needed outside counsel, and they could have pointed to a faceless document rather than disappointing the donor with a decision that seemed *ad hoc*.

Gift acceptance policies are key to upholding an organization's reputation, complying with laws and regulations, managing risk, defining financial procedures, and protecting donors. According to the Association of Fundraising Professionals' *Code of Ethical Standards*, "Nonprofit leaders must understand that the public trust is vital to the sector's mission, and their organizations must be accountable to donors, stakeholders, government agencies, and future patrons . . . Key to gaining that donor trust is keeping to established guidelines for handling donations . . ."[2]

A written gift acceptance policy defines the types of gifts an organization will accept, how their monetary value will be determined, and the conditions for acceptance. Forms of current giving beyond simple cash – such as securities, personal property and real estate, intellectual property, distributions from retirement accounts, and even gifts of cryptocurrency – may require special handling and documentation. Even large cash gifts ("large" as defined by the scale of an organization and its contributed revenue, but often $10,000 or more, given regulations to thwart potential "money laundering") warrant special procedures. Many donors support endowment through planned gifts (see Chapter 8) and while the great majority of these planned gifts will be simple bequests, other complex instruments such as various trusts and annuities may place burdens on the finance office.

Donors of charitable gifts must assign a value to their gifts if they intend to pursue a charitable income tax deduction. The tax regulations related to the valuation of charitable gifts are complex and may vary by state. Valuation and tax deductibility take into consideration how and when the donor acquired the asset, its current value, and the organization's use of the gift. Often, the current valuation must be established by a qualified appraisal obtained by the donor at the donor's sole expense, based on IRS regulations. Gift acceptance policies help to avoid misunderstandings or conflicts between the donor and the organization about the value or handling of the gift (see more about gift counting in Chapter 9). In addition, policies can encourage boards of directors to use windfall gifts to build the principal in the quasi-endowment. For example, many organizations' policies state that the amount of any realized bequest that exceeds $25,000 is automatically added to the quasi-endowment.

> Gift acceptance policies help prevent misunderstandings or conflicts between the donor and the organization.

Any organization that plans to manage its endowment internally or through an affiliated foundation must have sound gift acceptance policies that are periodically reviewed and refreshed by the board. Even when an organization plans to partner with a community foundation or other external partner that will have its own gift acceptance policies, the cause should have its own set that reflects organizational values.

There are several reliable resources that provide guidance – and even model standards – for gift acceptance, available to charities registered in the United States from organizations such as AFP, CASE (the Council for the Advancement and Support of Education), and CGP (the National Association of Charitable Gift Planners). Gift acceptance must conform to the legal, ethical, and financial requirements of their nation of origin. There are associations in many countries that offer such standards, such as Imagine Canada, the Institute of Community Directors (among others) in Australia, and the Charities Commission in the United Kingdom. Citations for links to the resources provided by these organizations are included in the Resources section in the back of the book.

Adopting a gift acceptance policy is not as simple as "rubber-stamping" any one of the industry models. The process should start with a standing committee of the board such as governance, finance, or development, or perhaps a task force with representatives from each. They may consult with professional advisors and engage senior finance or development staff throughout the process. While they may start with one of the model standards to provide a framework, it must be adapted to align with the values and mission and management capabilities of the cause. The involvement of key leaders not only results in a sound policy, but it also ensures that these leaders and, by extension, their peers on the board and in the C-suite, understand the rationale behind the acceptance or rejection of various forms of gifts. Even with a sound policy affirmed through a formal vote of the board, gray areas still emerge, so the policy should also designate who has the authority to deal with unforeseen circumstances.

The gift acceptance policy should also then be aligned with other important policies and procedures dealing with donor recognition and privacy, and procedures for receiving, recording, acknowledging, and managing gifts. Depending on the sector, it may also need to conform to regulations such as HIPAA in healthcare, or accreditation standards focused on the management of collections (see the American Alliance of Museums), higher education accrediting bodies, and increasingly stringent data management requirements. The "Resource: Considerations for Developing a Gift Acceptance Policy" sidebar can help organizations reflect on considerations when developing a gift acceptance policy.

Resource: Considerations for Developing a Gift Acceptance Policy

Who is authorized to accept gifts:

- Of cash less than $10,000?
- Of cash gifts of $10,000 or more?
- Via donor advised funds?
- Restricted to a purpose that has already been approved by the board?
- Restricted to a new purpose as designated by the donor?
- Pledged over a period of years?

Are there any gifts the organization will automatically reject, such as proceeds from legal (or illegal) gambling or cannabis, funds derived from actions contrary to the mission (such as resource extraction or predatory credit practices), or from donors with problematic reputations?

When should the organization consult with tax, legal, or other advisors on gift matters?

Will the organization accept current gifts (other than cash), and what are the procedures for acceptance, valuation, and management of gifts such as:

- Gift certificates and cards

- Qualifying charitable distributions from retirement accounts
- Public securities
- Closely held/private securities
- Cryptocurrency
- Personal property including artwork, collectibles, automobiles, and so on
- Real estate
- Intellectual property
- In kind gifts of goods or services

Will the organization accept deferred gifts, and what are the procedures for acceptance and management of gifts such as:

- The receipt of monies through a simple bequest?
- The management and/or receipt from various kinds of trusts?
- "Split-interest gifts" such as annuities?

Who is authorized to periodically review and amend the policy?

What is the minimum amount for establishing a named or designated endowment fund?

Endowment Growth via Responsible Investment

Prior to the adoption of the original UMIFA (see Chapter 1), nonprofit managers were held to a standard of management that ultimately weakened their cause: they could not expose any assets – including endowed funds – to the risks of the equity markets. Since 1972, organizations have been able to make wise investment decisions to allow endowments and other assets to benefit from the market and alternative forms of investment such as private equity.

The skills and experience required for management of endowment assets are different from those needed to oversee operating budgets, capital expenditures, or reserve accounts. Organizational leaders need to analyze the options available for the creation, implementation, and periodic updating of its endowment investment and spending policies. These leaders most often chose one of three paths for the management of their endowments:

- Internal
- An affiliated foundation
- An external manager such as a local community foundation

Each of these is discussed at length in the following sections.

Internal Investment Management

Organizations with sophisticated finance and development operations may elect to manage their own endowment. The endowment program: both attracting new gifts and managing the current investments is fully integrated into the organization's everyday operations, with specific responsibilities distributed to various departments.

While the development office is busy attracting contributions for operations, special programs, capital, and endowment, they are also responsible for the careful stewardship of relationships with those who have already given to the endowment, providing regular reports (at least annually) to inform the donor about both the financial performance of their endowed fund(s) and their impact.

The business office oversees financial aspects, including gift valuation and disposition; implements investment decisions based on the investment policies (assigned to a Chief Investment Officer if the endowment is large enough); makes disbursements to the operating budget based on spending policies; oversees reporting and payments if the organization has a charitable gift annuity program; prepares tax forms for the organization and its beneficiaries; and prepares periodic performance reports for the development office to share with donors, beneficiaries, and the board of directors.

Some of this may occur in-house, while other tasks can be assigned to an outside manager such as a bank, trust company, or a management firm. Even with the support of these vendors, internal management of the endowment can be daunting. It consumes time and expertise and places all of the risk and responsibility on the organization.

The benefits of internal management and administration of the endowment include cost savings, greater control over the ethical and social impact of investment decisions, the ability to align those decisions with the mission, transparency since all of the assets and decisions are in-house, and a long-term perspective. These benefits are realized only if the entity has the resources to manage the endowment well, including access to legal counsel with expertise in planned and deferred gifts, and wise investment management. In the absence of staff, time, or sophistication, it may be appropriate to consider a different alternative.

Investment Management by an Affiliated Foundation

Some nonprofit organizations establish separate 501(c)(3) affiliates (supporting organizations, as defined in Section 509(a)(3) of the Internal Revenue Code), which are commonly called *foundations*. These are a practical necessity when a publicly funded organization such as a library or public school seeks philanthropic support and must segregate private funding from government constraints. They are also popular with private organizations that receive substantial government funding (such as developmental disability organizations), have substantial risk (such as pediatric health centers), or are the local affiliate of a nationally incorporated agency. These foundations have their own boards of directors, separate bylaws, articles of incorporation, investment policies, and operational practices. The board members are usually appointed in part or entirely by the supported (parent) organization.

Sometimes the foundation is the fundraising arm for the parent organization and sometimes its sole responsibility is to manage the endowment (and other assets) for the benefit of the parent organization. The foundation's role should be made clear when it is established, because that decision will affect the responsibilities of board members and the job descriptions of staff. While the parent organization and supporting foundation are legally separate, there may be overlap in board membership, and the professional staff may be employed by either the parent organization or the foundation with some sort of cost-sharing model or memorandum of understanding.

Whether the foundation is responsible for fundraising or not, it is likely that the parent organization's board may mistakenly conclude that it no longer needs to participate in fundraising. In a healthy system, both the parent board and the foundation board recognize that they are partners in securing and allocating contributions. While the parent board focuses on the vision and guidance required to accomplish the mission, individual board members may be called upon to engage donors – and all should expect to contribute some amount personally. Foundation board members understand that their primary responsibility is to raise and manage funds for the benefit of the cause, yet they must also be fully aware of the parent organization's operations and strategic vision. The two boards need to be in conversation. This can be accomplished by having a certain percentage of members who serve on both boards, periodic joint board meetings, task forces composed of members of both boards for special initiatives such as a capital campaign, and frequent reporting to one another. A system in which the foundation raises all the funds and the operating entity makes all the decisions about deploying those funds can lead to disharmony.

In Practice: Fidelity to the Donor and the Organization

Although separate foundations can be practical, care must be taken to ensure that a cause and its foundation remain inextricably – and legally – linked. A historical society in the Rockies discovered the importance of this constraint when

> its foundation began to make unilateral decisions about the release of endowment assets, including distributions to unaffiliated historical sites across the state. Ultimately, the foundation amended its governance to separate from the historical society and act independently – in competition with the founding entity – to raise and distribute funds. All was legal (though contentious) because the founding documents and subsequent policies weren't sufficiently rigorous, even though some donors intended their assets to benefit the founding historical society.

A supporting foundation may elect to perform all of the tasks of endowment internally, as described previously. Or it may rely heavily on outside partners, as described next.

Investment Management by Community and Other Foundations

When an organization is nascent, the staff is small or inexperienced, the cause is volatile, or for myriad other reasons, an organization may turn to an external foundation – such as the local community foundation – to manage its endowment. Some enterprising unaffiliated foundations have popped up around the country to fulfill this responsibility, or the local affiliate of a national association may be able to turn to the parent organization for endowment management. Among these choices, the local community foundation is often sought for this partnership because of its deep roots and understanding of community needs. The community foundation's leaders and board members are often key influencers, and access to their acumen and authority may bring ancillary benefits to the nonprofit.

According to the Council on Foundations,[3] there are more than 900 community foundations in the United States that operate in urban and rural areas in every state. They hold assets ranging from $100,000 to multiple billions of dollars. The oldest community foundation was established as a "civic progress fund" in Cleveland in 1914, and the largest is in Silicon Valley with almost $10 billion in assets. Through separate component funds called organizational (or agency) endowment funds, local community foundations can oversee the investment of an agency's endowment, handle tax and regulatory reporting, and distribute a portion of the fund's year-end value back to the organization at least annually.

For example, an organization serving people with special needs (pseudonym SPSN) received a windfall of $3.5 million from philanthropist MacKenzie Scott. SPSN decided to allocate a portion of the gift to establish the Special People with Special Needs Endowment at their local community foundation. SPSN irrevocably deposited $2 million with the foundation to establish a permanent fund. The foundation will make annual distributions to SPSN subject to its spending rate, which is currently 4.5% of the endowment's value. In addition, the foundation charges a fee of 0.5% for administering the fund. So the fund will provide $90,000 to SPSN annually, which should grow through investing over time to maintain spending power in step with inflation. And the foundation will provide the board of SPSN with quarterly reports on the fund's investment performance and may allow the board of SPSN to select from a vetted list of investment options. They'll use the fees to support their own operations and programs, which include capacity building training for area nonprofits.

The benefits to SPSN in establishing an organizational endowment at the community foundation include the following:

- The foundation's board and staff are comprised of experienced endowment fund managers, freeing SPSN's board to focus on their cause.
- The investment choices increase with a large pool of resources, providing the potential for a greater return.
- The community foundation will accept, receive, and process gifts in accordance with its own gift acceptance policies, alleviating an administrative burden and shielding SPSN from

controversy or ill will resulting from the acceptance or rejection of certain gifts.

- The community foundation has the ability to accept complex gifts such as real estate or closely held stock that may exceed SPSN's capabilities.
- Gift acknowledgments that meet IRS requirements are provided by the community foundation to every donor to the SPSN endowment. Of course, SPSN will want to personally thank donors as well.
- The community foundation's investment oversight may provide additional credibility and confidence to SPSN's donors.
- The community foundation will list SPSN's fund on the giving portal of its website and in its annual report and may offer planned giving technical assistance to SPSN's donors.
- If SPSN ceases to exist in the future, its fund will remain at the community foundation and continue to benefit people with special needs by providing support to similar causes.

Some of these same benefits may be available from the national office for an organization's local affiliates or from a commercial endowment-management firm.

Selecting and Monitoring Investments

Endowment funds grow through prudent investment. Some organizations serve as their own investment managers, especially if the endowment is too small to attract the interest of institutional investment managers or endowment administrators and they've decided not to go the route of the local community foundation. Many independent fiduciaries require six- or seven-figure accounts, which excludes small and growing endowments from outside professional management. Generally, small organizations have lean staff and little experience or time for administering planned gifts or managing an investment portfolio, although they call on an investment committee from their board to provide the required acumen. If they elect to place their funds at the local community foundation, they will still be expected to select from several investment advisors and/or portfolios. At the other end of the spectrum, some large or sophisticated organizations want the flexibility and strategy associated with their own internal investment management, although complexity does not necessarily correlate with fund performance.

In Practice: Investing: Simplicity vs. Complexity

For many years, sophisticated institutions like Ivy League universities realized enviable endowment growth by hiring their own experts and utilizing complex instruments like hedge funds and private equity placements. Under the right kinds of economic growth, such as the bull markets after the Great Recession, their investments outpaced the equity markets and left envious fund managers wondering if they should emulate these risky practices. But when market conditions changed quickly, simplicity was rewarded. As the economy stumbled in 2022, endowments at universities like Harvard, MIT, Duke, and Vanderbilt declined, while those with simpler asset allocation strategies saw growth. Or, as John Rosenberg wrote in the January 2024 edition of *Harvard* magazine when the University's endowment returns of 2.9% fell far short of market trends:

Fiscal 2023 was the sort of year that vexed managers of large, diversified endowments like Harvard's. As common market indexes, like the Standard & Poor's 500 and NASDAQ (up 19.6 percent and 26.1 percent), soared . . . permanent endowments lagged. The more sophisticated their strategies and the more highly diversified their assets, the larger the gap. Smaller endowments and foundations, which tend to invest principally in publicly traded securities, appear to have earned 9 percent to 10 percent returns on average during the year. But somewhat larger institutions appear to have realized rates of return averaging 6 percent to 7 percent, reflecting the underperformance of private equity holdings—and the larger the endowment, the greater the penalty.[4]

The National Association of College and University Business Officers (NACUBO) issues an annual study of endowments in higher education. Their 2023 report[5] cited overall growth in endowments but found that those with simpler asset allocation strategies tended to outpace their complex peers once again.

Small organizations often must limit the kinds of gifts they accept and the gift vehicles they offer due to their limited staff and expertise. This may reduce their ability to attract some prospective donors. Despite these limitations, the organization may conclude that in-house oversight is their best option.

Whether the endowment is large or small, managed internally or delegated to fiduciaries, the board of directors should assign responsibility for reviewing management and custody of the endowment to a specific group, such as a subcommittee of the finance and/or development committees. This group then develops an investment management strategy, which may look something like Table 5-1.

The target portfolio may further define the split between growth and value stocks, the types of alternative investments allowed, such as hedge funds and private equity. They may also determine whether the investment portfolio should follow the values of the organization. For example, an addiction recovery organization will probably eschew investments in a beverage conglomerate that sells alcohol, while an organization that serves children may avoid tobacco products.

TABLE 5-1 Typical Investment Allocation

Asset Class	Target Percentage of the Portfolio	Acceptable Range
Cash and cash equivalents	5%	2%–10%
Bonds and fixed income	30%	25%–40%
Domestic securities	40%	35%–50%
International securities	20%	15%–25%
Alternative investments	5%	0%–8%

Beyond the avoidance of these investments that contradict the mission, some organizations go a step further and limit their portfolio to socially responsible investments that align with environmental, social, and governance (ESG) practices, as the California Endowment did with its entire $4 billion portfolio in 2024. This growing practice, a form of "impact investing" (see Chapter 5), is especially relevant if a cause hopes to attract donors born after 1981.

The committee will also establish benchmarks for assessing the performance of investment managers. For example, they may state that the portfolio's performance must perform within 5% of an established index such as mutual fund performance, S&P 500, or Russell 3000 Index.

A written investment policy will outline the investment objectives, portfolio allocations, and tolerance for risk. It might prohibit certain equity investments such as commodities or real estate, require socially responsible investing, and require a minimum rating for fixed-income investments. See the Resources section for links to samples of nonprofit investment policies.

Spending Policy

A prudent spending policy will sustain the purchasing power of endowed funds in tandem with judicious investments. Too often, the average lay person assumes that endowments spend the "interest" or "growth" that the funds produce – and too often, they also mean ALL of that interest or growth. The result will be wild fluctuations in the endowment draw, the risk that a year of poor investment performance will reduce the fund to less than the original value of the gift(s) that established the fund, and failure to keep pace with inflation.

Instead, most organizations have adopted a "total return" spending policy that is based on two factors:

- **Total return**, or a measure of the overall value of the endowment funds invested, based on principal (sometimes called *corpus*), earned income (dividends and interest), plus realized and unrealized changes in the market value (gains and losses).
- **Net assets released**. This is the portion of the endowment value that will be liquidated and released into the operating accounts for general use, fees, or for allocation to the activities designated by the fund's donor(s). Assets may be released annually at the start of a new fiscal year or quarterly depending on the size of the endowment and the cash needs of the organization.

Generally, the board adopts a spending rate that represents a predetermined percentage of the endowment's total value, averaged over the past 3 to 5 years (or "trailing 12 quarters" as professionals might state). The rate might be evaluated and adjusted periodically—perhaps once every 5 to 10 years—but not so frequently that trustees are tempted to match temporary market conditions. A rate of 4% to 7% is common, with many organizations settling at 4.5%. A smaller percentage may be attractive to risk-averse board members but could dissuade donors who wish to see their gifts accomplish more and therefore may decide to keep the assets in their own portfolio. A rate higher than 7% may violate UPMIFA and will certainly deplete the endowment's buying power over time. Table 5-2 shows how to calculate a total return draw.

The total return spending policy takes guesswork and emotions out of the equation. When the market soars, the draw remains at the set percentage and the board does not succumb to irrational optimism.

TABLE 5-2 Calculating a Total Return Draw

	Year 1	Year 2	Year 3	Year 4	Year 5	Year 6
A. Endowment value, start of year	$1,000,000	$1,260,000	$1,604,500	$1,939,838	$2,152,358	$3,178,720
B. Growth of investments (~8%)	$80,000	$100,800	$128,360	$155,187	$172,189	$254,298
C. Board-designated contributions	$100,000	$0	$75,000	$125,000	$187,000	$187,000
D. New gifts	$85,000	$250,000	$140,000	$0	$750,000	$25,000
E. Fees and expenses (~0.5%)	$5,000	$6,300	$8,023	$9,699	$10,762	$15,894
F. Endowment value, end of year	$1,260,000	$1,604,500	$1,939,838	$2,210,325	$3,250,785	$3,629,124
G. Total return draw				$57,968	$72,065	$85,450

Key to Total Return Calculations

A. Endowment value, start of year	The endowment value at the end of the preceding year, less any draws from the endowment (E-F)
B. Growth of investments (~8%)	The increase in value based on dividends, interest, capital gains, or other investment performance
C. Board-designated contributions	Any funds added to the endowment by the board (quasi-endowment)
D. New gifts	Any new gifts to the endowment designated by donors (true- or term-endowment)
E. Fees and expenses	The amount paid to investment advisors, etc.
F. Endowment value, end of year	The sum of A + B + C + D – E
G. Total return draw	The set amount (often 4.5%) of the average value of the fund at year end for the prior three years

When the market declines and trustees may lose confidence, the draw remains at the set percentage (unless it drops below the value of the original gift) and provides dependable resources in the face of economic headwinds.

Further, spending from the endowment as a whole, or from individual designated funds, is also influenced by UPMIFA (see Chapter 1) as well as prudent policies adopted by many organizations. UPMIFA (and prudence) dictates that a fund that is defined as "true endowment" cannot be depleted lower than the value of the original gift except under extraordinary circumstances. Many organizations apply this practice to all types of endowment. So if an original gift was $100,000, and the fund has grown through prudent investing to $120,000, then the excess (or a portion) can be withdrawn to be used for current purposes (in this case, a 4.5% draw would yield $5,400). But if poor investment performance or prior withdrawals (or both) have depleted the fund to less than $100,000, then no further withdrawals can be made until the investments restore the fund to its original value and beyond. To ensure that funds have sufficient value to support their designated purposes, many organizations adopt a policy that prohibits withdrawals for the first five years. Sometimes, donors will provide annual gifts that are equal to the proposed withdrawal amount for the early years so that the organization can deploy funding immediately. This practice of annual gifts serving in lieu of an endowment draw is sometimes referred to as "living" or "virtual" endowment.

Most boards assign the drafting and review of investment and spending policies to a finance committee, which then presents the policies to the full board for discussion and approval. As an alternative, an endowment management team consisting of knowledgeable board members, representatives from the business and development offices, and financial and legal advisors may be assembled to tackle policy development. While developing the endowment policies, they may also take into account the organization's other assets, such as the availability of reserves (see Chapter 6). Once adopted, the policies may be shared with fundraisers, donors, their advisors, and the community's financial professionals.

The appropriate policies for gift acceptance, investment management, and spending will vary based on each organization's mission, risk tolerance, and other factors. They also need to take into account management fees and other expenses. It's a balancing act. It may be helpful to think of the endowment as a "perpetual 18-year-old" so that the decision-makers treat the needs of today and the needs of the future equitably.

> Think of the endowment as a "perpetual 18-year-old" so that the decision-makers treat the needs of today and the needs of the future equitably.

Gift and Fund Documentation

Gifts to an endowment must be carefully documented in accordance with UPMIFA, especially if the gift results in promised recognition or the endowment draw is designated for a specific purpose. The three types of endowment described in Chapter 1 – true endowment, quasi-endowment, and term endowment – must be tracked separately, although funds can be comingled for investment purposes. Thus, each endowment gift should be categorized by type.

The organization should maintain records for each major endowment donor, and the finance office should maintain records of each component fund's performance and deployment. These digital or paper records are sensitive and must be protected with appropriate layers of security. To the greatest degree possible, they should be recorded in the CRM so that it can serve as a "single source of truth" for the organization, now and in the future. For each donor, the permanent record might include:

- Donor profile
- All correspondence to and from the donor, including substantiative emails and even text messages

- Contact reports describing each personal interaction with the donor
- Identification and information about the donor's professional advisors
- A link to all gifts, pledges, and planned gifts recorded in the database, documenting the date, amount, type, purpose, and gift restrictions
- Copies of gift agreements, transaction documents, and any board actions related to the gift

Endowment fund descriptions for named and/or designated endowments must be carefully documented, because the board and administration will be responsible for carrying out the terms of the gift both now and in the future. Some considerations included in the description of the endowed fund are as follows.

- The name of the fund.
- Full name of donors with contact information.
- A list of the assets transferred to the fund for outright gifts and planned gift arrangements that are expected to be received in the future.
- Donor restrictions on the use of the fund and alternatives should the intended use ever become obsolete.
- If the fund is established for a competitive purpose, such as a scholarship or named staff position, provide a description of the donor's selection priorities. Clearly document that the donor or their designee may be involved in an advisory capacity, but the final selection of recipients is determined by the organization or a panel it establishes.
- Provisions regarding future additions to the fund by the donor, family members, or the general public.
- Signatures of all parties including the donor, their spouse or children when appropriate, and someone with the capacity to make legally binding commitments on behalf of the organization.
- Donor recognition commitments.

A draft fund agreement in a donor's name can be introduced into discussions with a potential donor as a final and persuasive step toward securing the donor's commitment. Careful documentation is especially important for endowment and planned giving donors, because it often takes years to complete a gift. The funds may not be fully realized until after the donor's lifetime, and staff members involved at the beginning may have moved on.

Gift Administration

Decades after the gift is finalized, the absence of a living donor may encourage an institution to take shortcuts or fudge on the donor's intended purpose. This is a mistake. Failure to comply with the donor's intent is an ethical lapse (see the Donor Bill of Rights in the Resources section) and may create legal issues with donors and their heirs. It is also a strategic misstep, because today's living donors will begin to question whether their future intentions will be honored. For those reasons, the administration of the gift must function efficiently and fully in compliance with the terms of the gift agreement.

When an organization enters into a gift agreement with a donor, it is committing future staff and resources. Today's leaders must be certain that the gift will advance the mission, not just help them achieve aggressive fundraising goals. Decades from now, members of the development and finance teams may devote their time to transfer and valuation of assets; ensuring that appraisals are completed; working with banks, brokerage firms, and financial institutions; and many other tasks. All are worthwhile to ensure the donor's gift is carefully administered and devoted to a purpose that genuinely advances the organization's mission. See links to sample gift agreements among the resources listed at the end of the book.

To ensure that the donor's intent is honored and the endowment fund makes a difference, careful record keeping and meticulous follow-up is necessary. If regular payments are to be received from donors to pay life insurance premiums, for example, someone needs to be sure they are received in a timely manner and in the proper amount. Final gift documents must be prepared, reviewed by legal counsel, signed by the donor, and filed appropriately. These are not the most glorious tasks, but attention to detail makes the difference between a satisfied donor, who is likely to maintain their gift intentions and consider additional gifts, and an unhappy donor, who is unlikely to consider additional gifts and certain to tell others about their displeasure. It's what Patrick Madden, Executive Director of the National Archives Foundation, calls "invisible fundraising."

Summary and Next Steps

Responsible stewardship of assets, and especially endowment, honors the donor and elevates the future of the organization. It is an essential ingredient in successful endowment building. It ensures enduring relationships, as discussed in Part 2 of this book. And it leads to successful endowment building, which is measured through the factors described in the final chapter. Before exploring those topics, however, the next chapter discuss alternatives to endowment – especially reserves – and why they are an important component in financial resilience.

Notes

1. *Merriam-Webster's Collegiate Dictionary*, 11th ed. (2003) s.v. "stewardship."
2. "Code of Ethical Standards | Association of Fundraising Professionals," Afpglobal.org, 2014, https://afpglobal.org/ethicsmain/code-ethical-standards.
3. "Homepage," Council on Foundations, n.d., https://cof.org/.

4. John S. Rosenberg, "Financial Fitness," *Harvard Magazine*, January - February 2024. https://www.harvardmagazine.com/2024/01/jhj-endowment-2023

5. NACUBO and Commonfund, "2023 NACUBO-Commonfund Study of Endowments," *NACUBO*, February 15, 2024, https://www.nacubo.org/Research/2023/NACUBO-Commonfund-Study-of-Endowments.

6

Alternatives
to Endowment

This chapter enables you to:

- Appreciate how reserves and endowments are complementary.
- Learn about the different types of reserve funds and understand how to create and manage them.
- Understand why some donors prefer funds that are more nimble than endowment.
- Acknowledge other vehicles that can provide long-term financial resilience.

Endowment is one proven process for securing financial resilience, but it isn't the right path for every cause, especially those with a limited history or a short-term objective. Even an organization with a large endowment finds that other classes of assets provide necessary flexibility. For example, the Cleveland Museum of Art, with an endowment exceeding $1 billion, still maintains emergency and strategic reserves that can be deployed in the face of urgent crises, fluctuations in cash flow, or sudden opportunities.

Further, endowment does not appeal to every donor, especially those who created their own wealth and have realized the benefits of deploying financial capital quickly and creatively. Some have been influenced by the endowment criticisms explored in Chapter 1. Others saw organizations struggle through financial hardships such as the Great Recession or the disruptions of the COVID-19 pandemic because of limits on the use of endowed assets. Entrepreneurial donors are adept at leveraging financial resources in many imaginative ways and find the inflexibility of endowment to be a constraint. For these donors, and the causes they care about, there are alternatives.

Reserves are the primary alternative to endowment, and basic reserves are a prerequisite for any organization hoping to build endowment. Beyond reserves, nonprofit leaders can pursue other innovative strategies to ensure the resilience of their cause. Strategic partnerships with other causes, social ventures, impact investments, licensing and commercialization of unique innovations, and public funding all can provide recurring streams of revenue to advance the cause. These are all explored in this chapter, starting with reserves.

What Are Reserves?

Reserve funds are liquid cash resources that are available to an organization to sustain operations in the wake of temporary cash disruptions, such as the delayed payment of a major grant. Reserves may also fund specific initiatives that take place outside of the organization's ongoing operations, such as starting a new social enterprise or preparing for a transformational capital campaign. They function just as a for-profit enterprise might deploy working capital. Whereas endowments are usually held permanently, including those that are temporarily restricted (see Chapter 1), reserves are more fluid and may be expended – partially or fully – at any time. According to the website of Propel Nonprofits, a community development financial institution (CDFI, a sort of nonprofit bank) in Minnesota, "Reserves, on the other hand, are 'unrestricted' funds that can be used in any way that the nonprofit's management and board chooses."[1]

Reserves can provide an alternative to short-term borrowing, lines-of-credit, or draconian budget cuts and layoffs when an organization faces a temporary decline in cash flow. For example, many independent schools deploy their reserves when tuition revenue drops in the summer, then replenish the funds when deposits come in at the beginning of the new school year. In addition, some level of reserves can act as a "rainy day fund" to be accessed in an emergency. Many organizations relied heavily on emergency reserves to survive the early days of the COVID-19 pandemic, until various forms of federal aid arrived. These two examples are unlike a planned withdrawal from an endowment.

Thoughtful organizations may also build up *strategic reserves* in anticipation of some transformational event. For example, reserves might fuel the creation of a new social enterprise. That's how a "meals-on-wheels" organization was able to start up a boxed-lunch catering operation that eventually generated enough net revenue to cover its costs, replenish the reserves, and fuel expanded operations. A global women's empowerment organization quietly added to its reserves for several years in order to fund the preparation and early stages of a comprehensive campaign, with early proceeds from the campaign paying the organization back for campaign expenses (as allowed under accounting guidelines when properly communicated to donors).

This section explores both operating and strategic reserves: how they are created and expanded, when they might be deployed, and their appeal to certain types of donors.

How Much Should Be Held in Reserves?

How much should an organization have in its reserves? It depends. For operating reserves, most experts suggest an amount equal to *at least* three months of normal operations, and perhaps as much as 24 months but seldom more. Or, put another way, at least 25% of annual operating expenses averaged over the past three years and perhaps more than 200% of annual expenses. The amount increases with the urgency of the cause: an organization that provides lifesaving services, such as a hospital or residential facility, should lean toward the high end of the range. Nonprofits that elevate humanity – such as a museum or advocacy groups – may require less. Academic and journalist Amy Schiller differentiates these two ends of this spectrum ". . . physical life-and-death existence, or our larger capacities for imagination, creativity, cooperation, and excellence"[2] (p. 5).

The amount also depends on the volatility of an organization's sources of revenue, the seasonality of its activities, the risk tolerance of its leadership, the flexibility of spending, and the availability of a line of credit. Thus, as shown in Figure 6-1, consideration for the

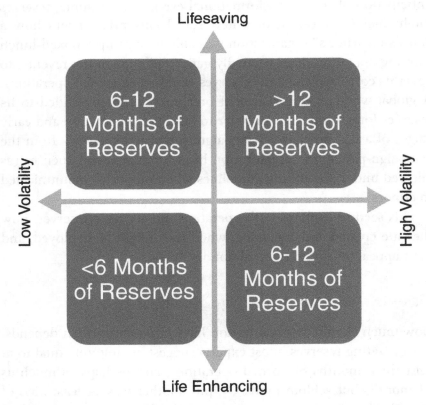

FIGURE 6-1 Matrix for estimating the need for emergency operating reserves.

amount of operating reserves might be calculated along two axes: urgency (from lifesaving to life enhancing) and volatility (from high to low).

The resulting calculations can lead to unexpected conclusions. For example, the Phoenix Children's Hospital held more than $1 billion in net assets without donor restrictions in 2022, an incredible amount of money by any standard. Some might suggest those assets could have been deployed to serve children right away. Yet, the hospital has an enormous responsibility to ensure that children who depend on it for lifesaving treatments won't experience an interruption in care due to unforeseen circumstances. Reserves of $1 billion will sustain the hospital's operations for approximately one year – a prudent and justifiable measure of security, which many hospitals relied on through the disruptions of COVID-19 and the soaring cost of providing healthcare – especially to maintain the salaries of essential personnel. Until needed, they can also be invested in ways that preserve liquidity (the ready availability of the funds) while generating a modest return.

There may also be *special purpose reserves*. If a nonprofit museum or university has an expansive campus, a maintenance reserve might be devoted to capital expenditures for major maintenance. An organization that relies heavily on reimbursements from major grants or government sources may rely on revolving program reserves to fulfill commitments to clients while awaiting payments.

Strategic reserve amounts depend on the organization's vision, preferably as outlined in a strategic plan. An institution that antici-pates a campaign for a new building may want to estimate initial costs that will be incurred before fundraising can begin, including architect's fees, possibly land acquisition, and fundraising assess-ments. Another envisions a new social enterprise that will need startup funding including one-time costs and supplemental funding until revenue covers all expenses.

The various types of reserves might be compared to the capital structure of a for-profit enterprise. Operating reserves are similar to working capital, which is a measure of operating efficiency and short-term financial health. Strategic reserves are analogous to growth capital that is specifically allocated for activities that will elevate the enterprise and are an indication of long-term potential. This comparison is one way to explain nonprofit reserves and make them interesting – even enticing – to those with business acumen.

Regardless of their purpose, reserves constitute *net assets without donor restrictions* and will therefore be mingled with other assets on the financial statements. This might be complemented with a separate dashboard so that they can be monitored easily. An organization's leaders must show discipline in understanding the different classes of assets held in this manner and manage them for their various purposes.

Creating Reserves

Groups such as the Council of Nonprofits and Nonprofit Finance Fund[3] report that fewer than half of all nonprofit organizations have more than six months of cash in reserve, and many reveal that they have less than three months. How can these causes create a less perilous existence?

Most operating reserves are built over many years through a disciplined process of planning, budgeting, and managing expenditures. At the end of the budget year, there may be surplus funds as a result of successful revenue generation through an unexpected contribution or wildly popular programs. Expenses may be lower than budgeted because a highly compensated position was vacant for part of the year or even because low snowfall diminished the cost of plowing. The irrationally exuberant manager may want to spend this bonanza in a rush of fiscal-year-end spending, while the prudent leader sees an opportunity to build a stronger fiscal foundation for the future.

Some organizations make the mistake of conflating quasi-endowment with reserves. However, as discussed in Chapter 1, donors can be dissuaded by the resulting tax reporting that implies the overall endowment may be poorly managed. If there is a likelihood that excess cash will eventually be deployed to support operations or expansion, then it should be held in reserves, not parked temporarily in the quasi-endowment.

> If there is a likelihood that excess cash will eventually be deployed to support operations or expansion, then it should be held in reserves, not parked temporarily in the quasi-endowment.

Any institution with fixed capital assets – mainly buildings or large pieces of equipment – must depreciate those assets at the end of each year, creating an expense on the statement of activities. Because this expense is not a cash transaction, some financial managers will simply subtract it on a subsequent line to reflect a balanced budget. Disciplined financial managers will maintain at least a portion of the expense, ensure it is covered by sufficient revenue, and shift cash from operations to designated reserves – this is how a *maintenance* or *capital* reserve fund is created to preserve and maintain the assets that are depreciated.

In Practice: What Is Depreciation?

de•pre•ci•ate, *verb*
   to lower the price or estimated value of property[4]
Depreciation is an accounting term. It acknowledges that the value of an asset may diminish over its useful life. For example, a vehicle that is purchased to deliver meals throughout the community declines in value as time passes and mileage accumulates. The vehicle might have been purchased for $60,000, but may be worth much less after five years and 150,000 miles of wear and tear. This decrease in value is recorded on an organization's balance sheet, and it is recognized on the income statement

(continued)

as a non-cash expense that reduces the organization's net income. Significant depreciation can appear to create a deficit budget, even though cash is sufficient to meet the annual budget for programs and operations.

One common practice among nonprofit organizations is to "zero out" depreciation below the bottom line of the Statement of Activities so that the budget appears balanced. Then they address deferred maintenance and capital expenditures through periodic capital campaigns. Other organizations budget to ensure that operating revenue covers some portion of the depreciation expense, which then allows them to shift that cash to a reserve fund, and eventually spend it to replace the vehicle or repair the building. Particularly prudent organizations may employ both tactics.

Budget discipline alone may not yield the desired results, especially in years of high inflation or diminished charitable giving.

The funding of *operating reserves* can be uninspiring, and therefore a tough sell for many donors. The leaders of a cause may explore other options, such as designating a portion of board giving or devoting otherwise unrestricted proceeds from a popular event. There may also be a policy that assigns a portion of undesignated realized bequests or windfalls to these reserves until they are fully funded (see links to policy examples in the Resources section) and only then redirects them to quasi-endowment once the reserve targets are met. That's exactly what several organizations did to attain financial stability when they received large unexpected and unrestricted grants from writer and philanthropist MacKenzie Scott. Sudden infusions of cash can come from many sources such as an unexpected bequest, insurance payout, wildly popular performance or exhibition, or legal settlement. Imagine if such funds went into a single year's operating budget, creating a spike that will not be repeated in future years and deploying the funds in ways that cannot be sustained. By allocating all – or a portion – of the largesse to reserves, a disciplined organization maintains a stable operating budget and provides a cushion for future years.

Strategic reserves are different because they may be deployed for visionary purposes, which is why they are sometimes called *opportunity* reserves. Consider the midwestern art museum that maintains a reserve of approximately $3 million. The funds are used periodically to create or acquire a blockbuster touring exhibition, produce award-winning publications, or develop educational curricula that are adopted nationally. These activities all elevate the museum's mission as well as its national stature. Donors are drawn to these "creative reserves," which may be replenished from the gifts of future donors or from the earned revenue produced as a result of these initiatives.

For many years, museum leaders positioned these funds as "covering deficits" and lamented their inability to fund a balanced budget from current museum activities. A former museum director met with donors and sheepishly asked them to replenish these "deficits," which they did out of a sense of obligation rather than inspiration. It was only when a new director pointed out that current operations did cover *basic* expenses – and that creative reserves elevated artistic excellence, visitor experience, and educational merit – that they embraced the model and repositioned it with their donors, who also found great satisfaction when they were told that their contributions to the reserve resulted in impactful programs and exhibitions. "Inspired giving is more impactful," observes Simon Bisson, a certified fundraising professional who has led large fundraising teams in human services, healthcare, and higher education. "Donors want to invest in the future, not replenish resources or cover deficits."

All reserves – emergency, operational, or strategic – should be relatively accessible to the organization. They should not be tied up in some of the investments that a long-term endowment could hold. For example, a 10-year bond may provide security and attractive returns, but the principal cannot be easily accessed when an emergency or sudden opportunity presents itself. Nonprofit managers should seek more liquid short-term investments that will provide some measure of growth and income while remaining available when needed, even though the income or appreciation may not be as great as some other investment options may offer. Over time, these investment returns can be reinvested to provide growth in the reserves and/or can be seen as an ancillary source of unrestricted income for operations.

The interplay between endowment and reserves also presents strategic opportunities. For example, generous donors may have endowed the mammogram program at a mobile health clinic. In any given year, the organization may have adequate unrestricted funding to provide the free mammograms to women in underserved areas and therefore be tempted to skip the annual draw on the endowed fund. To do so will deny the donor the gratification of seeing their gift put to use, and also miss out on an opportunity to build nimble reserves. Instead, the organization can deploy the endowed funds to provide the mammograms and shift the surplus programmatic funds into reserves (note that this is an option only if the programmatic funds are unrestricted). The donor is pleased, and the balance sheet is stronger. Moreover, donors who see that an organization has a healthy balance sheet with adequate reserves are more confident that their gifts to endowed funds will be deployed strategically, not merely to "cover deficits."

This process also results in the phenomenon of the strong getting stronger. As the balance sheet gains strength, the door to other financial resources may open further. An organization that can cite permanently restricted assets (endowment) or unrestricted assets (reserves) will be viewed more favorably when the time comes to borrow responsibly or pursue a merger with another organization. While one cause elevates as a result of years – even decades – of prudent management (the tortoise), others struggle to meet basic operating obligations despite the popularity of their programs (the hare) because their predecessors chose to spend all available revenue in the mistaken belief that nonprofit organizations shouldn't produce net revenue.

Deploying Reserve Funds

The objective of a plentiful reserve isn't solely to build a strong balance sheet. Ultimately, these funds are released to sustain or elevate the mission through a careful process defined in a reserve policy. A sound reserve policy answers these essential questions:

- What types of reserve fund(s) will the organization maintain (emergency, maintenance, strategic, or other)?
- What is the intended use of each fund?
- What is the target amount to be held in each reserve fund and how will it be resourced?
- Who has authority to draw on reserve accounts and under what specific circumstances?
- How will reserve funds be reported to the board and external stakeholders?
- What are the guidelines for investing reserve funds?
- How will the reserve policy be reviewed and amended periodically?

As with other policies (as discussed in Chapter 5), the creation of a reserve policy provides a valuable opportunity to engage and educate the board of directors and other stakeholders. As leaders wrestle with these questions, they will hold deep existential discussions about the organization, its mission, and its desired impact – all leading to both a strong policy and deeply engaged advocates. While they may start with a good policy template such as the one provided by PropelNonprofits (see the Resources section at the end of the book), their discussions and recommendations must take into account the specific nature of their mission.

Other Ways to Bolster Financial Resilience

Reserves are the foundation of financial resilience and should be a part of the resilience model for every cause. There are other strategies that can complement a nonprofit organization's business model. Some have gained popular cachet, while others are deployed by only the most sophisticated management teams. Any of these can provide reliable revenue to fund the mission or can become a costly distraction resulting in both wasted time and actual costs. Therefore, the decision to pursue any of these should be made carefully and with guidance from legal and business advisors, and only after the basic building blocks of financial resilience (reserves and endowment) are in place.

Social Ventures

A *social venture* – sometimes called a social enterprise – is an earned income venture selling goods or services that is fully owned and managed by a nonprofit organization. While the venture is run like a business, the net proceeds don't benefit private individuals; rather, they are reinvested in the core programs and services of the organization. In the best cases, the business entity reflects and furthers the cause.

Social ventures aren't new. Some of the oldest and most successful are so deeply embedded in our culture that the casual observer does not equate them with a newfangled concept. For example, Goodwill Industries was established in 1902 to collect, repair, and sell or donate gently used items. Today, there are more than 3,200 retail thrift stores across the globe. They spin off a profit to fuel Goodwill's services such as job training and supportive housing. Equally important, each Goodwill store provides opportunities for the organization's clients to gain important experience – working as a retail clerk, learning upholstery or other repair skills, managing logistics – all skills that will help them become more employable and self-sufficient.

The example of Goodwill Industries, where social enterprise is closely aligned to the mission, is a stark contrast to some other schemes. For a period of time, an ice-cream brand well known for inventive flavors and social activism waived the franchise fee for any nonprofit that wanted to open a retail "scoop shop." Yet nonprofits with completely unrelated missions found that dabbling in retail sales did not provide the automatic stream of revenue they had hoped for.

The most successful nonprofit social ventures link their revenue stream with the mission. For Thistle Farms in Nashville, Tennessee, that means the production of personal care products to provide employment for women who are escaping trafficking and sexual exploitation as they heal and gain the skills to pursue self-sufficiency. For National Church Residences, the largest nonprofit provider of senior housing in the country, a portfolio of market-rate (and even luxury) senior living communities helps to fund high-quality housing for those who are aging with inadequate financial resources.

Despite their long history, social enterprises gained cachet in recent decades through high-profile success and a few failures. One success, Kiva, provides a micro-finance platform that allows individuals to make loans to help people in struggling economies create or expand small businesses. On the other hand, Cause was a "philanthropub" that lasted only 14 months in the crowded Washington, DC dining scene. According to Eric Nee, an editor of *Stanford Social Innovation Review*, "Having a social mission does not insulate a business from the forces of capitalism. In fact, it can sometimes place an added burden on the company that makes it even more difficult to survive, let alone thrive."[5]

Hybrid business models such as B-Corps (benefit corporations) and L3Cs (low-profit limited liability companies) have blurred the lines between the private enterprise and nonprofits. Companies such as TOMS (a shoe brand) herald a triple bottom line: purpose, planet, and people. These initiatives may supplement or possibly supplant traditional approaches to fundraising and philanthropy as consumers and donors alike begin to view their purchasing practices as their primary expression of generosity. In his seminal article for *Nonprofit Quarterly*, titled "Social Entrepreneurship as Fetish,"[6] scholar Fredrik O. Anderson decries the assumption that businesses are more qualified to tackle social problems through capitalism than the governments and NGOs that have been tackling wicked problems for decades.

Nonprofit social ventures are just as risky as for-profit ventures. According to the World Economic Forum,[7] only 45% of social enterprises lasted more than three years, and 38% folded within a year of launching. Why? Many cite the same struggles any entrepreneur faces: lack of access to capital, inadequate skills, and a product that didn't connect with consumers. The difference is that a failure in a for-profit startup can be a platform for learning, and the loss of capital is a risk that initial investors willingly took. When a nonprofit venture fails, an organization faces reputational harm and an acknowledgment that funds were diverted from mission-critical activities.

Strategic Partnerships

Matthew Goldstein was succeeding in his career at a major corporation but struggled to find an outlet for his desire to serve others. He leaned upon his business and technology acumen to create Besa (an Albanian term for "keep the promise") to link motivated volunteers like him with opportunities to serve in their communities. Rather than concentrating on the volunteer aspect of the mission, he launched the platform by reaching out to corporations who saw the technology platform as a solution to their challenges in corporate social responsibility. These partnerships provided the earned revenue to launch the organization with steady funding; philanthropy is focused on connecting with the nonprofit organizations that are elevated through the efforts of the volunteers.

Other nonprofits find ways to connect with one another to improve efficiency or reduce costs. Examples abound: the nonprofit early-learning center that leases classrooms from a church at below-market-rates; the residential facility for people with intellectual challenges that contracts with a nonprofit meals-on-wheels agency for its food service; the history museum that hires part-time staff from the local college's history department. In each case, the organizations gain resources and expose new stakeholders to their mission.

Impact Investment Partnerships

When private equity is invested to achieve dual purposes, a financial return-on-investment and a social good (such as environmental remediation or poverty reduction), it often falls into a broad category called "impact investing." Impact investing in the United States is thought to approach $20 trillion, although only a fraction of the partnerships include a nonprofit partner.[8] While an impact investment may be one way for a nonprofit to fuel the startup of a social enterprise, the investor may impose restrictions on the use of the funds and will expect an eventual exit strategy that repays the investment, including growth in their original capital.

Impact investing – whether in the nonprofit or for-profit sector – is increasingly popular, especially among investors who want to "do good while doing well." It may be a bit of a misnomer, as "all investments have impact," according to Noell Laing, chief investment officer for Builders Vision, an impact investing platform founded by Lukas Walton, an heir to the founder of Walmart. "In 20 years, impact investing will just be called 'investing,'" she asserts, citing the combination of market-rate returns with compelling social impact.

Here can be found a link to endowments that might help to elevate their appeal among next-generation donors. When the Association of Art Museum Directors and Black Trustee Alliance asked Upstart Co-Lab to assess the investment practices of endowed art museums to better understand how they align their money with their mission and values, they found that 13% of museums deployed endowment assets in impact investing compared to 47% of colleges and universities and 51% of foundations.[9] One of the most thoughtful and active is the Walters Art Museum in Baltimore, whose "Impact Investment Due Diligence Framework" can be found in the Resources section.

Imagine the allure of this double bottom line: contribute to our endowment to make our cause more resilient, and we will in turn invest our endowment to have both a financial and social ROI.

Licensing and Royalties

Not every cause has a product that can make markets work on their behalf, but some have found great success in this arena. Have you ever eaten a Honeycrisp apple? If so, a portion of your purchase benefited the University of Minnesota (U of M), which has been licensing various apple varieties since 1920. Today, the U of M and many other major universities have established offices of commercialization that help to convert their success in research and development into a continual source of funding for their mission. Other organizations that have received the gift of a family farm may lease the property to nearby farmers while retaining the mineral rights for future additional income (if they are comfortable with the potential environmental impacts).

When a nonprofit organization's brand may add value to a commercial venture, the former may license their name and likeness to the latter. One example is AARP, which has licensed its name to various companies, including UnitedHealthcare, The Hartford, and ExxonMobil, according to CPA firm Olsen Thielen. The firm explains that such arrangements can provide a source of revenue but may also cause problems. For example, if a product "endorsed" by a nonprofit is found to be ineffective or harmful, the nonprofit may suffer by association. By the same token, a nonprofit mired in controversy could harm the public perception of a product or service bearing its name.

A newer variation on licensing is the sale of nonfungible tokens (NFTs). Gallery Belvedere in Vienna, Austria, used this approach with a prized work in its collection, Gustav Klimt's *The Kiss*. The art museum collected more than $4 million by creating and selling 10,000 digital representations (tokens) of a small portion of the artwork.

To ensure a license arrangement doesn't become a public relations problem, Olsen Thielen advises nonprofits to thoroughly research any potential partner's business, products, and its principals' backgrounds. Also, the nonprofit should confirm that the two parties' mission and values align. If a potential licensee's products or services have the potential to undermine the cause, they should take a pass – no matter how high the promised royalties.[10]

Single-Issue Donor Advised Funds

This common giving vehicle can give rise to management strategies that build resilience. A donor advised fund (DAF) is a charitable giving vehicle that allows donors to set aside monies, receive an immediate tax benefit, and then deploy the funds over a period of time to nonprofit recipients. Generally, DAFs are held by local community foundations or by national/global financial institutions. The oldest sponsor of DAFs is believed to be the Cleveland Foundation, while the largest is Fidelity Charitable, a nonprofit arm of the powerhouse investment firm Fidelity Investments. Donor advised funds have exploded in popularity, with combined assets thought to exceed $141 billion with distributions approaching $30 billion annually, according to the 2021 report from Giving USA©, *Donor Advised Funds, New Insights.*[11]

More recently, various causes have created their own "private label" DAF programs, allowing donors to realize all of the benefits of a donor advised fund while directing most of the DAF's assets to the cause that is their philanthropic priority. Also called "single-issue DAFs," they have been created largely by major universities and national religious organizations such as the Jewish Communal Fund or Presbyterian Church (U.S.A) Foundation. In a few instances these funds are administered by the 501(c)3, but more often they are legally administered by a partner such as the local community foundation, while offered to donors through the nonprofit that is the ultimate beneficiary of the funds.

For a cause with a large corps of donors, a single-issue DAF can be a strategic resource. Donors who place their funds (irrevocably) in the DAF must eventually distribute the monies to fuel various activities of the organization (although some single-issue DAF sponsors allow donors to distribute a percentage of their grants to outside charities). Moreover, the DAF-sponsoring organization can require that any monies left in the DAF after the donor's lifetime be transferred automatically to the endowment, thus preserving the donor's intent to support the cause in perpetuity.

While a single-issue DAF can be appealing, there are also drawbacks. There are widespread critics of the DAF model who see them as "hoarding" of philanthropic resources in a way that provides greater advantages for the donor and the sponsor with more meager impact for the nonprofit beneficiaries. As a result, regulatory bodies are being pressured to limit the use of and increase reporting requirements for DAFs, which could make the management of these funds even more complex.

Serve and Advocate

In their influential book *Forces for Good,* Leslie Crutchfield and Heather McLeod Grant identify "serve and advocate" as the first of six practices of high-impact organizations, stating that nonprofits "may start out providing great programs, but eventually they realize that they cannot achieve systematic change through service delivery alone" (p. 21)[12] to which observers would add that they cannot achieve resilience, either. Advocacy can lead to permanent funding from government sources. It's a lesson that is on full display in St. Louis, Missouri. In 1971, voters first approved a special taxing district that permanently provided substantial operating support to the zoo and several museums in or near Forest Park. In addition, a permanent fund of $230 million was created in 2023 through the settlement of a lawsuit brought by the city and county when the NFL football team relocated: the resulting endowment will be devoted to civic priorities.

Summary and Next Steps

A cause that is seeking financial resilience has a variety of strategies to choose from instead of or in addition to endowment. The principal method is one that every nonprofit organization should pursue: reserve funds. Whether used as an emergency fund or deployed for strategic opportunities, reserves are at the core of any sustainability strategy. More than a "rainy day fund," reserves provide credibility that reassures donors and long-term sustainability that encourages leaders to pursue innovation.

Once sufficient reserves are in place, more inventive strategies, such as social ventures, licensing, impact investing, advocacy for public funding, or even a single-issue inhouse DAF, can be explored. While care should be taken that these don't become gimmicks that distract from the core purpose, a mission-aligned social enterprise can diversify revenue and increase financial stability.

All of these models of resilience share a common trait: they are typically created and expanded by engaging supporters as donors, investors, or advocates. The coming chapters explore the role that supporters play in fueling causes, and the ways to build the enduring relationships that can help to pursue dreams and weather storms in ways that are equally important – perhaps even more essential – than a strong balance sheet.

Notes

1. "Operating Reserves with Nonprofit Policy Examples," Propel Non-profits, 2024, https://propelnonprofits.org/resources/nonprofit-operating-reserves-policy-examples/.
2. Amy Schiller, *The Price of Humanity* (Melville House, 2023).
3. "Survey," Nonprofit Finance Fund, 2022, https://nff.org/learn/survey#results.
4. "Depreciate," in *Merriam Webster's Collegiate Dictionary*, 11th Ed., 2020.

5. Eric Nee, "Learning from Failure," Stanford Social Innovation Review, February 2015.
6. Fredrik O. Andersson, "Social Entrepreurship as Fetish," *Nonprofit Quarterly*, April 11, 2012, https://nonprofitquarterly.org/social-entrepreneurship-as-fetish-2/.
7. François Bonnici, "Why Social Enterprises Need More Support," World Economic Forum, January 18, 2024, https://www.weforum.org/agenda/2024/01/social-enterprises-financial-policy-support/.
8. US SIF Foundation, "2022: Reflections on Sustainable Investing," December 2022, https://www.ussif.org/.
9. Upstart Co-Lab, Association of Art Museum Directors, and Black Trustee Alliance for Art Museums, "Cultural Capital: The State of Art Museums and Their Investing," June 2022, https://upstartco-lab.org/cultural-capital-the-state-of-museums-and-their-investing/.
10. "Your NFP May Want to Consider Licensing Your Name and Brand," Olsen Thielen CPAs & Advisors, October 13, 2020, https://www.otcpas.com/your-nfp-may-want-to-consider-licensing-your-name-and-brand/.
11. Lilly Family School of Philanthropy, "Donor Advised Funds: New Insights" (Giving USA, September 2021), https://store.givingusa.org/pages/giving-usa-special-report-donor-advised-funds-new-insights.
12. Leslie R. Crutchfield and Heather McLeod Grant, *Forces for Good* (Jossey-Bass, 2007).

PART 2

Enduring Relationships

en • dur • ing, adj.

Lasting. Durable.[1]

Introduction: Why Relationships Matter

For most nonprofit organizations, enduring relationships with donors are essential. The donor who gives year after year (or perhaps month after month) is the bedrock of a successful fundraising program. The magnitude of their gifts is less relevant than their dependability, and their years of giving are a strong predictor of a potential estate gift. An organization with a large cohort of repeat donors is resilient. Endowments, which also provide the assurance of financial sustainability, are often created by the transformational estate gift from loyal donors, fueled by assets they've accumulated over their lifetimes and/or inherited from earlier generations.

Yet this type of loyal donor is becoming less common as participation in charitable giving declines among American households. Whereas in 2002 a higher proportion of people gave to charity (68%) than voted, today fewer than half of all American households

155

participate in charitable giving according to the triennial Philanthropy Panel Study conducted by Indiana University's Lilly Family School of Philanthropy. While giving activity rebounded slightly in 2020 as donors responded to the extraordinary economic and social impact of the pandemic and racial reckoning, the long-term decline resumed thereafter. And there is a crisis of donor retention among America's nonprofit organizations. The Fundraising Effectiveness Project, a collaboration among several national groups that has been tracking giving data since 2006, reported in 2023 that donor participation and loyalty had declined among just about every type of donor.

Despite declining participation, giving grows because high net worth households have increased the amounts they give. Or, as Dr. Una Osili of Indiana University's Lilly Family School of Philanthropy says, "Dollars up, donors down." As a result, charitable giving – like many sectors of the American economy – has become more concentrated, with top-end donors representing a higher proportion of total giving. For some organizations, this trend is a part of their rationale for building endowment.

Why Should We Care?

Concerns about declining participation in charitable giving fall into at least three categories. Two illustrate the risks to the nonprofit sector and the broader economy. Because nonprofit organizations represent 5.6% of GDP and employ 10% of America's workforce, the health of the sector has a significant influence on overall economic vitality. A third category explores the widening wealth gap which, ironically, creates more pressures on the nonprofit sector; it explores intrinsic value of inclusive – rather than exclusive – models of social generosity that help make a cause fiscally resilient.

- *Donor concentration creates risk.* There is immediate risk to any nonprofit organization that relies on a diminishing number of donors to make ever-larger contributions. Just as a publicly traded company must disclose concentration risk if any customer represents more than 10% of its revenue, non-profit organizations should recognize the risk of ever-increasing concentration among their top-end donors. If any top donor abandons the cause, it may take years to nurture new supporters to provide comparable revenue. As an alternative, some organizations ask the (usually aging) major donors to include the organization in their estate plans so that a final endowed gift can replace the sums given annually during their lifetimes. For all of the reasons explored in Chapter 3, this approach may not resonate with many donors.

- *The eventual, inevitable decline.* Will growth in current charitable giving ultimately hit a ceiling as a result of the shrinking pool of donors? This bleak hypothesis is explored in the opening chapters of *The Generosity Crisis*,[2] which postulates that continued declines in donor participation could culminate in an end to all charitable giving by 2049. Although unlikely, this scenario is a call to focus on *all* donors, not just those who make the largest gifts. A growing pool of contributors is necessary for sustained growth in charitable giving, and a strong corps of engaged, loyal, "everyday donors" may be a better signal of eventual bequests, which are typically devoted to endowment.

- *Inclusive philanthropy is good for society.* "The etymology of philanthropy comes from the Greek philos (love) and anthropos (humankind)," observes fundraising and planned giving practitioner Joe Bull. "Literally it is the love of humankind. There is no dollar sign attached to the definition." That is why there are increasing questions about the very understanding of "philanthropy." For some, it conjures images of wealthy patrons writing large checks. Increasingly, its meaning is broadened to include other demonstrations of generosity for the benefit of society, such as gifts of time and talent. Younger generations and women particularly embrace this more inclusive definition.

Whether making formal gifts to a registered charity, or supporting a neighbor in need, giving is one of several prosocial behaviors that is a barometer of a society's durability. Stated another way by researchers at the University of Maryland's Do Good Institute, "individuals who ... donate build their community's social capital by working together with their neighbors, finding ways to cooperate and compromise, and becoming more aware and understanding of each of our differences."[3] That understanding is critical to the resilience of a cause.

Experts point to many possible causes for declines in donor participation:

- The widening wealth gap that constrains the giving of middle- and working-class households
- Media focus on big gifts, which implies that only major donors matter
- Declining attendance at religious worship, which is highly correlated with overall charitable giving
- Eroding trust in institutions
- Reduced tax benefits for "everyday" donors
- The growing popularity of informal ways of giving such as crowdfunding
- Unintentionally harmful practices among fundraisers

The first factors are beyond the control of average nonprofit organizations, although a variety of field-wide initiatives are seeking to redress them. The final factor – practices of fundraising professionals that can unintentionally harm relationships with donors – can and should be addressed by every organization and are explored in the chapters to come.

From the Field: Treating Donors with Respect

Consistency and respect to sustain relationships with donors is a lesson that I learned early in my career:

In the late 1990s, I joined the development team of The Ohio State University, which was then in the midst of its first $1 billion campaign. I had spent the prior 12 years with a national fundraising firm, where I had interacted with hundreds of donors and board members and encountered just about every fundraising strategy that existed at that time. I was an avid consumer of leading publications like *The Chronicle of Philanthropy* and especially *Giving USA©, the Annual Report on Philanthropy*. In short, I was pretty sure of myself.

Early in my tenure at Ohio State, I had a memorable encounter with Jerry May, who was then president of the university's foundation and is widely respected throughout the fundraising field. We were standing in the lobby of the Wexner Center for the Arts, where I was responsible for fundraising efforts. I don't recall my exact words to Jerry, only that I said something glib and vaguely amusing about one of our donors. I do remember Jerry's response. He turned to me and said quietly and with great dignity, "We don't talk about donors that way, Laura. The way we talk about donors reflects the way we think about them. And the way we think about them affects the ways we interact with them. At this university, we treat donors with respect, and that's how we talk about them."

Loyal donors are essential to fuel causes that serve the common good. It can be a fragile equation. Donors may be more valuable to nonprofit organizations than the cause may be to donors. That is why it is incumbent upon everyone who works within an organization to nurture relationships with donors, whether they have direct responsibility for fundraising, are implementing the programs that donors help to fund, or manage finances in a back office.

These final chapters are devoted to the factors that can help to engage donors, nurture relationships, and secure both loyalty and financial resources expressed through charitable giving.

Notes

1. "Enduring." In *Merriam-Webster's Collegiate Dictionary*, 11th Ed., 2020.
2. Crimmins, Brian, Nathan Chappell, and Michael Ashley, *The Generosity Crisis* (John Wiley & Sons, 2022).
3. Grimm, Robert T., Jr., and Nathan Dietz. 2019. "A Less Charitable Nation: The Decline of Volunteering and Giving in the United States." Research Brief: Do Good Institute, University of Maryland.

7

Who Gives, Who Gives to Endowment, and Why

This chapter enables you to:

- Understand who makes charitable gifts in America, and who is most likely to give to endowment.
- Identify the most common traits of individual charitable donors.
- Distinguish between donors making current gifts and those who give toward the future.
- Review the variety of methods that explore motivations for giving and how they can be applied to endowment fundraising.

Donors may provide all – or most – revenue for many causes. Museums, advocacy organizations, environmental causes, and other sectors typically rely on contributed revenue for more than half of their income, as illustrated in Figure 7-1. Sectors like healthcare and higher education that have a high proportion of earned revenue call on philanthropy to ensure access (through scholarships, for example) and pursue innovation. According to the Urban Institute's National Center for Charitable Statistics,[1] contributions account for slightly more than 20% of total revenue in the nonprofit sector, with wide variations depending on the cause.

161

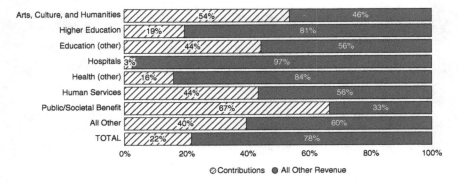

FIGURE 7-1 Proportion of contributed versus earned revenue by sector
Adapted from NCCS

Given this reliance on donors and the funds they provide, declining donor participation is alarming for nonprofit organizations in every sector and every region. And, because donors to endowments are generally those with longstanding relationships, this trend may have an impact on the ability to secure endowment gifts.

What is the cause of this decline? Is it that individuals have lost faith in the power of philanthropy, as evidenced by declining trust in institutions?[2] Are everyday households squeezed by inflation and stagnant wages? Do attention-grabbing headlines of charity wrong-doing crowd out positive messages from the vast majority of nonprofits doing good? Perhaps we should examine today's sophisticated fundraising operations that shower attention on big givers, with lip service for those of comparatively modest means. Or look more closely at other expressions of generosity, such as GoFundMe campaigns and mutual aid societies that are not counted in most philanthropic data. These factors may all be contributing to the decline in the percentage of American households that participate in traditional charitable giving.

This chapter is devoted to donors: understanding who gives, the traits common among donors to endowment, the team of advisors that may assist and influence donor's decisions, and what we know about donor motivations.

Who Makes Charitable Gifts in America?

Charitable giving in the United States first eclipsed $500 billion in 2022, according to *Giving USA, the Annual Report on Philanthropy*.[3] Giving usually represents approximately 2% of the American economy: that's about the same influence on the economy as major industries, such as mining or utilities. *Giving USA* data shows that the amount given to 501(c)3 organizations generally grows (it showed a decline in current dollars only five times between 1967 and 2023), although it does not always keep pace with inflation.

Giving USA identifies four sources of charitable gifts: individuals, foundations, corporations, and bequests (see Figure 7-2). Individual donors have given a majority of all charitable dollars ever since the annual study began in the mid-1960s. The influence of

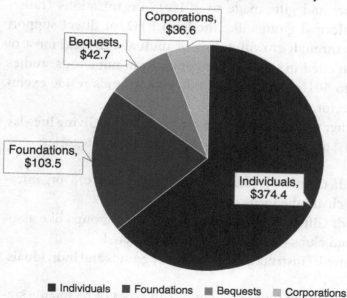

Sources of Giving ($ Billions)

Corporations, $36.6

Bequests, $42.7

Foundations, $103.5

Individuals, $374.4

■ Individuals ■ Foundations ■ Bequests ■ Corporations

FIGURE 7-2 Sources of charitable contributions
Adapted from Giving USA 2024, the Annual Report on Philanthropy for the Year 2023.

individual donors is magnified when gifts by bequest are considered, which – after all – come from individuals making decisions about the distribution of assets after their lifetimes. In addition, about half of all foundation giving is driven by closely held family foundations or donor advised funds: that is, individuals making decisions about money they have set aside for charitable giving. Taken together, these sources consistently provide approximately 85% of all charitable dollars. Corporations and the remaining foundations represent less than one-fifth of total charitable giving. These are promising statistics for endowment builders, since most endowment gifts come from individual donors.

> Most endowment gifts come from individual donors.

Most measures of charitable giving, chiefly the *Giving USA* report, focus on donors and gifts made to 501(c)3 organizations (rather than gifts to informal groups like the local PTO, or direct support for individuals through crowdfunding or mutual aid), and most of the information cited in this chapter comes from numerous studies about donors to 501(c)3 charities. Endowment funds reside exclusively in this sector.

There are other ways to categorize generosity. The GivingTuesday Data Commons[4] organizes gifts of money into three categories:

- **Registered:** Gifts to formally incorporated 501(c)3 organizations, which are the focus of this discussion.
- **Structured:** Gifts to organized and structured groups like associations and clubs that are not legally registered.
- **Unstructured:** Unstructured community groups and individuals.

Considerations of all types of giving to all types of recipients significantly expands the definition of "generosity." Because researchers have found that most donors who participate in "informal" philanthropy also give to incorporated charities – and vice versa – all expressions of generosity may be a harbinger of "formal philanthropy" and opportunities to engage donors who could eventually support endowments.

The Traits of Individual Charitable Donors

Anyone who seeks to raise funds can – and should – develop an understanding of the traits of people who give to charity by reviewing abundant studies and reports, some of which are listed in the Resources section. Few studies focus solely on donors who give to endowment, so the traits of donors who make planned gifts might serve as a proxy for understanding endowment donors. A summary of general research findings (as of 2024) is described in this section. Generally, researchers take into consideration various demographic traits and the resulting impact on the likelihood and magnitude of charitable gifts. As stated in the report *Changes to the Giving Landscape*,[5] researched and written by the Lilly Family School of Philanthropy:

Income, education, homeownership, marital status, and religious affiliation once largely shaped the likelihood and amount of giving. Today, these categories intersect with national trends that include economic shifts, workforce diversity, changing gender roles, and shifting demographics to alter philanthropic giving patterns (p. 5).

So, while demographic traits may provide generalities in charitable giving behavior, they are just a starting point and do not replace tailored relationship-building, as discussed in the final chapters. These general demographic traits are discussed fully in the following sections.

From the Field: The Limitations of Data

Approach data about charitable giving with caution. I've found that the vast majority of longitudinal studies in our sector (as well as most others) is based on white men only, and therefore can be very limited in its ability to predict future outcomes. When I was appointed director of development for the College of Nursing at a major university, I found that more than 90 percent of our graduates were women. Despite the sophistication of the university's database and modeling, rarely was a nursing alum lifted up as a donor worth pursuing for a major gift. With an understanding of these limitations in our data, I leveraged the expertise of the Lilly School to look differently at alumni and subsequently produced the three highest giving years in college history. We changed what we were looking for (longevity of giving vs. magnitude of gift, for example), how we communicated (more about collective impact than individual champions), and many other recommendations based on the research around women's giving. So I don't dismiss the existing data but also think critically about the limitations that exist and how it might impact my work.

—Katy Trombitas,
Vice President of Advancement, Columbus State
Community College

Generation

Donors' impact on the nonprofit sector varies with each generation (using the definitions developed by Pew Research Center). As of 2024, the giving of charitable dollars continues to be dominated by the generations born before 1965, due to the large population, affluence, and life-stage of its members – all of which make them candidates for charitable giving, especially through planned gifts. In particular, the "Baby Boom" generation, which was once the largest in the nation's history but is slowly declining in number, shapes the giving landscape in the early decades of the twenty-first century. Their influence will be eclipsed by the charitable giving practices and preferences of succeeding generations (especially Millennials, whose large population continues to grow through immigration) and their rising financial stature. It is important to note that these younger generations are expected to inherit wealth estimated to approach $72 trillion from their Baby Boomer and older parents. As a result, they may be the most influential donors in the history of American philanthropy.

Each generation has unique charitable behaviors that will (re) shape the charitable landscape. As Ryan Turner, Principal of Business English for Social Impact observed, "newer generations favor control as much as older generations favor legacies." A study conducted by the Blackbaud Institute in 2018 (*The Next Generation of American Giving*)[6] provided one barometer of each generation's charitable priorities, as explained in Table 7-1.

Scholars debate whether participation in charitable giving increases with age or if today's younger generations are simply less able or willing to make charitable gifts, or express their generosity in other ways, and will continue these behaviors as they age. The Blackbaud Institute study did provide one hint: a significant percentage of generations X, Y, and Z anticipate an increase in the amount they give (approximately 25%, 32%, and 42% respectively).

The Millennial Generation ("Gen Y") has been the focus of considerable philanthropic research because of the size of its population and their distinctive approach to social issues. The Case Foundation has supported longitudinal research about this generation's interactions with causes since 2009. Among their findings: Millennials care about issues rather than institutions; support causes through multiple channels, not only charitable giving of money; and show a tolerance for risk in employing innovative approaches to solve wicked problems.

TABLE 7-1 Charitable Giving Practices By Generation

Generation	Population in 2022/ Estimated Percentage That Give	Top Five Charitable Giving Priorities
Pre-Baby Boomer (born prior to 1945)	19 million/78%	Worship*, Local Social Service, Emergency Relief, Health, Children
Baby Boomers (born 1946–64)	69 million/75%	Local Social Service, Worship*, Health, Emergency Relief, Children
Gen X (born 1965–1980)	65 million/55%	Health*, Local Social Service, Animal, Children, Emergency Relief
Millennials (Gen Y) (born 1981–1996)	72 million/51%	Worship*, Children, Local Social Service, Health, Animals
Gen Z (1997 – 2012)	70 million/44%	Children, Animal, Health, Worship*, Local Social Service

*Indicates the sector that receives the most dollars when respondents were asked to prioritize.

"Next Gen" giving behavior has also been studied by groups like the Dorothy A. Johnson Center for Philanthropy at Grand Valley State University and the nonprofit group 21/64. Their groundbreaking 2022 report *Next Gen Donor Learning* states:

> In their book *Generation Impact: How Next Gen Donors Are Revolutionizing Philanthropy*, Sharna Goldseker and Michael Moody make the somewhat grandiose claim that "next gen donors" are in the process of becoming the "most significant donors ever" (p. 3). But there are a lot of reasons why this is the case. For one thing, major donors of Gen X and later generations will have an historic amount of resources to give – both because of the vast wealth transfer happening right now, and because of the continuing trend of considerable wealth creation at younger ages (*Next Gen Donor Learning*, p. 8).[7]

While endowments have been viewed as the purview of older generations, succeeding generations also have the capacity to give if nonprofit organizations can secure their loyalty and adapt to their distinctive approach to charitable giving.

In Practice: Planned Giving Prospects in "The Middle"

It is common to focus attention on "major" donors who have shown their affinity to an organization through very large gifts, based on the hope that they may also make a very large bequest to support endowment. However, it is a mistake to exclude other donors from conversations about endowments and planned giving.

A series of studies on mid-level donors produced by Sea Change Strategies and Edge Research documents the opportunity to engage these individuals in a discussion about a potential planned gift to support endowment. The fourth study in their series[8] found that mid-level donors:

- Are likely to have net worth (excluding the primary residence) between $1 million and $5 million.
- Donate more than $1,000 annually to an average of 5.7 different organizations.
- Have often been involved with the organizations they support for a decade or more.
- Are aware that making a bequest to an organization is an option; more than half have either made a bequest to an organization (31%) or say that they plan to make one in the future (23%).

Wealth and Its Source(s)

It is not surprising that wealth correlates to formal charitable giving. Since 2006, the Indiana University Lilly Family School of Philanthropy has conducted a periodic study of charitable giving by affluent households, now sponsored by Bank of America.[9] They define affluence as "households with assets of $1 million or more (excluding the value of their primary home) and/or an annual income of $200,000 or more," which represents approximately 3% of all American households that account for approximately 65% of all charitable dollars given. The study has consistently found that affluent households are more likely to give to formal charities compared to the general population (85.1% vs. 48.8% in 2018) and that their average annual giving amount is considerably higher ($34,917 vs. $2,581). They are no more generous as a *proportion* of household income – in fact, households at the lowest end of the income spectrum (<$50,000) give a higher percentage of their overall income. Contrast this display with the reasons that some affluent households claim when they *do not* give to charity, citing "my priority was to take care of my family's needs" (44%) and "I did not have the resources" (25%) as their top two reasons, despite their apparent wealth.

The source of wealth also appears to correlate to the ways that households give. According to the study *Entrepreneurs as Philanthropists* conducted in 2018 by Artemis Research for Fidelity Charitable,[10] the average annual gift from entrepreneurs (those who earned their wealth through various enterprises) is four times higher than gifts from others ($50,359 vs. $11,151), although this distinction is moot among families in racial classes whose ancestors were largely denied opportunities to create businesses or generational wealth.

Professional fundraisers affirm that the distinction between inherited and earned wealth aligns with their experience. They share many anecdotes suggesting that those with inherited wealth, who may view themselves as multi-generational stewards of a family's assets, proceed with greater caution, while entrepreneurs may be bolder in their giving habits, perhaps bolstered in the belief that they always have the capacity to create more wealth. However, these same professionals also report that the qualities that made the entrepreneur successful – like intellect, risk tolerance, using money as leverage, the ability to solve a problem – may become a meddlesome hindrance with entrepreneurial donors who tie strings to their giving based on the assumption that the same qualities apply equally to the work of a cause.

Education

Several academic studies have shown a correlation between educational attainment and giving amounts. Put simply, "college-educated households are more likely to donate compared to those households with an incomplete high school education. The percent of income given also increases with level of educational attainment."[11] Of course, educational attainment is closely related to household income. Households with less education are more vulnerable during economic disruptions, inhibiting their capacity to participate in formal philanthropy – although evidence is emerging that indicates modest households demonstrate their generosity in other ways.

Race and Ethnicity

While "generosity is inherent in all cultures," according to Dr. Una Osili of Indiana University, "it is expressed and carried out in different ways in different communities." The comparison also extends to rates of participation in charitable giving (considering charitable gifts to formal charities), which are declining across all races. Among the various causes cited earlier, communities of color – and their capacity to give – are especially impacted by wealth disparities.

According to a study by the Lilly Family School of Philanthropy:

Asian Americans have the highest average income between 2000 and 2018, followed by White Americans. However, despite having one of the lowest average household incomes, Black Americans gave a higher percentage of their income to charity than Asian Americans and Hispanic Americans in most of the years between 2000 and 2018. Between these years, Black Americans donated 3 to 4 percent of their income to charity on average (*Everyday Donors of Color*, p. 21).[12]

The study also points out that consistent constraints on the ability of some racial groups to build intergenerational wealth hamper their capacity to give. One can surmise that this dynamic may be especially influential in decisions to pass wealth to heirs through estate plans as a higher priority than making charitable bequests to charities.

The Donors of Color Network concluded that "philanthropy always sounds like someone else" in their report of the same name.[13] They cite that there are at least 1.3 million high net worth households in America led by a person of color, yet a high proportion face structural barriers to giving. They are often the first generation – if not the first individual – in their family to create wealth. Therefore, they feel a responsibility to give informally to family and friends (78%) in addition to registered charities. Yet nearly one-third of the study's participants had a bequest in place to support a charitable beneficiary.

Gender and Sexual Orientation

The Women's Philanthropy Institute at Indiana University (a part of the Lilly Family School of Philanthropy) has studied the distinct giving patterns of women versus dominant cultural assumptions based on the charitable giving behaviors of men. They have further studied behavior based on marital status, race and gender, household composition, and other factors, with the reports available on the website philanthropy.iupui.edu/institutes. Among the conclusions they've drawn are the following.[14]

- **Women's wealth is rising.** Women's share of wealth has risen considerably over the past 50 years and today they hold around 40% of global wealth.
- **Women are more likely to give.** Across income levels and generations, women are more likely to give, and they give more than their male counterparts. Their giving is also more likely to be based on empathy for others, whereas giving by men is often more about self-interest.
- **Women give differently.** From motivations to causes to behavior, women and men demonstrate different giving patterns. For example, about 70% of giving circles are women.

Sexual identity can also influence giving behaviors. Several studies suggest there may be less wealth in the LGBTQ+ community but confirm that there are still many prospects for major gifts and shining examples of extraordinary generosity. In her essay on "the Gay and Lesbian Donor" for *AFP Advancing Philanthropy* magazine, Donna Red Wing summarized several studies and surveys to conclude that members of the LGBTQ+ community donate more than the average American. They are more likely to give to causes they are passionate about, organizations that are seen as lesbian/gay friendly, and places where they volunteer (Oct. 1, 2018).[15] A 2021 essay by Casey J. Saunders, CFRE in the same journal shed light on the opportunity: "Understanding that an LGBTQ+ person is more likely to be philanthropic makes them likely a 'better' prospect for some revenue lines. Further understanding that LGBTQ+ people are less than half as likely to have children and possess more wealth to distribute to charity notably though planned gifts may make them an even 'better' prospect for the planned gifts that are often devoted to endowment."[16]

Engagement

There is a strong correlation between those who volunteer with an organization and those who give, and vice versa. In the University of

Maryland's 2024 study *Social Connectedness and Generosity*,[17] "People who volunteer in the previous year are more likely to give in the current year, by 14.5 percentage points, and people who give in the previous year are more likely to volunteer in the current year, by 9.3 percentage points" (p. 3). This finding was reinforced in the *Giving USA* Special Report *Leaving a Legacy*,[18] which found that the prospects who had the highest likelihood of making a planned gift include those who served on the organization's board, were longtime committed volunteers, and/or were longtime dedicated employees.

The adage "involvement leads to commitment" has long been applied by fundraising practitioners, and it appears that the inverse is also true (although the data supports correlation only, not necessarily causation).

Conclusions About Who Gives

All of this research into the demographic traits common among generous donors could lead a fundraiser to seek out only affluent, entrepreneurial, highly educated white females who volunteer for the organization and identify as LGBTQ+, which would be an obvious mistake. While demographic traits may be one clue to charitable behaviors, in reality donors reflect the larger trends in America's society. It may be that those who are most frequently singled out as "philanthropists" are simply those who support charities in the most public and traditional ways, display the most obvious indications of wealth, and/or who are pursued most vigorously by front-line fundraising officers. Demographics can help to organize and prioritize an unwieldy list of prospective donors, but over-reliance on demographics will result in many missed opportunities to inspire generosity.

Who Gives to Endowments?

An understanding of the general charitable giving landscape is a place to start, then successful endowment-building requires an appreciation for the specific traits of donors who are most likely to support endowment and other future-looking funds, and why and how they give. The latter informs the former: many nonprofits with established endowments report that planned gifts – especially bequests – account for a large percentage of their corpus. Research such as the *Giving USA* Special Report *Leaving a Legacy* can help to pinpoint those who are likely to make planned gifts, which may serve as a proxy for those who are likely to support endowment. They found that the average age for writing a first will is 44 years old (p. 17), and the average age for making the first charitable planned gift is 53 – much younger than conventional wisdom has suggested.

To understand who might give to *endowment*, practitioners also rely on their own experience, historic patterns of giving to their organization, and guidance from peers and consultants. Additional research and observations about donors to endowment provide the following insights.

- **Current gifts** to endowment can come from just about any donor. However, an organization's endowment policies may dissuade donors of modest means from participating – intentionally or unintentionally, explicitly or subconsciously. For example, if the policy requires a minimum gift of $25,000 to endow a programmatic fund, many "everyday philanthropists" may feel priced out of participation. Prominent recognition for donors who create large, endowed funds may send the message that extraordinary wealth is a prerequisite. There are alternative strategies that can provide avenues for participation of all donors, like giving circles, as described in Chapters 3, 4, and 9. Nevertheless, donors who give cash or other current assets to endowment follow many of the patterns discussed earlier: wealthy and well educated. Why? Because wealth is required to meet common minimum requirements to establish an endowed fund; and well educated because endowment is most likely to appeal to a donor with a sophisticated understanding of nonprofits and financial models.

- Deferred gifts, on the other hand, can come from a wider range of donors. While there are many kinds of deferred gifts that appeal to a wide variety of donors as discussed in Chapter 8, more than 80% of donors' arrangements are simple bequests included in their will. Whether a donor specifies that their bequest be permanently restricted (or "endowed" – see Chapter 1) or the organization's policies automatically place the funds in quasi-endowment (see Chapter 5), bequests are believed to be the source of funding for most endowments.

An annual survey by the website for seniors and their caregivers, caring.com, found that only one in three adult Americans has a will and, among them, Black and Hispanic Americans are even less likely to have a will (29% and 23%, respectively). A report from online estate planning firm GivingDocs.Com affirmed this finding and found that "lower rates of charitable planned giving among communities of color are primarily correlated with lower rates of estate planning itself and not with lower rates of charitable intent."[19] The caring.com study also found that the likelihood of having a will increases with educational attainment (54% with a post-graduate degree have a will versus just 26% with a high school education). When asked why they had not drafted a will, all sectors cited procrastination as the primary reason – suggesting that nonprofit organizations have an opportunity to encourage estate planning, including a charitable bequest, using the tactics described in the next chapters.

Even if a donor has already prepared their will, it is not too late to add charitable bequests: the majority of people update their will at least once if not several times. A simple addition to a will is called a *codicil*. Many nonprofit organizations include sample language for a codicil on their website (see sample language in the Resources section at the end of the book).

Whether a donor is making a current or deferred gift that is large or small, there is agreement on one trait that is almost universal among donors to endowment: they have been loyal to the organization for a long time. Their affinity may have led them to serve on the board, volunteer, or attend programs frequently; or it may be expressed simply through consistent giving over many years – even decades. They may be beneficiaries of the cause themselves, such as a proud graduate, grateful patient, or avid member of the audience. Any cause can identify these prospects in their midst by looking through the organization's history and donor records – it does not require a fancy or expensive process. According to a survey of donors conducted for the *Giving USA* Special Report *Leaving a Legacy*, 78% of planned gift donors responded that they had supported the recipient of their largest bequest for 20 years or more, half at relatively modest levels with lifetime giving less than $25,000 (p. 21).

Who Doesn't Give to Endowment?

It is *un*common for corporations or foundations to make grants for endowment. Why? A common reason is that these funders may view their resources as equivalent to endowed funds, which they prefer to manage internally and deploy as current gifts. Others cite their preference for the accountability that comes from a nonprofit organization's annual funding cycle, which requires an organization to make its case and demonstrate its impact each year. Or they point to restrictions imposed by a foundation's founders or preferences expressed by the shareholders of a public company. On the rare occasions that a foundation or corporation makes a significant gift to a nonprofit endowment, it is generally for one of two reasons: to fund a scholarship or other workforce development initiative that will expand their workforce pipeline, or because a member of the C-suite or board serves on the nonprofit's board or campaign committee.

According to Janelle Coleman, a corporate philanthropy veteran who has worked with and for multiple Fortune 500 companies, "there are several reasons why corporations typically won't make a gift to a nonprofit's endowment. Most corporations prefer annual gifts because they ensure accountability and annual updates from the cause. We want to determine the way that the cause will deploy resources in our name. And we want to avoid the complicated accounting that can result from a long-term pledge or a transfer of assets from our balance sheet to the nonprofit's." A search of foundation directories reveals that fewer than 2% of all foundations list "endowment" among their grant-making priorities.

When the Center for Effective Philanthropy explored foundation funding for endowments in their 2024 report *Funding Nonprofit Endowments,* they found that "just under a third of foundations provide endowment grants, and these represent a small fraction of their total giving" (page 6).[20] The report goes on to observe that few foundations that do not currently fund endowments plan to adopt the practice because they do not believe that such funding is aligned with their mission, funding strategy, or size.

There are a few exceptions. Among the most notable is the Lilly Endowment, an independent foundation created in 1937 by the founder of pharmaceutical giant Eli Lilly and Company. Because of the stellar performance of the stock donated by the founder, the Lilly Endowment is now approaching the scale of another heavyweight, the Gates Foundation. Unlike the Gates Foundation, Lilly has focused on increasing the endowments of community foundations throughout their home state of Indiana, and of HBCUs across the country.

Why Do People Give?

Nobel Laureate Richard Thaler described the study of economic behaviors as "behavioral economics – which holds that imperfect humans do not fit neatly into classic economic models." So any exploration of the reasons for charitable giving must be tempered with an understanding that the motivations for giving vary widely among donors – and may even differ for any single donor depending on the cause and the day. Few studies distinguish giving to an endowment from other giving. Nevertheless, it's helpful to understand – and apply – some of what has been learned from the many studies on this topic.

Understanding of donor behavior has been investigated in multiple ways, with different outcomes given the strengths and weaknesses of each method.

Surveys

Surveys ask donors why they give. While their feedback is informative, this self-reported data is particularly prone to response bias. It turns out that human beings often do not fully understand the reasons for their own actions and tend to assign credit to the factors that make them look socially acceptable. Survey data should be just one element in a larger consideration of charitable giving behavior. An example of a broad philanthropic survey is the online polling conducted by the research data company YouGov.[21] They asked survey participants about their charitable giving motivations in a 2022 poll; the responses are outlined in Table 7-2.

The same survey found that only 13% of respondents felt it was important to know that they would receive public recognition for their donation. Yet, as explained in the "Donor Surveys" sidebar,

TABLE 7-2 Responses to a Poll About Why People Give

Motivation for Giving	Percent of Responses
I believe in the cause	48%
I believe you should give to charity	31%
Giving to charity is part of my religious beliefs	15%
I don't feel the state does enough to help people in need	13%
I have a personal experience benefiting from the charity	11%
I always give to charity	11%
I want to support a friend	8%
Other and not sure	4%

these self-reported reasons for giving differ from the results of other types of studies.

In Practice: Donor Surveys

Giving data or online metrics can be analyzed extensively, but this alone will not uncover the essential question: Why does a donor support a cause? Loyalty, motivation, or intent cannot be measured without attitudinal data. To truly understand these critical elements, a solid approach is to combine transactional data (such as giving patterns) with attitudinal data (like survey responses).

The science behind surveys is complex and could easily fill a book. The first chapter of that book would probably state that most surveys have limited effectiveness. To design meaningful, predictive surveys, it is advisable to consult with an expert. However, a straightforward action that will enhance understanding of donors is a simple "commitment" survey, as described by Roger Craver in *Retention Fundraising: The New Art and Science of Keeping Your Donors for Life.*[22]

This type of survey assesses the strength of the relationship between a donor and the organization. When integrated with actual giving data from the CRM, it creates a scoring system that identifies the greatest areas of potential.

Three affirmative statements can measure commitment when asked consistently across multiple communication channels:

- I am a committed donor to [ABC Charity].
- I feel a sense of loyalty to [ABC Charity].
- [ABC Charity] is my favorite nonprofit.

> Ask respondents to rate each statement on a 10-point scale. The commitment score is derived from the average of these three ratings. Highly committed donors score 8-10, medium commitment donors score in the 5-7 range, and low commitment donors score 5 or below. This score, combined with their past giving history and giving capacity, offers a reliable method for pinpointing the most promising prospects.
> —Steve Beshuk, Nonprofit Technology Advisor

Analysis of Large Datasets

Analyzing large datasets, like the Philanthropy Panel Study or Current Population Study (CPS), can demonstrate correlations – such as links between volunteering and giving – but economists are cautious about citing specific causation. The University of Maryland's Do Good Institute used CPS data to demonstrate a strong link between volunteering and giving, although it did not speculate on the reasons that an individual might choose to do either.

Similarly, the Lilly Family School of Philanthropy at Indiana University mines their periodic Philanthropy Panel Study for a variety of explorations, including the links between giving behaviors and gender cited earlier.

Organizations that have accurate data about their donors and gifts dating back many years can apply similar inquiries to better understand the charitable giving behaviors specific to their cause. For example, a query into the specific donation patterns of their donors who have given to an endowed fund may reveal that there are numerous "look alike" donors with similar traits. These "look alike" donors are among the best prospects for future gifts to the endowment, although care must be taken to ensure that this practice will not simply reinforce any bias in the organization's historic fundraising practices.

Behavioral Economics

The emerging field of *behavioral economics* relies on "natural experiments" and other observed behaviors to postulate the factors that influence giving. Most of this work focuses on large groups of donors making comparatively modest gifts, so they have limited application to the larger gifts that have come to dominate charitable giving totals and are relevant in building endowment.

The nonprofit think tank ideas42 compiles a periodic list of behavioral research studies. Their recent literature review cited more than 21 papers on topics such as "Social Norms," "Avoidance," and "Emotion and Giving."[23] Work in this field has provided valuable insights such as:

- **When a person is unsure, they look to others.** For example, knowing the amount that an early donor gave to an endowed fund may increase others' donation amounts. This is called "social norming" or the "follow the leader" effect.
- **The "follow the leader" effect is much stronger than "crowding out,"** meaning that a celebrated large gift from one donor is more likely to encourage giving from others, not discourage it.
- **Matching gifts, challenge gifts, and seed funding (an initial large gift) all have a positive impact on giving.**

However, the application of behavioral economics to charitable giving is a niche in a field where there has been a greater focus on other behaviors such as consumer choices. Some of that work can also be applied to help understand the charitable giving environment.

Neuroeconomics

Neuroeconomics uses technology such as functional MRIs to observe the brain activity of individuals as they consider their charitable giving. This has led to the concept of the "warm glow of giving," or stated another way, that giving decisions take place in a different part of the brain than consumer choices, and giving makes people feel good. Researchers such as Doctors John List and Uri Gneezy conclude in their book *The Why Axis* that ". . . in the end, giving to charity is nothing like purchasing a Snickers bar; it's more about doing the right thing and joining a fight, and feeling good about what you give" (p. 195).[24]

This field has benefited greatly from the work of Dr. Russell James, whose research is particularly applicable to planned giving and endowment. Much of James' research is readily accessible on his website encouragegenerosity.com. He has found a large "behavioral gap" between current giving and planned or bequest giving (*Inside the Mind of the Bequest Donor*, p. 17).[25] He notes that most people try to avoid mortality reminders, which discourages them from planning their estate – but also observes that this defense mechanism can be overcome with symbolic immortality emphasizing that some part of a donor's achievements can exist beyond their lifetime (p. 25). The best means to leverage this "autobiographical heroism" is through story, but not just any story. James' extensive exploration of the role of the "hero myth" provides specific guidance for those who engage donors in conversations about their charitable giving, yielding more gifts, larger gifts, and a better experience for the donor. It is a relatively simple equation as illustrated in the *Epic Fundraiser* (p. 10):

Initial Identity → Challenge → Victory = Elevated Identity

Perhaps it is deceptively simple because James spends another 283 pages and three other books unpacking each element of this equation and the role of the donor, the beneficiary, and various other characters in developing a story with a compelling plot that is most likely to resonate with donors. See Table 8-3 in Chapter 8 for a further exploration of the donor's journey as the "hero myth."

The Action-Reaction Model

Finally, in addition to or instead of all these research methods, practitioners may intentionally or subconsciously apply a form of *praxis* (also known as an *action-reaction model*). With time and experience, fundraisers gain a greater understanding of their donors as they evaluate the response to different engagement and solicitation methods, and perhaps share their experiential learning through conference presentations or discussions with their peers. Their successful strategy with one donor solicitation may be applied to future appeals. Experiential learning can be relatively easy and affordable with broad base appeals, where a/b testing can reveal which email subject line resulted in the highest rates for opening the email, clicking through to the website, and making a donation. However, it is less applicable in the world of major gift fundraising: a development officer cannot take the risk of "experimenting" with a donor if failure might result in the loss of a large gift and important relationship. Conclusions can also be drawn from a single donor's gifts year-after-year under a variety of solicitation techniques and economic conditions, but it is impossible to run a comparison with bequest giving since it "is not a series of gifts made year after year, but rather we have only one gift" (James, 2013, p. 9).

Translating Research to Practice

The insights gleaned from all these methods, and summarized in the *Giving USA* Special Report *Leaving a Legacy*, reveal several factors that seem to correlate to making a planned gift (p. 23):

- Not having heirs, or having successful heirs
- Having a pragmatic attitude toward death
- The individual or family members have benefited from the organization
- Displaying a personal value of generosity and a history of charitable giving
- Feeling financially secure enough to support heirs and others
- Having legal and financial advisors who encourage giving

Factors that appear to be common among those who are reluctant to make a planned gift include concerns about late-in-life healthcare costs, the (often mistaken) belief that assets are insufficient to make a meaningful gift, and especially simple procrastination.

While surveys might suggest that donors give because "I believe in the cause," and data analysis points to links between donor behavior and other actions such as volunteering or voting, behavioral economics and neuroscience tell us that people give because of the "warm glow" they get – it makes them feel good. All of this learning can – and should – be harnessed to design the most effective strategies for donor engagement and endowment building. For the professional gift officer, nurturing a relationship between a donor and a cause may unfold over many decades, where the intimate knowledge of a singular donor's interests and behavior trumps any generalizations that can be read in studies or heard in conference presentations.

Summary and Next Steps

Most charitable gifts, including gifts to endowment, come from individual donors making decisions about their own money – how it will be deployed during their lifetime or after. An understanding of the traits of charitable givers, including their age/generation, race, gender, religious belief, and other factors can help to pinpoint those who are most likely to support a cause. On the other hand, an over-reliance on demographic segmentation may also be one reason that a lower percentage of American households made charitable gifts in 2022 than did in 2002, as fundraisers continually mine the same data for ever-smaller subsets of donors.

Finally, emerging science is helping to pinpoint the factors that motivate people to make current or planned gifts, providing practitioners with insights to strengthen the bonds between a donor and a cause. The intended output of the donor + motivation equation is a gift. As the next chapter reveals, there are many types of donor journeys that result in a variety of different gift types.

Notes

1. Urban Institute, "National Center for Charitable Statistics Data | Urban Institute," www.urban.org, accessed March 6, 2024, https://www.urban.org/tags/national-center-charitable-statistics-data.
2. Independent Sector, "Trust in Civil Society," September 26, 2023, https://independentsector.org/resource/trust-in-civil-society/.
3. Giving USA, *Giving USA 2023*, 68th ed. (Giving USA, 2023).
4. "GivingTuesday Data Commons," GivingTuesday, accessed March 6, 2024, https://www.givingtuesday.org/data-commons/.
5. Lilly Family School of Philanthropy and Vanguard Charitable, "Changes to the Giving Landscape," 2019, https://blog.philanthropy.iupui.edu/2019/10/24/changes-to-the-giving-landscape-giving-before-and-after-the-great-recession/.
6. Blackbaud Institute, "The next Generation of American Giving," 2018.
7. Sharna Goldseker and Michael Patrick Moody, *Generation Impact: How Next Gen Donors Are Revolutionizing Giving* (Hoboken: Wiley, 2017).
8. Alia McKee and Mark Rovner, "The Missing Middle Part Four" (Sea Change Strategies and Edge Research, 2024), https://seachangestrategies.com/resources/.
9. Lilly Family School of Philanthropy, Indiana University, "The 2023 Bank of America Study of Philanthropy: Charitable Giving by Affluent Households," *IUPUI Scholarworks*, October 2023, https://scholarworks.iupui.edu/items/31aafdfd-a6a6-486e-978c-35c705409f2c.
10. Fidelity Charitable and Artemis Research Group, "Entrepreneurs as Philanthropists," 2018, https://www.fidelitycharitable.org/insights/entrepreneurs-as-philanthropists.html.
11. "Changes to the Giving Landscape," page 13.
12. Lilly Family School of Philanthropy, "Everyday Donors of Color: Giving Trends by Race and Ethnicity," November 2023, https://philanthropy.indianapolis.iu.edu/research/latest/donors-of-color.html.
13. Hali Lee, Urvashi Vaid, and Ashindi Maxton, "Philanthropy Always Sounds Like Someone Else: A Portrait of High Net Worth Donors of Color," *Donors of Color Network* (Donors of Color Network, 2022), https://www.donorsofcolor.org/resources/philanthropy-always-sounds-like-someone-else-0c68d.

14. "Research," Lilly Family School of Philanthropy, accessed March 6, 2024, https://philanthropy.indianapolis.iu.edu/institutes/womens-philanthropy-institute/research/index.html.
15. Donna Red Wing, "The Gay and Lesbian Donor," *AFP Advancing Philanthropy*, October 1, 2018.
16. Casey Saunders, "Fabulous and Philanthropic," *AFP Advancing Philanthropy*, June 1, 2021.
17. Nathan Dietz, "Social Connectedness and Generosity" (University of Maryland School of Public Policy Do Good Institute, January 11, 2021), https://dogood.umd.edu/research-impact/publications/social-connectedness-and-generosity-look-how-associational-life-and.
18. Elizabeth J. Dale PhD, "Leaving a Legacy: A New Look at Today's Planned Giving Donors" (Giving USA, September 2019), https://store.givingusa.org/products/leaving-a-legacy-a-new-look-at-planned-giving-donors-digital-edition?variant=39331664658511.
19. Jade Bristol, J.D., "Can Planned Giving Advance Diversity, Equity and Inclusion?," *GivingDocs.com* (GivingDocs, 2024), https://www.about.givingdocs.com/post/dei-in-planned-giving-part-3-recommendatons-to-increase-diversity-in-planned-giving.
20. The Center for Effective Philanthropy, "Funding Nonprofit Endowments: Foundation Perspectives and Practices," 2024, https://cep.org/report-backpacks/funding-nonprofit-endowments-foundation-perspectives-and-practices/?section=intro.
21. Oana Dumitru, "Half of Americans Say They Have Donated Money to Charity in the Past Year | YouGov," today.yougov.com, August 15, 2022, https://today.yougov.com/society/articles/43435-half-americans-donate-money-charity-past-year-poll.
22. Roger Craver, *Retention Fundraising: The New Art and Science of Keeping Your Donors for Life*, 2 ed (Civil Sector Press, 2014).
23. "Behavior and Charitable Giving: 2023 Update," *Ideas42*, April 2023, https://www.ideas42.org/publications/giving/.
24. Uri Gneezy and John List, *Why Axis: Hidden Motives and the Undiscovered Economics of Everyday Life* (New York: Public Affairs, 2016)
25. Russell James, *Inside the Mind of the Bequest Donor* (CreateSpace, 2013).

8

How Endowment Donors Give and How They Are Engaged

This chapter enables you to:

- Help donors navigate the myriad decisions they must make when giving to endowment.
- Gain basic familiarity of the types of current and planned gifts that donors may employ in supporting endowments.
- Be introduced to the team members who influence giving decisions.
- Understand the actions that may elevate or undermine a donor's generosity.

Charitable giving can be as simple as the spontaneous decision to drop a $20 dollar bill into a firefighter's boot on Labor Day in support of the Muscular Dystrophy Association or it may be far more complex and considered, with many individuals advising the donor who is making the contribution. Gifts to endowment give a donor great flexibility because they can fall anywhere within this continuum, although they tend to be more of the latter, as they often require some amount of planning and consultation. Many of the same planning considerations can apply when a donor gives to an organization's strategic reserves. This chapter provides insights to help an organization guide a donor through that planning process.

How Donors Give to Endowment

Donors decide to support endowment (or reserves) for all of the rational and subconscious reasons explored in the previous chapter. It may be a spontaneous act or explored thoughtfully over months or even years. Once the conclusion has been reached, donors still have many decisions to make.

> Once the decision to support endowment has been reached, donors still have many decisions to make.

Determining the Amount to Give

Gifts of any amount can and should be accepted into a general purpose (unrestricted) endowment or reserve fund. In the best case, the amount is driven by an understanding of the desired impact: a $20,000 gift may not produce a sufficient draw (at approximately $900) to provide a meaningful scholarship, but the same gift could endow a fund to buy supplies for an early learning classroom. Donors can be encouraged to make gifts of *any amount* to an existing field-of-interest-fund that the organization has designated for a broad purpose, such as "innovation" or "youth development."

However, an organization may want to set a minimum contribution amount if the donor elects to be prescriptive in the allocation of the eventual withdrawals from the fund. An endowed gift of $10,000 with a narrowly defined purpose will result in an annual draw of $450, which is likely too little to have a significant impact or warrant the administrative burden associated with endowment. Too often, small, endowed funds go unused – the staff member doesn't take time to make a budget allocation; the development office has no way to enforce the donor's wishes; and the donor is disappointed. These missteps can be avoided if the same donor adds $10,000 to an existing fund, raising the collective impact and gratification in concert with the fund's earlier donors.

The amount that must be given to establish a fund for a purpose designated by the donor will be determined by parameters set by the receiving nonprofit, such as the minimum amount to endow a scholarship or outreach program. The amount may be calculated based on the annual operating cost of the program that is endowed: how much is necessary to fund the chaplain's salary or to feed the zoo's animal collection? In the case of a new fund with a specific purpose, the donor must be fully informed if the purpose can be achieved only when others' gifts are added to the fund. These decisions are then codified in the policies described in Chapter 5.

It is the responsibility of the nonprofit organization to engage the donor and then to match the donor's interests and capacity with the right gift. This includes reminding the donor that they can likely make a much larger gift (and therefore impact) than they realize through a multi-year pledge and/or a planned gift. The fundraising team can rely on prospect research to estimate the amount a donor might be able to give and rely on the methods cited throughout this book to inspire the largest gift that will have the greatest impact possible.

Deciding the Terms of the Gift

Will it be a one-time gift, a monthly or multi-year pledge, a gift paid solely from the donor's estate after their lifetime, or some blend of these techniques? A one-time gift can be documented with a simple gift acknowledgement and tax receipt (which should generally be two separate documents). Larger gifts and more complex terms require greater documentation, especially if a pledge is meant to be legally enforceable during the donor's lifetime or as a part of their estate. It is common for organizations to permit donors a period of 5 or even 10 years to meet the minimum requirements to endow a specific purpose, such as a scholarship, as long as the donor makes regular payments. Planned gifts might be documented, counted, and recognized in a variety of ways (see links to the National Association of Charitable Gift Planners and their "Model Standards for Reporting and Counting Planned Gifts" in the Resources section). Furthermore, keep in mind that true endowment requires the donor to specify that the gift is intended to be permanently restricted (see Chapter 1), so it is especially important to document the donor's intent regardless of the payment terms.

In Practice: Can (Should) Pledges Be Legally Enforced?

A properly executed gift agreement is a legally enforceable contract, meaning that an organization can go to court if the donor doesn't fulfill the gift. This can be a source of anxiety and indecision for the donor and can depict the nonprofit as overly adversarial if not handled with care. There are many reasons that a nonprofit organization may desire a formal pledge: for example, they may be hiring staff or awarding scholarships that depend on the draw once the endowment is established. Or perhaps they are engraving the donor's name on a building based on the promise of a large future estate gift. There are equally compelling reasons why a donor might be reluctant to sign a pledge: perhaps they do not want to burden future generations with the fulfillment of the gift, or perhaps the assets will be drawn from a donor advised fund that precludes the ability to pledge. All must be thoughtfully weighed and balanced in negotiating the donor's journey.

Even if the pledge *can* be enforced, should it? It depends on the reasons. If the donor has suffered a reversal of fortune and their ability to make payments is disrupted – hopefully temporarily – then empathy and a renegotiated pledge payment schedule might be a better path. But what if the organization secured a loan based on the donor's promise, or recognized the gift in public, only for the donor to die and remaining family members want the money for themselves or learn that there's not enough in the estate to fulfill the donation? It's a decision Duke University faced in 2016 when Aubrey McClendon died before a $10 million pledge could be fulfilled. They initially filed a lawsuit that brought critical news coverage, only to withdraw it quietly when it became clear that the estate was insolvent. In other cases, nonprofit hospitals and universities have sued successfully when there are sufficient funds yet payment is resisted by reluctant heirs.

Identifying the Source of Funds

Regular gifts or monthly contributions tend to come from the same household accounts that pay for groceries and housing, generally provided by the donor's income. Consideration of other resources can substantially increase a donor's capacity. Financial resources that have been built up over time include savings, certificates of deposit, and investments; ownership stake in privately held corporations; donor advised funds; real property such as a valuable collection or an interest in a vacation home; retirement accounts, life insurance, or even the proceeds of intellectual property can be utilized for charitable giving, often resulting in a larger gift than the donor realized they could make. (A deeper exploration of planned giving vehicles appears later in this chapter.) In some cases, the source of funds will dictate the terms of a gift: for example, the IRS prohibits a donor from fulfilling a legally enforceable pledge with funds from their donor advised fund.

Specifying the Use of the Gift

While an organization's chief financial officer may crave the flexibility of unrestricted reserves or endowment, most donors will want to specify how the proceeds will be used. This designated purpose might be as broad as a field of interest fund designated for "educational outreach" or "personal care supplies," or the donor may wish to establish a new fund that will be used more narrowly in accordance with their wishes: strategic reserves to launch an upcoming social enterprise or an endowed fund for a specific position or program. Gentle nudges from the organization can help to ensure that the purpose is relevant and evergreen, and prudent policies (see Chapter 5) can help to ensure that the size of the gift is sufficient to fulfill the designated purpose.

Establishing Recognition for the Donor

Will the organization recognize the gift with a "named" faculty position or scholarship program? With a plaque in a prominent location? It all depends on the organization's policies, the wishes of the donor, and the extent to which public recognition might encourage others to give. Donors may desire recognition for many reasons: to immortalize their values, to inspire peers and future generations, or to honor a loved one. Commemorative recognition has long been an effective tool for capital campaigns: Tom Mitchell, who retired from the University of Florida after a storied career in fundraising, observes that endowment recognition can be just as powerful, describing it as "putting your name on knowledge." Donor recognition can also be strategic for the organization, especially if it triggers a "follow the leader" effect among other donors. But it is also a strategy that can be overemphasized by a fundraiser who focuses on the transaction rather than the relationship. These aren't "naming rights" that are being "sold." A discussion about recognition may motivate the donor and influence the gift amount, but it is rarely the sole factor.

The Donor Journey

All of these decisions to support endowment take time, a process that is often described as a "donor journey." The donor may wish to consult with advisors. Representatives of the nonprofit organization will need to have their own counsel. They must demonstrate both patience and persistence through the numerous conversations that will maintain the donor's interest while determining the specifics of the gift.

Types of Gifts

When most donors first think of giving, they calculate an amount that they can fund immediately with readily available resources. But as illustrated, there are many ways that the same donor can support the cause and help build its reserves and endowment, most of which will yield a far larger gift than a spontaneous act. This intentionality is often referred to as the realm of "planned gifts." Many planned gifts aren't realized by the organization immediately; the transfer of funds will occur in a period of years (often decades) or at the end of the donor's life. Deferred gifts are particularly relevant when building endowment, whereas raising funds for reserves generally relies on current gifts.

Planned giving and endowment are not synonymous. Not all planned gifts are designated for the endowment, and not all gifts to the endowment are planned. However, many gifts to endowment, especially the largest contributions, are planned gifts. A planned gift generally comes from the donor's accumulated assets and/or estate. These gifts are fueled by resources that have been accumulated over the donor's lifetime – or even many generations of a family. That is one reason why the permanence of endowment appeals to these donors. Each type of gift is treated differently, as illustrated in Table 8-1, later in this chapter.

Planned giving and endowment are not synonymous.

Bequests

The simplest form of a planned gift is a *bequest*: a donor includes a statement in their will that a set amount of money or a percentage of their assets is to be given to designated charities. There are variations: the donor might designate that a percentage of assets be distributed to charity(ies) only after children, grandchildren, or other heirs have been taken care of (called a *remainder bequest*), or only in the event that other heirs are no longer living (called a *contingent bequest*). Sample language for all of these is included in the Resources section at the end of the book. Donors who arrange a bequest can always change their wills (and frequently do as described later in this chapter, although they seldom remove nonprofit beneficiaries altogether), so this type of gift is considered *revocable*. There is an exception: a donor may provide an "estate note," which is an irrevocable pledge to make a payment out of the estate's assets to the designated nonprofit recipient. The difference between irrevocable and revocable gifts is an important distinction, as discussed later in this chapter.

Beneficiary Designations

Another simple form of a planned gift is a *beneficiary designation*. A donor may indicate that one or more nonprofit organizations receive a distribution from their retirement assets or life insurance after their lifetime. These are fairly simple for the donor to execute; they simply complete or update a form provided by the investment or insurance company. However, these gifts are also revocable because the donor can change their mind, withdraw their assets, or cancel the insurance policy. Some enterprising vendors may work with the donors to a nonprofit organization to establish insurance policies that are owned by the charity, thereby guaranteeing that the proceeds will eventually benefit the organization so long as the donor – or the nonprofit – maintains the policy payment schedule. Care should be taken to ensure that such an arrangement brings greater benefits to the organization or its donors than to the insurance salesperson.

Complex Planned Gifts

More complex planned gifts generally fall into three categories – current gifts, life income, and charitable trusts.

- **Current gifts.** Some would define any purposeful act of giving a "planned gift," although generally the term is reserved for gifts that involve the donor's overall financial and/or estate planning. Current planned gifts are received by the charity in the near term, and may be deployed for programs, operations, or reserves; or deposited into endowed funds immediately upon receipt. The kinds of current gifts that are generally recognized as planned gifts include:
  - **Qualified Charitable Distributions (QCD),** in which a donor who is at least 70.5 years of age can make a charitable gift directly to a cause from their IRA without it affecting their taxable income. The amount a donor can give in this manner is limited by the IRS to $100,000 annually (indexed to inflation beginning in 2024). Typically, the donor contacts their financial planner to arrange the transfer of funds or fills out a simple online form provided by the investment manager. Because many people roll their 401(k) or 403(b) retirement assets into an IRA when it is time to take income from the retirement plan, this can be a sustainable source of giving.
  - **Appreciated Assets** can be an advantageous way for a donor to give, since the value of the gift, its tax-deductibility, and its beneficial impact on the cause are based on today's value

and the donor avoids paying tax on the capital gains. While the most common application is gifts of stock, personal property, real estate, cryptocurrency, and other assets can also be utilized to fund gifts with similar advantages. Every organization should have a process to accept gifts of stock or cryptocurrency, and a policy to sell the asset immediately upon receipt (see Chapter 5).

Once these gifts are received by the cause, they cannot be "clawed back" and so they are considered irrevocable.

- **Life income** (sometimes called split-interest) gifts include a variety of charitable vehicles that allow a donor to receive income for a period of years (up to the remainder of their lifetime) with

In Practice: Determining the Value of Donated Property

When a donor wants to give a non-cash asset that has a value greater than $5,000, such as real estate, artwork, or collectibles, the IRS requires that the donor obtain a qualified appraisal at the donor's sole expense. "Qualified" because the professional appraiser must meet the IRS' requirements to be "qualified," which generally means they have earned the designation from a recognized organization of appraisers such as a state appraiser board. The acknowledgment of the gift that is provided by the nonprofit organization should include only a description of the property being given (for example, "20 acres of pasture located in Mingo County"), never an estimated value. If the donor wants to claim a tax deduction, the tax-deductible value is determined and documented by the appraiser, and the appraisal is attached to IRS Form 8283 when the donor files their taxes.

the residual going to the charity. Some types of life income gifts include the following:

- **Charitable Gift Annuities (CGAs)** allow a donor to make a gift today, with the charity contractually obligated to pay the donor a fixed amount for the remainder of their life (and perhaps the lives of their spouse or one other person). CGAs can be appealing to donors who want to support a cause while simplifying their finances and allaying fears that they will outlive their money. And because the annuity fund is controlled by the nonprofit (or an intermediary they have designated), the arrangement cannot be changed by the donor – it is *irrevocable*. But CGA donors tend to make smaller gifts[1] and there is potential risk for the careless nonprofit: consider the cultural organization in North Dakota that provided a donor with annuity payments based on the value of an illiquid asset – a building next door that the museum coveted for its expansion – only for the donor to live well past the age of 100 and the annuity payments to far exceed the actual value of the building. Proceed with caution. The risk is diminished if there are numerous annuitants. Many organizations that are just starting CGA programs will want to partner with a local community foundation or their national association to spread the risk across a larger pool.

  The payout rate for charitable gift annuities is fixed, depending on the age of the donor when the fund is established and the contemporaneous interest rate environment. While each cause can set its own payout rates, the American Council on Gift Annuities calculates suggested maximum annual payout rates that are adopted by most organizations, and which are designed to ensure that the cause receives approximately half of the amount that originally funded the annuity. ACGA research shows that the median residual amount received by charities is 82%, well in excess of the 50% residuum targeted by the ACGA's suggested maximum rates.

- **Pooled income funds** are analogous to a mutual fund, where contributions from multiple donors are pooled into a common fund. Each year the pooled income fund pays its income to its members (donors) with each member receiving a *pro rata* share of the distributed income. As a result, the payout to the donor can fluctuate based on investment performance. Gifts into the pooled income fund are irrevocable. These have fallen out of favor with donors because of the relatively low payouts generated during the historically low interest rate environment of the first two decades of the twenty-first century.
- Two types of **charitable remainder trusts (CRTs)** can be established by a donor. Either type of CRT provides an income tax charitable deduction for the donor, and the donor can avoid capital gains tax on appreciated assets contributed to the CRT. The two types of CRTs differ in the calculation of annual income paid to the donor or others over the course of a fixed number of years (no more than 20) or the beneficiary(ies)' lifetime(s). At the end of the term of years or beneficiaries' life, the CRT's principal is distributed to the organizations identified by the donor. A CRT is an *irrevocable* instrument; however, it is possible for the donor to change the trust's nonprofit beneficiary(ies) before the trust's end date.
- A **Charitable Lead Trust** (CLT) is the mirror image of the CRT. A CLT pays a fixed amount to the cause(s) identified by the donor generally for a fixed number of years, then the assets revert to either the donor or to the beneficiaries designated by the donor. The CLT is an irrevocable gift.
- In a **Retained Life Estate,** the donor transfers the title of their primary residence or vacation home to the nonprofit organization but retains the right to occupy it for their lifetime. Upon the donor's death, the charity can sell the home and use the proceeds for its charitable purposes. This is also an irrevocable gift.

> Donors with charitable lead trusts tend to make the largest planned gifts by value.

TABLE 8-1 Types of Gifts and Their Treatment

Type of Gift	Current	Deferred	Revocable	Irrevocable
Gift or pledge of money	X			X
Gift from a donor advised fund	X			X
Simple bequest		X	X	
Bequest with estate note		X		X
Beneficiary designation		X	X	
Qualified charitable distribution from retirement accounts	X			X
Gifts of appreciated assets	X			X
Charitable gift annuity		X		X
Pooled income fund		X		X
Charitable trusts	X	X		X
Retained life estate		X		X
Bargain sale	X			X

Although this may seem complicated, remember that bequests through wills account for more than 80% of testamentary gifts to endowments at most institutions.

According to *Giving USA*, charitable bequests have represented an average of 8% of all charitable giving since 1967. And this amount is likely to increase: a study by *The New York Times* identified more than $84 trillion in cash and assets will transfer from Silent Generation and Baby Boomer households to their heirs –*as well as to their non-profits of choice*.[2] Experts believe that $12 trillion of this monumental sum will be contributed to nonprofits by the year 2045. There is ample opportunity for every organization to pursue these gifts.

Most nonprofit organizations should be equipped to manage simple planned gifts by providing staff with the necessary training and providing donors with the necessary guidance and forms. Donors who pursue more complex arrangements will generally depend on their own team of advisors, as described in the next section. When donors express interest in complex gifts, an organization that lacks a planned giving specialist may want to retain their own outside counsel, avail themselves of the resources offered by the national office if they are a local affiliate, or consider partnering with the local community foundation.

The Donor's Team

All types of fundraising are a "team sport." Pursuing large, complex gifts for reserves or endowment requires group cooperation on the part of multiple roles within the nonprofit organization (as described Chapter 3) as well as various allies and professional advisors supporting both the organization and the donor. It is a markedly different process than dropping loose bills into a Salvation Army kettle or sponsoring a friend's walkathon. Successful organizations will secure gifts for endowment (and sometimes reserves) by engaging the donor's entire team.

The Donor's Immediate Family

Start with the donor's inner circle: the immediate family. Does the donor have a spouse or partner, children or grandchildren, or other close relatives? Several studies have documented that couples tend to make their giving decisions jointly. According to IUPUI's 2021 study *How Households Make Giving Decisions*,[3] ". . . more than six out of ten couples make charitable giving decisions jointly (61.5%). When one partner makes decisions for the household, women are slightly more likely to do so than men (15.3% and 12.1%, respectively). The remaining couples (11.1%) decide separately."

Other studies document even higher joint decision making among affluent couples. With older donors, the inner circle may extend to adult children or grandchildren. A devout donor may consult with a spiritual advisor such as a pastor, rabbi, or imam. Those who implement donor engagement strategies should seek permission from the donor to engage all members of the inner circle who will influence donors' decisions.

In Practice: Endowment Giving and Family Dynamics

A successful entrepreneur and his wife gave quietly and generously throughout the community. She served on the board of their children's independent school, which was in the midst of a campaign. When it came time to discuss the couple's gift, he deferred to her, but the school's leaders insisted on a joint meeting. The husband repeatedly declined, citing his wife's service on the board and her independence in making the decision. After months of wrangling, the couple finally met jointly with school representatives to discuss their gift. They pledged $1 million: less than their capacity, less than the school had sought, and the experience left the husband and wife disenchanted with the school and less likely to make future gifts.

Any major gift decision should take into consideration family dynamics and follow the donor(s) lead, including:

- Do couples make their giving decisions independently or jointly?
- Among older donors, is there any indication that decision-making capacity is diminished? If so, who can assist the donor(s) and ensure that a gift is appropriate?
- Are there adult children or grandchildren? If so, are they supportive, or would they prefer to keep resources within the family for the benefit of future generations?

> Those who implement donor engagement strategies should seek permission from the donor to engage all members of the inner circle who will influence donors' decisions.

Beyond the Donor's Family

Building on the groundbreaking research of Nobel laureate Richard Thaler described in Chapter 7, donor behavior and the role of the donor's advisors can be seen as the highest level of charitable giving akin to the most sophisticated financial transactions (see Table 8-2). The result is a transformational gift. The term "transformational" can be (mis)applied to connote only the magnitude of a gift. It is better to consider all of the ways that a truly thoughtful and generous gift can be transformational for the donor and their inner circle. And magnitude alone does not define "transformational" for the receiving organization: does the gift stretch the donor's capacity, break new ground, or inspire others? If so, it can be described as "transformational."

As illustrated by Thaler and experienced by fundraising professionals, when a donor makes a complex planned gift, other advisors will enter the picture. In fact, a nonprofit organization should *encourage* or even require donors to seek their own legal and financial counsel and welcome the opportunity to provide information and assurances to the advisors when asked.

- Donors may work with their **financial planners** to execute a gift of stock or similar assets, and perhaps to determine which stocks to transfer from the portfolio. (Note: In order to receive the most generous tax treatment for their gift, donors should always be encouraged to give the stocks, bonds, or cryptocurrency directly rather than selling the asset and giving the resulting cash.) A qualified charitable distribution from a donor's IRA (also known as an "IRA charitable rollover") may require the

TABLE 8-2 Applying Thaler's Hierarchy to Charitable Giving

| Level | Type | Behavior | | Relationship | Interaction | Message Hierarchy | Message Examples |
		Consumer	Donor				
1	Spontaneous	Buying socks online	Responding to a disaster with a one-time donation	Awareness	Little/no human interaction	Need: The cause needs a donation	Give now. Fight back. We need your gift to make a difference.
2	Meaningful	Buying a car or appliance	Making a recurring gift or joining a donor society	Interest	Online research; single interaction at transaction	Serve: The cause needs donations to serve the needs of others	Our track record proves that every gift makes a difference. Let us show you how your gift can protect women and girls.
3	Major	Episodic purchase such as a house	Multi-year campaign pledge of assets	Engagement	Intense involvement of one or two advisors (realtor/ major gift officer)	Impact: Donors give to the cause so that it can solve wicked problems	It isn't every day that we get to build a movement. With your partnership, we can. We are excited to share the details with you.
4	Transformational	Sale of a business	Endowment gift (especially planned/ deferred)	Ownership	A team of advisors	Change agent: Donors solve wicked problems by giving through the cause	You've worked a lifetime to make a difference such as this. Your leadership now will make a difference for lifetimes to come.

financial advisor to transfer the funds or provide instructions for the donor to handle the transaction themselves through their online fund management platform.

* Even in the case of a simple bequest, it is likely that an **estate attorney** is involved (although more and more online services offer free or low-cost will services and some actively encourage charitable bequests – see the In Practice: "The Emergence of Online Estate Planning" sidebar). If the donor already has a will, new charitable bequests can be added later, and frequently are. The donor will need to instruct the attorney to add the charitable recipients, which is a relatively simple process.

In Practice: The Emergence of Online Estate Planning

Creating a will once occurred almost exclusively in the hushed conference rooms of law offices, borne from deep conversations between attorneys and their clients. This practice remains for many thoughtful individuals, especially those with larger assets, multiple heirs, or complex financial structures. But even this revered process has now become the subject of online services that help people prepare a simple will. Many of these online services – even those that are primarily commercial – encourage charitable bequests. Others, such as freewill.com, provide free resources and specifically encourage charitable bequests. Another example, givingdocs.com, charges a small fee (generally to the nonprofit organization deploying their tool) in exchange for a higher degree of functionality and donor engagement. More and more, nonprofit organizations are creating partnerships with these services and providing a link to online estate planning on the giving pages of their website.

- **Attorneys** will also be involved in the creation of various trusts. Often there will be at least two legal counselors: an estate attorney and tax counsel. Depending on the complexity of the donor's finances, an **accountant** may be consulted as well. These professionals will ensure that the trust serves the best interests of the donor and fulfills intentions for any charitable distributions.

- If the donor plans to leverage real property such as a home or farm to fuel their charitable and financial plans, then **real estate professionals** may be involved in the creation of the plan, appraisal of property values, and eventual conversion of properties through sale. Experts will also be consulted to determine the value of artworks, antiques, or valuable collections.

- Very wealthy donors may also engage a **philanthropy advisor**: someone who understands various giving vehicles and can also guide the donor in achieving their charitable goals through the selection of charitable recipients and designated purpose of the donation. Many of these advisors have earned the C.A.P. designation (Charitable Advisor in Philanthropy) through a rigorous professional development process. Donors of any means might secure the same guidance through a local community foundation, which often will provide education and resources to donors who intend to support local charities.

Professional advisors are generally a great help when a donor is motivated to be charitable. On the other hand, advisors are unlikely to promote giving when their client is disinterested, and they are unlikely to suggest a specific cause or organization for the donor to support. Rather, they will facilitate the donor's decision process and then develop a plan to achieve the donor's wishes. Their propensity to encourage charitable behavior follows the donor's lead. Their advice can be informed by nonprofit organizations, employing the tactics to engage professional advisors described in Chapter 9.

The clear objective of all of this teamwork is a transformational gift. As described earlier, too many in the field of philanthropy equate "transformational" with mega-gift. However, "transformational" is better understood through the lens of the donor: is the gift deeply meaningful due to its purpose, impact, and magnitude as a proportion of the door's overall financial circumstances? Using these criteria, the gift of Oseola McCarty described in Chapter 4 is certainly "transformational," while a multi-million dollar donation from a billionaire might not be.

How Fundraisers Can Encourage (or Discourage) Gifts to Endowment

As the earlier chapters have demonstrated, there is abundant research about philanthropy and charitable donors, somewhat less that addresses endowments and reserves specifically, and even less about the effective behaviors of professional fundraisers. However, the way that a member of the fundraising team engages a donor will have significant impact on the likelihood that a donor will support the organization's long-term financial resilience. "Fundraisers at resilient nonprofits integrate estate and deferred giving opportunities into their overall fundraising activities," observes Paul Yeghiayan, CFRE, CSPG. "Doing so builds more profound and thoughtful relationships that consider the donors' financial planning goals and the nonprofit's long-term financial stability." Even the fundraiser's title can be relevant (see the sidebar From the Field: "What Is the Right Title?").

From the Field: What Is the Right Title?

Fundraising professionals go by many different titles. "Development" is often part of the title, indicating the staff person's role in developing relationships within both the organization and the community. "Advancement" is also common, especially in higher education, because of the role of contributions in advancing the organization's mission.

Dr. Russell James explored the merits of fundraisers' job titles in a series of experiments conducted in 2022.[4] His premise: that many people avoid including "fundraiser" in their job title because there is stigma and misunderstanding associated with the job. But, as James pointed out in a LinkedIn post, euphemistic job titles like "Development Director" or "Chief Advancement Officer" may diminish giving because they convey the benefits for the organization rather than what the professional offers to donors.

When James tested people's willingness to contact a charity employee about making a gift, he found that the worst-performing job titles included Director of Advancement, Chief Advancement Officer, Director of Development, and Chief Development Officer – four of the most common job titles in the profession. Titles that conveyed the help that employees offered to donors performed much better, titles like Director of Donor Guidance or Gift Planning Advisor. After all, donors want guidance, planning, and advice when giving.

It is this gap that authors Joshua Birkholz and Amy Lampi sought to address in their 2023 book *Benefactors: Why Some Fundraising Professionals Always Succeed.*[5] They called on their decades of cumulative experience, delved into their client's fundraising metrics, and extrapolated from plentiful studies of fundraising tactics to identify eight traits, or "factors" that effective fundraising officers have in common:

- **Data-driven:** They use data as an asset for building stronger relationships with the right people and asking for the right gift.
- **Innovative:** They have a commitment to adopt "next practices" through continual learning and improvement.
- **Collaborative:** Effective fundraisers rarely "go it alone;" they successfully engage volunteers, subject matter experts, the

donor's advisors, and anyone else who can help to engage and educate a donor.

- **Authentic:** Experienced donors can discern the difference between someone who embraces the organization's mission and acts in accordance with their true self versus the shallow "cheerleader" type of performative fundraiser. These are fundraisers who ask powerful questions and listen to the response rather than engaging in idle chit-chat. The donor will respond much more enthusiastically to the former.
- **Confident:** More than bravado, confidence derives from preparation and planning, which bolsters the conviction to inspire donors to make their best gift.
- **Advocacy:** A culture of excellence is rooted in a professional's willingness to encourage their peers, their organization, the broader cause, and the practice of philanthropy.
- **Tech-savvy:** Whether navigating the donor database or employing a donor's favored communication channel, modern fundraisers understand the role of technology and know how to employ it to their advantage.
- **Leadership:** It's not enough to simply raise a lot of money. Strong fundraisers model excellence, learn continuously, and bring the best out in others.

Leadership in fundraising is not about being "the best." It is a commitment to character, knowledge, innovation, and inclusion with which a fundraising leader derives the best from their team and their donors.

> Leadership is a commitment to character, knowledge, and innovation, driving a fundraising leader to derive the best from their team and their donors.

According to Adam Fazio, who helps organizations find fundraising staff, endowment building requires professionals with both financial acumen and the capacity to articulate a vision for the future. "The most effective fundraisers have both experience and an extensive set of both hard and soft skills to navigate this complex terrain," he states. Johnny Cooper of Cooper Coleman shares similar insights. "Endowment fundraisers are translators of opportunity and impact. Endowment solicitations are data-driven, meticulously prepared, and strategically aligned with the donor's desire for the organization's or program's perpetual sustainability." Perhaps most importantly, they are skilled at listening.

Sadly, not every organization is served by this level of staff. The missteps of poorly trained (or inexperienced, or overworked, or otherwise inadequate) fundraising professionals have been documented repeatedly. In their book *Philanthropy Revolution*[6] Lisa Greer and Larissa Kostoff lament about Greer's experiences with philanthropy before and after her family gained sudden wealth through the success of her husband's technology start-up. Greer tells of awkward fundraising staff or volunteers whose poor behavior could be dismissive, inauthentic, shallow, and entitled. She shares experiences when organizations requested a gift while simultaneously ignoring clear statements about the family's philanthropic priorities. This lack of listening may be the most common and detrimental trait of weak fundraisers: failing to listen closely for the donor's interests, capacity, and affinity.

If *listening* is the key competency for fundraising professionals, then the ability to ask powerful questions is essential. Advancement Resources, a global firm that provides research-based professional development for those engaged in fundraising, has conducted interviews with thousands of generous donors. Based on their research, they advise development staff and their colleagues (such as volunteers, program staff, academic deans, or healthcare clinicians) to use questions like these to engage donors' hearts and minds.

- What would you like to accomplish with your money that would be meaningful to you?

- How do you see yourself making a meaningful impact in the area of work we have been discussing?
- What do you see as your legacy?

Powerful questions such as these reveal the deeply held convictions of a donor. They are a far more revealing and compelling way to connect a donor with a cause when compared to the superficial discussions some poorly trained fundraising professionals might pursue. Questions about the weather or the latest athletic contest will not connect deeply with donors. Worse yet is the organization whose fundraising ambassadors fail to ask any questions and describe the organization's latest initiatives as if reading from a prepared script, hoping to "sell" the donor on the idea.

In addition to considering the questions to ask donors, experienced development professionals consider the questions that donors will be asking of themselves, of the organization, and the project. These are the questions and concerns that donors will ultimately need to satisfy before they consider making a significant contribution. A trained development professional will consider these questions as they prepare and determine how to address them in partnership with the organization's leadership. Through their donor focused research, Advancement Resources further determined the unspoken questions many donors consider. These may include several of the following:

- Does this organization respect and value me?
- Do I respect and value this organization?
- Will this organization protect, honor, and enhance my reputation and legacy?
- Will my family members support this decision?

When it comes to permanently endowing a fund, these questions are even more pressing, and so the donor seeks certainty due to the length of the future relationship. When recognition is involved, the question of respect and legacy are in the forefront. Donors will consider past gifts to the organization, their relationship with the development professional, and their trust in leadership to guide their internal decision-making process. The best fundraising organizations recognize that these deliberations will take place and thoughtfully consider how they can effectively steward past contributions while building strong trust-based relationships.

Asking powerful questions and engaging in meaningful conversations helps to create the "radical connection" that authors Nathan Chappell, Brian Crimins, and Michael Ashley describe as the antidote to declining donor participation in their book *The Generosity Crisis*[7] (p. 26). "Radical connection" is an unbreakable emotional bond that aligns with – and then transcends – rational thinking. The authors go on to define the "Four Rules of Radical Connection" (pp. 138-140) followed by guidance to implement the practice:

- Generosity follows radical connection.
- Authenticity and inclusion are critical for success.
- Transparency and accountability are indispensable.
- It's about the organization and mission, not you.

These principles, combined with the thoughtful questions described earlier, demonstrate that the most effective fundraisers seek engagement rather than a one-time gift, which is the journey that most donors travel on their way to a meaningful endowment gift.

Summary and Next Steps

When donors decide to support an endowment, they still have many other decisions to make: how much to give, what gift vehicle(s) to employ, and who to consult among their own advisors and the organization's representatives. This is the donor journey, which is strikingly similar to the universal hero myth explored in Chapter 7. Drawing on Professor James' work and informing it with others as cited throughout this book, the role of the donor, the fundraising professional, and the giving process can be summarized in Table 8-3.

TABLE 8-3 The Donor Journey as Universal Hero Myth

Universal Hero Story	Endowment Donor Journey
Initial state	Longtime loyal donor
Challenge	To make a meaningful gift to endowment
Initial resistance	Fear about money, mortality aversion, procrastination
Journey	Navigating decisions about why, how, how much, use of the gift, source(s) of funding, etc.
Helpers and their archetypes	Fundraising professionals as guiding sage, tax and estate advisors as magicians, family members as co-explorers
Victory	A transformational gift
Elevated state	Heroic radical connection to the cause

This is the highest expression of fundraising, culminating in gifts that ensure the long-term resilience of a cause that has captured the donor's heart and mind. Organizations can take many steps to encourage such expressions of generosity and measure their progress along the way, as described in the final chapter.

Notes

1. Elizabeth J. Dale PhD, "Leaving a Legacy: A New Look at Today's Planned Giving Donors" (Giving USA, September 2019), https://store.givingusa.org/products/leaving-a-legacy-a-new-look-at-planned-giving-donors-digital-edition?variant=39331664658511. Page 19.
2. Talmon Joseph Smith and Karl Russell, "The Greatest Wealth Transfer in History Is Here, with Familiar (Rich) Winners," *The New York Times*, May 14, 2023, sec. Business, https://www.nytimes.com/2023/05/14/business/economy/wealth-generations.html.
3. Women's Giving Institute, "Women Give 2021: How Households Make Giving Decisions" (Lilly Family School of Philanthropy, 2021), chrome-extension://efaidnbmnnnibpcajpcglclefindmkaj/https://scholarworks.iupui.edu/server/api/core/bitstreams/717cd2b8-45f9-4133-a3be-f41a2c713329/content.

4. Russell James, JD PhD, "Introducing the Epic Fundraiser to the Public: What's Your Job?," *LinkedIn* (blog), August 9, 2022, https://www.linkedin.com/pulse/introducing-epic-fundraiser-public-whats-your-job-russell/.

5. Joshua M. Birkholz and Amy S. Lampi, *BeneFactors* (John Wiley & Sons, 2022).

6. Lisa Greer and Larissa Kostoff, *Philanthropy Revolution: How to Inspire Donors, Build Relationships and Make a Difference* (HarperCollins, 2020).

7. Crimmins, Brian, Nathan Chappell, and Michael Ashley, *The Generosity Crisis* (John Wiley & Sons, 2022).

9

Achieving and Measuring Success

This chapter enables you to:

- Define success for endowment-building efforts, using both leading and lagging indicators.
- Learn how current and planned gifts are generally acknowledged, reported, and counted.
- Understand how to budget and allocate the resources needed to raise funds for endowment.
- Develop a holistic strategy and organizational commitment to achieve success.

Success in building endowment or strategic reserves might be measured in many ways: the total size of the reserve or endowment, the number of endowed funds, the number of donors, or the percentage of the budget that is covered. These are all important factors to be considered and measured. However, it is important to keep in mind that they are all in service to the most important measure of all: *impact*. Do the resources – and the resilience they provide – enable the organization to provide enduring benefit for the common good? Are they deployed in service to the mission, whether that is meeting basic needs, enhancing a community or region, advocating for an important cause, or otherwise elevating the human condition? Funds that sit idly in investment accounts or are deployed with negligible benefit can't be considered a success, no matter how great the sum.

This chapter discusses ways to define success and how to measure the return on an investment in efforts to build endowment or reserves. Because the benefits of these efforts may not be realized for many years, it can be difficult to assess performance and impact in the short term. Indeed, merely counting the number of people served or dollars raised is rarely an effective measure of success for any program or fundraising initiative. Counting the number of people served is an output, not impact, and dollars raised is a lagging indicator. An over-emphasis on "dollars raised" may result in unsatisfactory progress in the early years, causing an organization to abandon the initiative. It can incentivize counterproductive behavior on the part of fundraisers, who rush to secure gifts in pursuit of an annual goal regardless of the donor's timeline. And it fails to provide forward-looking indications of progress that can inform strategic decisions and predict future results.

Measuring Impact

Successful endowment building, as defined in the following pages, is rooted in a case that resonates with donors. The case resonates when donors believe that their contributions will achieve their own goals for philanthropic impact and advance the nonprofit organization's mission and sustainability (see Chapter 4). That is one reason for any organization to have a process to measure the impact of funds deployed from endowment or reserves. Beyond donor relations, measuring impact provides essential information for the responsible distribution of resources, which is a core responsibility of the organization's leaders.

Measuring impact is hard. Consider an early learning program with a reading specialist whose work is funded by an endowment. It is fairly simple to answer the question "how many children does the teacher serve annually?," which is a measure of output, not impact. It might even be possible to measure outcomes such as "what improvements did we see in our student's reading scores?" or "did participation in the reading program increase students' attendance?" It is much more challenging to determine the true impact of early reading intervention: did the students flourish throughout elementary school? Were they more likely to graduate? Did the intervention have benefits for the entire family?

The difference between outputs, outcomes, and impact can be illustrated in Figure 9-1 through the classic "teach a person to fish" analogy:

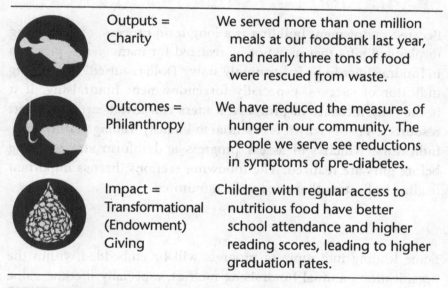

	Outputs = Charity	We served more than one million meals at our foodbank last year, and nearly three tons of food were rescued from waste.
	Outcomes = Philanthropy	We have reduced the measures of hunger in our community. The people we serve see reductions in symptoms of pre-diabetes.
	Impact = Transformational (Endowment) Giving	Children with regular access to nutritious food have better school attendance and higher reading scores, leading to higher graduation rates.

FIGURE 9-1   Outputs, Outcomes, and Impact.

Few organizations have the resources to perform long-term longitudinal studies that measure impact (although impact research and measurement could be the focus of an endowed fund!). Many will turn to respected field-wide research; in the previous example, the cause may have relied on the Chicago Longitudinal Study or other academic research published in peer-reviewed journals to show how similar methods have achieved impact in other settings. They might turn to a national trade association or accrediting body.

Or they may cite internal data, combined with stories of their students' success – an anecdotal approach that may resonate with donors. Regardless of method, the organization has a responsibility to its donors and its program participants to ensure that resources are used effectively.

To complement measures of programmatic impact, it is important for those who are accountable for endowment fundraising to monitor fundraising performance to ensure that it is achieving the desired financial goals.

Fundraising Performance Indicators

Because endowment building is a long-term process, often leading to planned gifts that may not be realized for many years, progress in fundraising can be frustratingly slow. "Dollars raised" is a *lagging* indicator of success, especially for endowment fundraising. If it is the only measure of progress, leaders can lose heart and divert resources. That is why it is essential to identify *leading* performance indicators, which will assess progress and inform strategy long before gifts are realized. The following sections discuss important leading indicators that need to be monitored.

Donor Retention

Some leading indicators of progress will be embedded within the organization's annual fundraising metrics, especially lifetime value (that is, the total amount a donor is expected to give over many years) and the overall donor retention rate, which is defined as the percentage of donors who continue to support the organization from year to year. Donor retention is the single most important fundraising metric. Why? For several reasons: donor loyalty is a signal that the organization's programs and services are continuously seen as worthwhile and relevant, that the donor feels appreciated, and that fundraising systems are operating effectively. Organizations that nurture loyal relationships are also more efficient because they reduce the expense of constantly acquiring a large corps of new donors.

> Donor retention is the single most important fundraising metric.

Yet, many organizations are experiencing a precipitous decline in donor retention, especially among the everyday donors who make gifts less than $250. In a typical organization, a high proportion of donors fall into this "small donor" category – perhaps 75% to 90% of all donors. These gifts may represent only a small proportion of total dollars contributed – often less than 10% – while a small number of donors who make very large gifts account for 90% of revenue. Donors may leave an organization for many reasons, regardless of the magnitude of their giving: their gift(s) weren't acknowledged promptly, the organization didn't provide any information about the difference their contribution made, their personal circumstances changed, or maybe another cause captured their attention. Or perhaps they always intended to give only once because their gift was in memory of someone, as is often true with hospice organizations. A nonprofit organization that is paying attention to donor retention rates will see evidence of shortcomings early and take steps to respond.

In Practice: How and Why to Calculate Donor Retention

Monitoring donor retention rates is essential when building endowment because most donors who support endowment – especially through a planned gift – have been loyal supporters for years or even decades.

Some organizations make the mistake of using a simple formula such as last year's number of donors divided by this year's number of donors. An organization that received contributions from 1,200 donors last year and 1,000 donors this year may be tempted to celebrate an

(continued)

83% donor retention rate. There are two serious problems with this equation. First, it doesn't indicate whether this year's 1,000 donors are the same people who gave last year, or if a portion of them are new donors who are replacing donors who failed to give. It also fails to acknowledge and respond to the fact that the donor pool is shrinking.

The correct way to calculate donor retention requires an organization to identify their specific contributors. Using this example, the organization must determine how many of last year's donors gave again this year:

Formula	Example
('This Year' / 'Last Year') *100	(800 / 1200) * 100 = 67%

If 67% of last year's donors gave again this year, then the organization with 1,200 donors will need to acquire almost 400 new donors to replace the lost donors – what fundraising leader Shannon Spencer refers to as the "leaky bucket" of fundraising. Because acquisition is much more expensive than retention, the result on net fundraising proceeds is diminished when retention rates are lower.

While there are many national standards for donor retention, an organization's best benchmark is its own historic performance. Are retention rates increasing or decreasing over time? Which donor cohorts perform best, as defined by giving amount, years of giving, graduation year, or some other indication of affinity? Most organizations find that retention rates are lowest among new donors making small (less than $250) gifts and increase as the amount and longevity of giving rise.

Declining donor retention has been documented by the Fundraising Effectiveness Project as well as in Indiana University's Philanthropy Panel Study. Although this research doesn't pinpoint the cause, there are many possibilities, as described in the opening pages of Chapter 7. These declines are concern for organizations seeking to build endowment or reserves, regardless of the generosity of loyal major donors, for the following reasons:

- **It is more expensive to acquire new donors,** so a fundraising operation that is constantly refreshing a high percentage of its donor pool will have a lower return on fundraising investment than one that retains a high percentage of its donors. This results in fewer dollars for endowment-building efforts (or mission).
- **A shrinking pool of donors creates risk.** As the organization counts on fewer donors making larger gifts, the loss of any single donor can leave a revenue gap too large to replace quickly or easily.
- **Engaged donors amplify an organization's voice.** When donors stop giving, they may also stop being an advocate for the cause, and they may send negative signals to other donors who then question their own commitment.
- **Long-term, loyal donors tend to increase their giving over time,** so a shrinking donor pipeline may ultimately reduce the number of donors rising to the ranks of major giving.
- **If endowment is built primarily through realized bequests and other planned gifts, and most planned gifts come from small and large donors with a long history of involvement in the organization, then the premature departure of donors reduces the number of prospects to support endowment.**

Any organization that aspires to build endowment or reserves must first look at its ability to retain donors, just as any runner preparing for a marathon should start with a basic health checkup. Given rising concerns about donor retention, a variety of resources have emerged to help organizations address shortcomings and can be found in the Resources section at the end of this book.

Measures of Donor Behavior

While donor retention is an indication of overall fundraising health, other leading indicators are specific to the endowment-building and/or planned giving effort. Some measures of *donor behavior* that are important to track, depending on the fundraising strategy being employed (see Chapter 3), include the following indications of donor engagement:

- The number of people who declare themselves eligible for membership in the legacy society by providing a written affirmation of their intention to provide a planned gift.
- The number of giving circles, the number of people who participate in giving circles, and the average (or median) amount each donor and each circle provides.
- Attendance at events, especially any gatherings that are intended to engage current and potential donors of planned gifts and/or endowment gifts.
- Social and digital media metrics, such as open rates for email, interactions with Facebook posts, or visits to the pages of the website describing ways to give and the role of the endowment.
- Inquiries about endowments and planned giving via a response form on the website, a mail-in reply device, or even an old-fashioned in-bound phone call.

Measures of Fundraiser Performance

Still other metrics help to quantify the effectiveness of the *fundraising team* that is tasked with raising funds for the future. The appropriate metrics should be integrated into the job description and performance evaluation for the position, which will vary based on the type(s) of donors the gift officer is engaging and the tactics the organization is implementing. It is essential to identify a single individual (usually a senior member of the development team) who is responsible for endowment building, coordinates the efforts of others, and tracks these performance metrics. Regular progress is reported to the CEO, who supports the effort in the ways described in Chapter 3. Tasks distributed among members of the team include the following, summarized in Table 9-1.

- **Gift officers** are tasked with managing a portfolio of major gift prospects and are generally expected to have a meaningful engagement (typically a personal meeting) with a specified number of donors and prospects each month (perhaps 10 to 15). They hold multiple meetings with a high percentage of the people in their portfolio over the course of 12 months; secure ongoing annual support from a high proportion (greater than 80%); and secure a set number of gifts to the endowment each year. Each gift yields a high proportion of the amount requested based on the donors' estimated capacity. In other words, the metrics are donor engagements, portfolio penetration, retention and upgrade, and yield. Accomplished fundraising leader Simon Bisson describes these as "activity metrics" (are gift officers seeking the right type and number of activities to maximize fundraising potential) as opposed to "productivity metrics" (dollars raised).

    If the organization's donor CRM has the capacity to assign a donor a "stage" (and it should), then an additional measure of progress can be the movement of donors from stage to stage as their affinity for the cause strengthens. For example, how many people in the portfolio moved from identified to qualified, qualified to interested, interested to engaged, and so on, and how quickly did they rise through the ranks toward an inspired transformational gift?

    In an organization where some members of the fundraising team have been assigned specific responsibility for planned gifts, additional metrics include the estimated value

TABLE 9-1 Performance Metrics for the Fundraising and Endowment Building Team

Measure of Success	Major Gift Officers	Annual Fund, Membership, etc.	Marketing	Fundraising Operations
Donor retention and lifetime value	x	x	x	x
Average (or median) gift amount	x	x	x	x
New prospects identified	x	x	x	x
New donors acquired	x	x	x	x
Donor survey scores	x	x	x	x
Growth in the legacy society	x	x	x	x
Value of new current and planned gifts	x	x		
Personal visits/engagements	x			
Portfolio penetration (% of assigned prospects engaged per year)	x			
Yield (amount given/amount asked)	x			
Event attendance		x	x	
Event donors (# and $)		x	x	
Digital metrics (visits to the planned giving pages of the website, email opens, etc.)			x	
Accuracy and timeliness of gift acknowledgments				x
Volume of prospect research		x	x	x
Collaboration	x			x

of planned/deferred gifts, the number of new members of the legacy society, and perhaps the engagement of professional advisors.

- Staff who manage **broader outreach** such as general membership, giving circles, donor societies, or fundraising events have performance metrics that reflect their responsibilities. Their retention numbers will be lower than the major gift officers' because donor acquisition is a key responsibility, and the relationship with a new donor is fragile. For these staff members, donor acquisition, retention, and average (or median) gift size are paramount. Other leading indicators of endowment-building success might assess donor engagement through attendance, volunteering, increasing life-time value among the donor pool, or referrals from members and donors that result in new gifts.

- **Marketing** works closely with the fundraising team to ensure that donors receive consistent compelling messages that encourage support of the organization's reserves or endowment. The messaging calendar should include a steady rotation of updated impact stories featuring both donors and beneficiaries, engagement such as surveys or calls for advocacy, invitations to small informational gatherings or large-scale events, with periodic calls-to-action (giving, volunteering, and so on). All platforms should be coordinated so that donors are receiving congruent messages, whether online, in social media, on site, or through the mail. Their metrics might include giving circle participants, audience size, email opens and click-through rates, and social media engagements.

- The **fundraising operations team** supports all this effort. They acknowledge all gifts and pledges promptly, maintain accurate records in the donor database, conduct periodic research to identify promising prospects for endowment among the existing donors, coordinate with the finance office, and create periodic reports to demonstrate the growth of the funds and their beneficial impact. Performance is measured by accuracy and timeliness of acknowledgments, volume of prospect research, and the resonance of stewardship efforts.

These measures are all important ingredients in an effective performance management plan, and they can apply to both general fundraising and specific endowment fundraising. But over-reliance can create unintended consequences. If a major gift officer hasn't yet met their goal for endowment gifts, they might be tempted to ask for a gift before the donor is ready, resulting in a smaller gift and less-inspired donor. Membership managers might be reluctant to encourage donors to increase their gifts to the amounts that move credit for the donor's giving into a major gift officer's portfolio. That is why it is important to also track and measure collaboration – how many times did the team member share credit with multiple colleagues in securing meaningful gifts to the organization? Each team member should have a specific, numeric goal for this activity, too.

The behavior of donors and actions of the fundraising team all roll up to answer important questions such as:

- How much can we expect to add to the funds' balance this year?
- What is the estimated value of gifts that we might receive in the future through donors' estates?

While current gifts and gift expectancies are a lagging indicator, they too are an important indicator of success in endowment-building. However, the value of future gifts such as realized bequests should *never* be incorporated into an annual budget. Because these gifts are realized after the donor's lifetime, the timing of receipt is unpredictable, and to incorporate specific amounts at a specific time is both risky and unseemly.

All of this may suggest that endowment can be pursued only by nonprofit organizations that are large enough to warrant a full development team and sophisticated enough to track multiple variables simultaneously. In reality, the majority of nonprofit organizations have a smaller team, but they can still raise funds for endowment. Each member of the fundraising team will wear multiple hats, and more of the responsibility and accountability will be taken on by the CEO and members of the board or other endowment-building champions.

Performance metrics are pared to an essential few. Partners including professional advisors or the local community foundation can meet occasional needs for gift planning advice. Outside vendors might be asked to create or refresh the annual endowment-building plan, provide coaching and guidance, or design endowment-specific marketing materials. Annual goals will be adjusted so that they are realistic given the constraints but still ensure steady progress.

Financial Performance Indicators

The leading indicators described previously eventually result in the clearest – although lagging – indicator of endowment-building success: dollars raised. "Lagging" because it is the result of activities that took place in the past, as compared to leading indicators, which predict future outcomes.

Knowing the amount in each endowed fund and the amount that can be disbursed today to fuel programs and operations is essential as an organization develops annual plans and budgets. Being able to predict the funds' future value is important for long-term planning but more difficult because the estimate is based on multiple variables: new cash contributions, realized estate gifts, allocations designated by the board, spending rate, and investment performance. Each must be taken into consideration as an organization assesses its financial resilience. The financial factors that affect the value of endowment funds include the following.

> The clearest – although lagging – indicator of endowment-building success is dollars raised.

- **Endowment value, start of year** may be slightly different than the assets that are included on the organization's balance sheet. For planning purposes, the endowment value in this illustration

should include only the assets that have been received uncon-
ditionally by the organization (that is, a "cash accounting"
approach). Organizations that follow the accrual accounting
method may have booked the anticipated value of certain irrevocable planned gifts such as the remaining years of pledge payments. Because these funds are dependent upon a future event
and the timing or amount are uncertain, they are not yet available to disperse resources for the nonprofit's activities and should
be excluded from the calculation.

- **Investment growth.** As described in Chapter 5, nonprofit organizations and/or their endowment managers invest endowed
funds to create earnings that allow for disbursement and also
maintain purchasing power against inflation. An average rate
of return can be used to project future investment earnings.
For example, a balanced endowment portfolio of 60% equi-
ties and 40% bonds has provided an average return of 9.3%
from 1950 to 2023, according to JP Morgan (although there
are large fluctuations from year to year). The nonprofit organization's finance office and/or endowment managers should be
consulted to determine a conservative estimate to use for this
calculation.

In Practice: Monitoring Investment Performance

Even an organization that carefully follows a prudent investment policy cannot simply "set it and forget it." Financial
officers and board committees should regularly evaluate
investment performance.

Some organizations compare their endowment's investment gains (or losses) with benchmarks for each asset class,
such as the following:

Asset Class Benchmarks

Asset Class	Benchmark
Public equity	MSCI All Country World Index
Hedge funds	HFRI Fund Weighted Index
Private equity	Venture Economics All Private Equity Index
Real assets	CPI +5%/factors such as commodity indices
Fixed income	Barclays Aggregate Index
Cryptocurrency	NASDAQ Crypto Index
Cash	Citigroup 90-Day T-bill Index

In addition to (or sometimes instead of) benchmarking against these market indexes, some organizations will compare their performance with others in their subsector. For example, a college or university may strive to fall between 50% and 74% of the median endowment performance as reported by NACUBO (the National Association of College and University Business Officers).

- **Board designated contributions.** Will the board elect to allocate some of the organization's spare money to the endowment from year to year? There might also be the allocation of realized bequests that were not designated by the donor, the sale of an asset such as real estate, or excess revenue generated by a successful fundraising event. These can be episodic and unpredictable occurrences, so projections tend to be conservative – and perhaps even $0.
- **New gifts** indicate the anticipated value of cash that will be infused into the fund, not the anticipated value of future planned gifts. These can also be difficult to predict, although the leading indicators suggested above can provide a target amount for new current (cash) gifts to the endowment, while historic

averages might be used to estimate the planned gifts that will be realized in any given year. This is also a place for conservative estimates and should never be based on the presumption that planned gifts from specific living donors will be realized during the time period.

- **Net assets released** are generally calculated using the total return spending policy described in Chapter 5: a set percentage (commonly 4.5%) of the funds' total value averaged of the past three to five years.
- **Endowment management expenses** may include fees paid to investment advisors, attorneys, or accountants and auditors. Note that this is not meant to include all estimated fundraising expenses (explained later in this chapter), although some institutions do impose a small fee that is allocated to the expense of raising future funds for the endowment, a practice that must be disclosed to donors who generally find it unpopular, as illustrated in Chapter 1. The typical costs associated with endowment management generally account for less than 1% of the funds' value.
- The **endowment value, end of year** is the calculation of planned additions to and withdrawals from the funds and becomes the starting point for the next year's endowment value. See Table 9-2.

TABLE 9-2 Projecting Endowment Value

Year	1	2	3	4	5
Endowment Value, Start of Year	___	___	___	___	___
+ Investment growth	___	___	___	___	___
+ Board designated contributions	___	___	___	___	___
+ New endowment gifts	___	___	___	___	___
(less net assets released)	___	___	___	___	___
(less management expenses)	___	___	___	___	___
= Endowment value, end of year	___	___	___	___	___

Other factors might be considered when evaluating the effectiveness of endowment-building efforts. These include earned media: how many times was the organization mentioned in print or digital media? When events feature messages about the endowment, it is important to count the number of attendees and the resulting number of new donor inquiries to determine whether the message resonates. Board members may want to know how many of their peers have supported the endowment personally and/or have introduced other potential donors to the organization's mission.

The Value of Future Gifts

The previous example will be helpful to organizations as they plan for future activities based on an estimate of the resources that will be available. In addition, a nonprofit's leaders should monitor the number and potential value of deferred gifts that will be received in the future, whether they appear on the balance sheet or not. A deferred charitable gift that has been documented by the donor is called an *expectancy*. Expectancies may include bequests, beneficiary designations, or any of the other types of gifts explored in Chapter 8. It is important for an organization to track the number of expectancies; the identity of donors; and whether the anticipated gifts are revocable or irrevocable, unrestricted or designated for a specific purpose. This information will inform both current stewardship of donors and long-term financial planning.

For the organization, the anticipated value of deferred gifts is an important consideration for multiple reasons. The performance of the fundraising team – and possibly a portion of their compensation – may be evaluated based on the future value of planned gifts, and the identification of planned gift donors requires careful stewardship of relationships. For the donor, an accurate accounting of a planned gift's future value can provide assurance of the gift's intended impact, as well as eligibility for some forms of donor recognition and benefits. When an organization is in the midst of an endowment-building campaign, understanding the future value of planned gifts is an important measure of progress toward the campaign's goal.

The National Association of Charitable Gift Planners first established national standards for the valuation of planned gifts in 2004 and updates the standards periodically. They state: "Valuation is the process of determining, in today's dollars, what a planned gift will accomplish when received and used for its intended purpose." A link to the entire *Valuation Standards for Planned Gifts* is included in the Resources section at the end of this book.

Jeff Comfort, who chaired the task force for valuing planned gifts, notes that these valuation standards are different from other guidelines such as IRS Regulations or FASB procedures, saying that:

"These methodologies are valid and useful for their intended purposes. However, none are intended to estimate the ultimate value of a planned gift to the charity that will receive it. In many cases, the accepted methods for accounting, counting, and determining the charitable deduction substantially underestimate the value of planned gifts. The valuation standards help charitable organizations and donors understand the value of a planned gift in terms of its present purchasing power. That present value is reached by considering real-world data, including the standards of the Prudent Investor Rule and historical indices of investment performance and inflation."[1]

This points to the importance of distinguishing between counting, accounting, credit, and recognition when considering planned/deferred gifts. In fundraising circles, there is often healthy tension – and sometimes outright conflict – between the finance office, advancement services, major gift officers, board members, and others who may have divergent ways to look at the same gift. Even a well-crafted gift acceptance policy can leave gray areas.

It helps to understand the purpose of each treatment of this gift as described here and illustrated in the sidebar In Practice: "Four Ways to View One Gift."

- **Accounting** is the systematic process that determines how the financial transactions of an organization are recorded and reported. Accounting practices must conform to accepted standards and will be reviewed by an external auditor.

• **Counting** is the allocation of a gift toward a goal, such as a campaign or annual fund. Counting practices should conform to standards such as those provided by AFP, CASE, and CGP. (Links to each organization's website are included in the Resources at the end of this book.)

• **Gift credit** describes how the gift is recorded in the donor's file, which may determine the donor's eligibility for benefits. At institutions with metric-driven prospect management, credit also defines which development officer(s) will be acknowledged for securing the gift.

• **Recognition** is the public acknowledgment of the gift. While an institution may have guidelines to ensure consistent recognition, there is usually some flexibility based on the donor's overall relationship with the institution.

In Practice: Four Ways to View One Gift

Imagine this scenario. Mary Smith, a trustee, has given $25,000 consistently for several years. She is also active on the steering committee for the Foodbank's endowment campaign. Today, the gift officer delivered her signed agreement to make a blended gift of $500,000, consisting of $50,000 per year for five years and an irrevocable promise that the organization will receive $250,000 from her estate. The donor instructs that the gift should be allocated to annual operations and/or the endowment in whatever manner best suits the organization.

• After consulting with the CEO and chief financial officer, the chief development officer recommends allocating

(*continued*)

half of the current pledge of $50,000 per year to annual operations (that is, maintaining her current giving level) and half to the endowment. All of the deferred gift will be allocated to endowment when it is received.

- The major gift officer who manages the relationship with Mary wants to count $375,000 toward the campaign now and $25,000 toward the annual fund each year for the next five years.
- The finance office wants to account for the current $250,000 pledge, in accordance with accounting guidelines, noting that all is unrestricted. They will not account for the bequest until it is realized after Mary's lifetime.
- The campaign chair wants to give her recognition with a $500,000 campaign naming opportunity, while the stewardship office wants to credit her $25,000 annual contribution to membership in the donor society each year.

Who is right? They all are.

So long as an organization exercises transparency, a single gift can be viewed from several different perspectives. The counting and accounting of the gift are governed by external guidelines, while credit and recognition are based on internal principles such as abundance and gratitude, informing the stewardship of a deeper relationship with the donor.

Keep in mind that most gifts are the result of many variables, such as the organization's history and reputation, brand awareness, relevant and resonant programs and services, and the work of successive generations of board and staff members in engaging donors for an extended period. Attention to each practice for managing gifts and nurturing relationships will increase the likelihood of continued gifts from that donor.

Gifts are the result of many variables, such as the organization's history and reputation, brand awareness, relevant and resonant programs and services, and the work of successive generations of board and staff members.

Return on Investment in Endowment Building

Endowment building requires the involvement of staff and volunteers, fees paid to vendors and professional advisors, costs for creating marketing materials, and myriad other activities that require the investment of an organization's resources. Budgeting the total expenses associated with endowment building can be a challenge. These questions need to be answered in an attempt to create a replicable system for estimating expenses annually:

- What percentage of development staffers' salaries should be allocated to endowment building, based on the percentage of time each devotes to the effort?
- What specific expenses are related solely to endowment building, such as planned giving brochures, online platforms, or planned giving contractors?
- Is endowment building integrated into a larger campaign and, if so, what proportion of those costs should be considered?
- If an annual report includes stories about endowment impact, should a proportion of the production cost be allocated to the endowment effort?
- What about the annual audit, given the increased complexity of the task as endowment assets grow?

A consistent, repeatable formula for estimating endowment-building expenses permits an organization to evaluate the return on its investment, following the formula in Table. Because endowment gifts can be unpredictable and volatile, ROI should be averaged over several years – perhaps even a decade. This will provide a clearer picture than looking at a single year at a time because a single large bequest can distort the picture. Mature planned giving and endowment-building programs often find that their total expenditures are 5% to 8% of gifts received annually and less than 1% of the total value of the endowment. It takes many years to achieve this level of maturity and efficiency.

New endowment programs are different. In the earliest years, expenses may outpace revenue, as is the case in almost any new business model. That is why it is essential for board members, endowment champions, and members of the C-suite to understand the long-term benefits of the endowment and leading indicators of progress and not waver from the program even when there are financial headwinds. Sometimes, the commitment to build endowment can be bolstered with a capacity-building grant meant specifically to fund the endowment-building activities. Or the board may decide to allocate a windfall to that purpose, which is what many organizations did when they received unexpected gifts from MacKenzie Scott or other "mega-donors." Other organizations find themselves the beneficiary of such a large bequest that they can more easily justify the expenses associated with engaging future donors.

Budgeting for Endowment Building

A commitment to build endowment will necessitate some one-time startup expenses, which could include retaining a consultant to conduct an assessment and design the plan, utilizing legal counsel to create templates of gift agreements and policies, screening donor data to identify potential endowment or planned giving donors, adding functionality to the donor CRM to track endowment metrics, training staff and board members, or designing and producing print and digital materials meant to last several years. These expenses might be funded through a capacity-building grant designated for the purpose, strategic reserves, or "bootstrapped" through the annual budget (although this last method will likely slow the process).

Annual expenses include the following.

- **Personnel with benefits,** including the percentage of time devoted by gift officers, finance and marketing staff members, the president or CEO, and so on.
- **Training** for staff and volunteers.
- **Marketing** costs to produce, distribute, and maintain print and digital resources to be used by the fundraising team and/or donors. Include any costs associated with donor **recognition** in this category.
- Allocation of a portion of the annual subscription for the **donor CRM.**
- **Events and gatherings,** ranging from an annual legacy society reception to small workshops or leadership briefings in private homes.
- **Travel** for members of the fundraising team to visit far-flung donors personally.
- Fees for ongoing **professional services** from attorneys, accountants, fundraising counsel, and others.

With this information at hand, an organization can calculate and track the return on their investment in endowment building over time using a variety of metrics to monitor performance. The formula is shown in Table 9-3.

TABLE 9-3 Calculating Returns on Endowment-Building Investments

1. Average value of current gifts received for the endowment (five years)
2. Average endowment value, end of year (five years)
3. Average value of endowment + expectancies (five years)
4. Direct expenses of endowment program
    = Cost per dollar raised (4 divided by 1)
    = Cost per dollar of endowment value (4 divided by 2)
    = Cost per dollar of endowment + expectancies (4 divided by 3)

An alternative is to measure the return, not the dollar, according to Shannon Spencer, who has deep experience as a higher education fundraiser and community volunteer. "I prefer to measure the return, not the cost. Each dollar invested in the expenses of the endowment program yields $\_x\_$ in cash added, $\_y\_$ in endowment value added (includes investment returns), and $\_z\_$ in endowment plus expectancies. Especially in smaller organizations, the annual 'cost' can sometimes drive decision-makers away from investments that are vital to its future."

By calculating these formulae each year and tracking progress over multiple years, the organization can see progress, identify factors that accelerated (or slowed) endowment-building progress, and maintain a commitment to the effort.

Going Forward

"Behold the turtle who makes progress only when he sticks his neck out," observed James B. Conant, who held an endowed chair in chemistry before becoming the president of Harvard University during the Great Depression.

Moving a cause forward is often marked by turtle-like progress, and success is attained only when an organization's leaders join together to take risks that demonstrate conviction for the long haul. As Conant experienced over his 30 years at Harvard University, this shared commitment can build resilience evidenced by a corps of committed supporters and a reservoir of resilient financial resources. Any organization can take this path, not just large and sophisticated ones. And, as explained through the previous chapters, success in engaging stakeholders, shoring up reserves, and building endowment results from a holistic approach that weaves together intersecting elements, including:

* Relevant mission
* Clear vision for the future articulated in a strategic plan

- Stories and data that illustrate impact for the common good
- Leaders who are knowledgeable, prudent managers, and team members who are equipped with the right tools
- Loyal stakeholders who embrace the organization's cause

Each element is tied to all of the others. Stakeholders' loyalty is earned through prudent management, transparency, impact, and evocative storytelling. A clear vision is crafted by leaders who are grounded by the relevant mission. And so on. All of the ingredients must be present and tended: this is the challenging and rewarding work of building endowment and nurturing relationships.

Note

1. Jeffrey Comfort and Robert Sharpe, "Valuation Standards for Charitable Planned Gifts | NACGP," charitablegiftplanners.org, June 2011, https://charitablegiftplanners.org/standards/valuation-standards-charitable-planned-gifts. Accessed March 5, 2024. Find a link to the most recent valuation standards in the Resources section at the back of this book.

About the Author

Laura MacDonald has worked professionally in fundraising and philanthropy for more than 40 years, although her interest in serving the common good may be traced to childhood experiences in church, clubs, and a large active family.

When she joined a fundraising consulting firm in the early 1980s, she drew on skills learned in television production and corporate communications to tell the stories of hundreds of nonprofit clients. Her fundraising acumen was sharpened in the late 1990s when she served alongside a remarkable corps of dedicated professionals during The Ohio State University's first billion-dollar fundraising campaign. Building on these experiences, she established Benefactor Group in 2000; a firm that has applied its founding principle of "serving those who serve the common good" by helping hundreds of organizations fuel their cause with powerful fundraising, people, and systems. As founder and principal of the firm, her counsel is sought by leaders in arts and culture, higher education, healthcare, human services, and other nonprofit causes.

MacDonald has served the sector through involvement in the Association of Fundraising Professionals, American Alliance of Museums, and especially her service on the boards of the Giving Institute and the Giving USA Foundation. She chaired the latter from 2020 to 2022, helping to steer the organization through a period of extraordinary disruption, and advancing the understanding of philanthropy's role in society. She is frequently called upon as a speaker, writer, panelist, commentator, and facilitator.

When not traveling extensively or fly fishing, Laura and her husband, Kirk, split time between their primary residence in Columbus, Ohio, and a home in Atlanta, where their daughter, Amber, lives with her husband and five children.

Acknowledgments

Like endowment building, writing a book is a team effort. It starts with a large circle of family, friends, colleagues, and clients who have provided invaluable support and lessons over the course of a career. Much of that career has been spent with teammates at Benefactor Group who have been generous with their time, talent, and wisdom as we've learned together and sought to do good work in a field that is deeply meaningful. A special note of thanks goes to Diana Newman, who helped us all learn more about endowments and the donors who build them. As leadership of the firm transitions to my fellow principal Steve Beshuk, I am confident in the team's capacity to serve the common good for generations to come.

I am grateful to all those in client organizations that invited me to join them as they engaged donors, raised funds, built endowments, and served their cause. Among the hundreds of experiences with clients who have enriched my understanding of philanthropy, a handful merit special recognition, such as colleagues at The Ohio State University in the late 1990s and my work with the World YWCA and Global Fund for Women, led by the incomparable Musimbi Kanyoro. There are many other professionals and volunteers – serving in the trenches of best-in-class hospitals, influential museums, scrappy human service and animal welfare agencies, and every other type of cause – whose generosity and creativity are endlessly inspiring.

The community where I live and work has a strong philanthropic culture, thanks in part to the leadership of The Columbus Foundation. Nonprofit trailblazers, generous donors, and committed trustees across the region have been generous with advice and guidance that have shaped my understanding of philanthropy and enriched my vocation.

Another source of valued insights has come from my involvement in the Giving Institute and Giving USA Foundation, where colleagues such as Josh Birkholz, Nathan Chappel, Rick Dunham, Wendy McGrady, Kate Roosevelt, and other peers encouraged the writing of this book and helped deepen my understanding of the trends shaping the nonprofit landscape. Giving USA's partnership with the Lilly Family School of Philanthropy at Indiana University provided opportunities to learn from Drs. Una Osili, Anna Pruitt, and their colleagues. Participation on the Giving USA Foundation board and in the production of the *Annual Report* has been a highlight of my career.

Finally, I am grateful to colleagues across the country and around the world who provided resources, time, and encouragement during the writing process. In particular, I thank those who reviewed early drafts of the chapters and helped make them better, especially JD Beiting, Steve Beshuk, Simon Bisson, Susan Brekelmans, Joe Bull, Johnny Cooper, Clare Flynn, Ben Golding, Christine Gomez, Musimbi Kanyoro, Parker MacDonell, Steven Moore, Diana Newman, Chad Paris, Susan Rector, Megan Simmons, Shannon Spencer, Katy Trombitas, and Paul Yeghiayan. Their insights will contribute to readers' ability to build endowment and elevate the common good.

Appendix: References and Resources

The following resources and references may be helpful to those who plan to implement the guidance found throughout the book. The references are arranged by general topic and include links to templates, sample policies, and other useful documents. Most are freely available online, although some may require users to create a free or paid account, and several provide periodic email updates to those who register. The resources include templates that are referred to in various chapters.

All are current as of the writing of this book (2024), but be sure to check for updated versions. Care should be taken to verify any information, especially that provided by for-profit organizations serving the social sector and anything sourced from a broad community of contributors (e.g., Wikipedia, Investopedia). The resources cited in this section are generally understood to be credible sources for information about endowments, fundraising, governance, and other nonprofit management topics. They do not replace the need for guidance from accredited legal, accounting, and financial advisors.

General References

- **The Association of Fundraising Professionals (afpglobal.org):** AFP offers extensive tools, resources, and training. Some of the most helpful require an AFP membership for access (an AFP membership is well worth the investment for development staff). In addition to online tools and resources, AFP offers periodic webinars, a library of "micro-learning videos," education programs in most cities, and an annual international conference.

- *Chronicle of Philanthropy* (philanthropy.com): As self-described, "for nearly 35 years, the *Chronicle of Philanthropy* has been the premier source of news, information, analysis, and opinion in the rapidly growing nonprofit world." The Chronicle is a nonprofit organization itself. Its flagship publication is the now-monthly newspaper, complemented with a content-rich website, special reports, and webinars.

- **Independent Sector (IS, independentsector.org)**: A convener of nonprofits and other organizations working to strengthen civil society, IS is a membership organization that provides research and education to inform practice and policy.

- **Lilly Family School of Philanthropy at Indiana University (philanthropy.iupui.edu/about/index.html)**: One of the oldest and most respected academic centers that conducts research and professional education to advance the understanding and practice of philanthropy. Hosted at Indiana University's campus in Indianapolis, IN. Signature projects include Giving USA, the Annual Report on Philanthropy (published by the Giving USA Foundation), the Philanthropy Panel Study, and the study of Charitable Giving by Affluent Households (in partnership with Bank of America).

- **National Council of Nonprofits (councilofnonprofits.org/running-nonprofit)**: This is another resource for a wide variety of tools, research, and resources that nonprofit organizations can consult to operate more effectively, efficiently, and ethically. The organization states that "to advance equity, we make . . . materials available for free to all nonprofits."

- **Nonprofit Financial Commons (https://nonprofitfinancials.org/)**: Several organizations have come together to create a platform where nonprofit organizations can share resources and templates, learn from one another, and engage peers around the challenges of financial management.

Data on Charitable Giving and the Nonprofit Sector

Large datasets provide insights about trends in charitable giving to help practitioners better predict results and target fundraising efforts.

- **Fundraising Effectiveness Project** (https://afpglobal.org/fep reports): Since 2006, a consortium of organizations – including AFP, the Center on Nonprofits, the Urban Institute, and several nonprofit data partners – have tracked anonymized donor transactions to discern trends in giving. They issue quarterly and year-end reports that include fundraising gains and losses recorded in their datasets (which reflect the characteristics of the organizations that utilize the participating data management platforms) that can be applied to any nonprofit's fundraising performance metric.

- **GivingTuesday Data Commons** (givingtuesday.org/data-commons/): As an outgrowth of the #GivingTuesday initiative, the organization works with hundreds of collaborators and global data labs to collect comprehensive datasets from across the social sector.

- **Giving USA** (givingusa.org): This is the seminal annual report on the sources and uses of charitable gifts given to 501(c)3 organizations in the United States. Topline data is freely available, and deeper insights can be accessed with an annual subscription. The *Annual Report* is supplemented with an exploration of each source of charitable gifts and each recipient sector, with references to curated studies and research. Giving USA also publishes periodic *Special Reports*, some of which are referenced in the bibliography.

- **National Center on Charitable Statistics** (urban.org/tags/national-center-charitable-statistics-data): President Lyndon

B. Johnson established the Urban Institute in 1968 to provide "power through knowledge." NCCS is a program of the Urban Institute. Its searchable databases provide data on the nonprofit sector.

Diversity in Endowment Building

While support for endowments has leaned heavily into "traditional" donors (older, white, wealthy, male), new efforts and resources have identified the missed opportunities among donors of color and provide guidance in effective engagement of these communities.

- **Donors of Color Network (donorsofcolor.org):** This cross-racial network has established "a space for donors of color to learn, strategize, and act . . ." Their website provides abundant resources, especially the report "Philanthropy Always Sounds like Someone Else" with insights about the giving behaviors of high- and ultra-high-net-worth BIPOC donors including attitudes toward endowment and planned giving.
- **Giving Docs (about.givingdocs.com/dei):** As a partner to nonprofit organizations, Giving Docs provides tools to help donors create estate plans with legacy commitments. Their emphasis on stewardship leads to effective implementation. Their commitment to diversity, equity, and inclusion in planned giving is demonstrated through three research reports and a resource library that can be freely accessed.

Information Clearinghouses

Any nonprofit organization with $200,000 or more in gross revenue or $500,000 or more in assets is required to file an informational tax return called an IRS 990. When endowed funds are held by the organization, they are reported on "Schedule D." The IRS 990 filings are publicly available. Many organizations post their 990 on their websites along with their audited financial statements. In addition, individual organizations' 990 filings and other data can be found in the following locations.

- **Candid/GuideStar (guidestar.org):** GuideStar began in 1994 with a goal of making basic information about nonprofit organizations readily available to donors. The organization merged with The Foundation Center in 2019, with the new entity known as Candid. In addition to a searchable compilation of IRS 990 data, the organization provides an overview of financials, people, mission, and impact, as well as rating the transparency of each organization. Much information including 990 filings can be accessed by creating a free account.
- **Charity Navigator:** By providing free access to data, tools, and resources, Charity Navigator strives to guide philanthropic decision making. Their rating system, which once emphasized "overhead," now focuses on more relevant measures of impact, stability, efficiency, and stability.
- **Nonprofit Explorer (projects.propublica.org/nonprofits/):** In addition to searchable IRS 990 filings, this resource provided by ProPublica also provides audits of nonprofit organizations that spent $750,000 or more in federal grants, summaries of nonprofit data by state and sector, and summaries.
- **Bridgespan:** As a nonprofit strategy, consulting, and think-tank entity, Bridgespan provides a variety of resources that inform the sector. They have a particularly helpful entry that helps to navigate the availability of nonprofit financial information at https://www.bridgespan.org/insights/where-to-find-nonprofit-financial-information.

The Science of Donor Behavior

Behavioral economics combines insights from psychology, neuroscience, and economic data in an attempt to better understand donors' behaviors.

- **EncourageGenerosity.com:** This website is curated by Dr. Russell James III and contains a wealth of links to open access books, videos, and articles. Dr. James' early career focused on charitable gift planning. More recently, he has authored a variety of resources about the neuroscience of donor behavior, especially the role of the universal hero story.

- **ideas42 (ideas42.org/giving/):** As a nonprofit organization dedicated to behavioral science, ideas42 has several initiatives that focus on giving with three goals: to help more people give, and give more effectively, and to translate their giving into social impact. They produce a particularly helpful literature review periodically, capturing insights from a wide range of behavioral scientists working on philanthropy and generosity.

- **The Science of Philanthropy Initiative (spihub.org):** The goal of SPI is to "develop a deeper understanding of the types of social preferences that shape philanthropic giving and to apply this knowledge to both practitioners and policymakers interested in philanthropy and the private provision of public goods." The website includes links to video resources from past conferences and presentations. The organization's funding ended in 2015, so more current resources may be found at the University of Chicago's Department of Economics website.

Federal and State Laws

State and federal laws that govern fundraising and nonprofit management are proliferating. So are requirements for nonprofit organizations and their fundraising consultants to register in many of the states where they solicit gifts. The most up-to-date information may be available from each state's Attorney General's office and the IRS.

- **Giving USA State Law Annual Survey (https://store.givingusa. org/collections/annual-updates-on-state-laws):** For a summary of the laws governing charitable solicitations and registration requirements, Giving USA provides an annual update available at a modest price for purchase, or included in an annual subscription.

- **Nonprofit Law Blog** (https://nonprofitlawblog.com/): The NEO Law Group regularly publishes blogs and short articles on this website, although their location in San Francisco leads to a focus on California State Law.
- **UPMIFA** (https://www.nacubo.org/Topics/Endowment-Management/UPMIFA-Resources): A quick web search will provide multiple resources for understanding the Uniform and Prudent Management of Institutional Funds Act (UPMIFA). The link from NACUBO (National Association of College and University Business Officers) is brief and helpful, with links to other sites and the text of the act itself.
- **State Associations of Nonprofits and State Attorneys General Offices:** These resources exist in most states and may have helpful guidance on their websites.

Reserves and Reserve Policies

Success in developing and managing reserve funds requires board engagement, disciplined fiscal management, and effective policies, which are offered by several organizations on their websites.

- **National Council of Nonprofits** (councilofnonprofits.org/running-nonprofit/administration-and-financial-management/operating-reserves-nonprofits): Questions such as "how much should we have" and "how do we develop policies" are answered briefly on this page, with links to instructional videos and policy examples.
- **Nonprofit Operating Reserves Institute** (https://www.nonprofitaccountingbasics.org/nonprofit-reserves): A working group sponsored by the Greater Washington Society of CPAs has created a variety of resources with a mission to "define, promote, and facilitate the practice of building and maintaining operating reserves . . ." Their publications include an extensive document library with helpful policy templates, which are updated regularly.
- **Propel Nonprofits** (propelnonprofits.org/resources/nonprofit-operating-reserves-policy-examples/): Community

Development Financial Institutions (CDFIs) are a sort of nonprofit financial institution. Among them, Propel Nonprofits provides particularly relevant information about reserves and several sound examples of reserve policies.

Broad-Based and Middle Giving

Much of the research on broad-based giving is provided by for-profit enterprises that offer fundraising and management services to nonprofit organizations. They may rely on data from their clients, which can create idiosyncrasies.

- **Blackbaud Reports** (https://www.blackbaud.com/industry-insights/resources/nonprofit-organizations/blackbaud-luminate-online-benchmark-report-2022 and https://www.blackbaud.com/industry-insights/resources/nonprofit-organizations/blackbaud-peer-to-peer-benchmark-report-2022): A major software technology company serving the social sector, Blackbaud provides several reports based on an analysis of charitable giving transactions among subsets of organizations that utilize their technology. While the subsets provide large quantities of data, they cannot be considered representative of the entire sector because they reflect the types of organizations that utilize only their products.
- **Classy** (classy.org/why-america-gives/): This technology platform is a part of the GoFundMe family of companies, with a focus on nonprofit fundraisers and supporters. Their reports are rooted in data from users of their platform, complemented with other research from sources such as GivingTuesday and Indiana University.
- **M+R Benchmarks** (https://mrbenchmarks.com/): M+R is an online marketing and public relations firm that works with organizations and movements to "engage the masses and raise money" for causes. Their annual benchmark report relies on data from clients (more than 200 in 2023) to provide insights

about donor engagement and giving through online, social media, and direct response media.

- **Missing Middle (seachangestrategies.com/insights/):** A series of four research reports detail the challenges and opportunities in engaging donors described as "mid-level."

Middle giving has been largely neglected, overshadowed by the major gifts that attract attention from fundraisers and the media. A prominent exception is the work done by Sea Change Strategies in partnership with Edge Research.

Endowment Policies and Management

Many of the sources listed throughout this resource directory provide guidance on endowment policies and management, especially the National Council of Nonprofits and the Association of Governing Boards. Organizations that are the local affiliate of a national or global organization may find that the parent organization provides resources and guidance. In many communities, the local community foundation may also be a source of information and policy templates. The following resources may be helpful as well.

- **American Alliance of Museums (https://www.aam-us.org/ programs/resource-library/financial-stability-resources/gift-acceptance-policies/):** Any organization that collects art, objects, or even living collections has special considerations in accepting gifts. The American Alliance of Museums offers sound guidance.
- **Council on Foundations (https://cof.org/foundation-type/ community-foundations):** Most local community foundations can be located using the locator feature on the Council's website. In addition to policy templates, many local community foundations offer support and training.
- **National Council of Nonprofits (https://www.councilofnonprofits. org/running-nonprofit/fundraising-and-resource-development/ gift-acceptance-policies):** In addition to policy examples, the

Council provides guidance for the process of developing and adopting policies, including investment, endowment management, and gift acceptance.

- **National Association of College and University Business Officers** (nacubo.org/topics/endowment-management): While NACUBO's resources and information are tailored to higher education, their research may help to inform a wide range of nonprofit organizations and donors. They publish an annual study of higher education endowments in partnership with TIAA.

- *The Sustainable Endowment:* Written by James E. Demmert, this book offers "10 principles to Make Your Foundation or Nonprofit Last for Decades." Published by New Insights Press in 2019, it is available wherever books are sold.

Governance and Strategy

Boards play a key role in developing strategies and policies for the creation and management of reserves and endowments, and individual board members are called upon to nurture the relationships that yield loyal donors. Many organizations seek guidance from their local community foundation, a national office (if the organization is a local affiliate), or a sector-specific professional association.

- **The Association of Governing Boards of Universities and Colleges** (https://agb.org/about-us/): AGB is "the premier organization focused on empowering college, university, and foundation boards to govern with knowledge and confidence." Some of their resources, such as the publication *Endowment Management for Foundations and Nonprofits*, have been adapted for broader application and are available for purchase.

- **BoardSource** (boardsource.org): BoardSource is a membership organization that provides research, leadership, and guidance for board members and the staff who support governance. Many resources are free, although some are locked behind a membership paywall. In particular, the organization provides guidance for content and examples of the policies explored in Chapter 5.

- **Responsible AI (https://fundraising.ai/):** As the use of artificial intelligence increases, responsible organizations will seek resources to ensure that applications prioritize and build trust. This collaborative offers a "Framework for Responsible Use" as well as resources and convenings to learn more about the practical and responsible use of AI tools in fundraising.

Planned Giving

An online search of the phrase "planned giving" returns millions of results. Many are the planned giving pages of nonprofit organizations, or local/regional planned giving councils. It will also provide links to credible planned giving consulting and marketing firms, as well as myriad entities hawking financial products that may (or may not) be effective at meeting the needs of donors and the nonprofits they wish to support. Care should be taken to vet the latter category of providers.

- **Leave a Legacy (https://charitablegiftplanners.org/leave-a-legacy)** is a public awareness campaign designed to inspire people to make a charitable bequest. Public domain resources can be downloaded from the website and utilized by any organization that is starting on a planned giving and/or endowment building program.
- **Leaving a Legacy: A New Look at Planned Giving Donors (https://store.givingusa.org/collections/special-reports-spotlights/products/leaving-a-legacy-a-new-look-at-planned-giving-donors-subscriber-edition?variant=39331665182799):** In this 2019 special report from the Giving USA Foundation, author Elizabeth Dale interprets survey results to shed light on key trends in planned giving.
- **National Association of Charitable Gift Planners (charitablegift planners.org/about):** This professional association helps to

advance members' work through education, resources, and advocacy. Local chapters provide education and networking opportunities while the national conference gathers practitioners and experts from around the world. Of particular merit are their widely accepted guides and standards, found at https://charitablegiftplanners.org/standards, including:

- Reporting and counting charitable gifts
- Model standards of practice
- Valuation standards
- Performance metrics

Global Philanthropy and Endowment Building

As societies around the world translate their cultural expressions of generosity into more formalized structures for charitable giving, many country-specific professional associations, governing laws, and regulatory bodies have emerged. Those seeking to build endowments should confer with these prior to adopting policies or allocating funds. Additional information about the global state of charitable giving may also be useful.

- **Charities Aid Foundation (https://www.cafonline.org/international-giving/caf-network):** In their effort to accelerate philanthropy in support of a fair and sustainable future, the Charities Aid Foundation has created an international network of partners.
- **Charities Commission (https://www.gov.uk/guidance/charity-commission-guidance)** website includes a "guidance" section with numerous topics that can be easily searched.
- **Citi GPS (https://www.solutions.citi.com/insights):** Beginning in 2021, the global research team at Citibank produced an annual report on the state of global philanthropy, citing sources such as the World Bank and the Charities Aid Foundation (UK) to better understand the global philanthropy landscape.

- **Global Philanthropy Forum** (https://www.philanthropyforum. org/): Through conferences, research, and other forums, GFF links funders, donors, and investors committed to issues that transcend borders. There are affiliate groups focused on Africa, Asia, and other geographies.
- **Global Philanthropy Tracker** (https://globalindices.iupui.edu/ tracker/index.html): Just as Indiana University's Lilly Family School of Philanthropy contributes to the general understanding of philanthropy, their global giving initiatives provide insights about fundraising globally and are complemented by reports and studies that focus on specific countries and regions.
- **Imagine Canada** (https://www.imaginecanada.ca/en) works with and for the nonprofit sector across Canada, in pursuit of a more just and fair society for all.
- **Institute of Community Directors Australia** (https://www .communitydirectors.com.au/about) provides insights to support the sector, including an extensive "policy bank" that is freely available.

Philanthropy in History

- **HistPhil** (https://histphil.org/about/): This web publication includes regular updates from scholars who study the history of philanthropy and the nonprofit sector, with a particular emphasis on how history can shed light on contemporary philanthropic issues and practice. Their home page includes extensive links to recent publications about philanthropic practices and influences around the world.

Just for Fun

- *The Counting House:* Gary Sernovitz' absurdist novel (published in 2022 by University of New Orleans Press) follows the trials and tribulations of an anonymous chief investment officer who manages the $6 billion endowment of an unnamed private university. Witty and profanity-laced, it pulls aside the veil of mystery around alternative investment strategies and their relative merits (or lack thereof) for endowed funds and the causes they serve.

Resources

These resources are templates you can use for your own work; they are referenced in the various chapters.

Endowment Readiness Test

(Referenced in Chapter 2.)

Consider this checklist, adapted and updated from Jacquelyn B. Ostrom's presentation at the Association of Fundraising Professionals 2004 International Conference.

Endowment Readiness Test

Score Range	Endowment Readiness Factor	Your Nonprofit's Score
0–20	Board commitment to endowment	_____
0–20	Stable, knowledgeable leadership	_____
0–15	Strong organization, including reserve funds	_____
0–15	A clear vision that resonates with supporters	_____
0–10	Solid fundraising fundamentals	_____
0–10	A corps of loyal and/or major donors	_____
0–5	Effective marketing and stewardship	_____
0–5	Current endowment policies exist	_____

Your Organization's Score: _____

100 is the maximum score. The criteria listed first are the most important. Usually, a score of 70 is necessary to successfully launch an endowment-building effort. An organization with a lower score, or with "0" in any category, should address weaknesses before proceeding.

Sample Resolution to Build Endowment (or Reserves)

(Referenced in Chapter 2.)

WHEREAS Any Cause, Inc., an Ohio not-for-profit corporation was established on September 16, 1954 for charitable, educational, and public purposes; and

WHEREAS the mission and vision of Any Cause, Inc. are vitally important to the people served by Any Cause, Inc.;

NOW THEREFORE BE IT RESOLVED that Any Cause, Inc. will establish [or expand] a permanent endowment [or reserve fund], named the Any Cause Fund, to provide an ongoing source of support to enhance stability and stature, allow for expansion and innovation, provide financial independence, and to allow flexibility for its leadership; and

RESOLVED FURTHER that Any Cause, Inc. shall allocate resources – both time and money – to the growth of the endowment [or reserves]; and

RESOLVED FURTHER that Any Cause, Inc., shall adopt the endowment [or reserve] building strategies attached hereto and integrate them into all fundraising programs and activities, and shall actively educate clients, members, volunteers, donors, gift planners, and other constituents about the endowment and methods to contribute toward its growth.

DULY ADOPTED by an affirmative vote of the trustees on [date].

Endowment Action Plan Example

(Referenced in Chapter 3.)

Any Cause, Inc.

(year) Endowment Action Plan

Goals for the year:

Personal prospect visits: 24

Number of new gifts: 3 named funds; many smaller gifts

Current dollars raised: $100,000

Board participation: $25,000 in new gifts; participation in ¼ of visits
New expectancies: $250,000
Long-range goal: Assets of $_____ by the year _____

Sample Endowment Action Plan

Donor Identification and Cultivation	Marketing	Special Events	Professional Advisor Engagement
Develop a list of 100 prospects through research and referral	Develop an endowment case and donor-facing materials	Host informal gatherings for four small groups of current donors	Identify board members' professional advisors and host a gathering for them
Identify contact person for each prospect	Celebrate all endowment gifts (with donor's permission) in earned and owned media	Endowment donors receive special experiences at annual events (examples: a VIP donor lounge, special name tags)	Ask interested donors to add their advisors to the contact list
Train five volunteers to seek visits and accompany staff	Integrate endowment stories into social media, website, and e-news	Host a lunch for professional advisors	Seek two speaking engagements at gatherings of estate attorneys, financial planners, CPAs, and similar
Schedule and complete two personal visits per month	Integrate endowment giving into the online giving portal		Meet one-on-one with four of the community's most respected advisors
Establish a legacy society	Send targeted endowment messages to all donors who have given 7 of the last 10 years		

Sample Language for a Simple Bequest (or Codicil)

(Referenced in Chapters 4 and 7.)

In order to make a bequest, donors should speak with their attorney. Often a cause will provide some basic bequest language to assist donors and their legal counsel, such as the following:

Bequest of a Specific Dollar Amount:

I hereby give, devise and bequeath _____ and No/100 dollars ($DOLLARS) to Any Cause, a nonprofit organization located at [address], Federal Tax ID #_____, for the general endowment of Any Cause.

Bequest of Specific Personal Property:

I hereby give, devise and bequeath DESCRIPTION OF PROPERTY to Any Cause, a nonprofit organization located at [address], Federal Tax ID #_____, for the general endowment of Any Cause.

Bequest of Specific Real Estate:

I hereby give, devise and bequeath all of the right, title and interest in and to the real estate located at ADDRESS OR DESCRIPTION OF PROPERTY to Any Cause, a nonprofit organization located at [address], Federal Tax ID #_____, for the general endowment of Any Cause.

Percentage Bequest:

I hereby give, devise and bequeath ____ percent (___%) of my total estate, determined as of the date of my death, to Any Cause, a nonprofit organization located at [address], Federal Tax ID #_____, for the general endowment of Any Cause.

Residual Bequest:

I hereby give, devise and bequeath to Any Cause, a nonprofit organization located at [address], Federal Tax ID #_____, ALL OR A PERCENTAGE of the rest, residue and remainder of my estate to be used for the general endowment of Any Cause.

Contingent Bequest:

If (primary beneficiary) does not survive me, then I hereby give, devise and bequeath to Any Cause, a nonprofit organization located at [address], Federal Tax ID #_____, DESCRIPTION OF PROPERTY to be used for the general endowment of Any Cause.

Restricted Bequest:

If the donor wishes to designate the use of the proceeds from the endowed fund, encourage the addition of the following language:

If, in the judgment of the Board of Directors of Any Cause, it shall become impossible to use this bequest to accomplish the specific purposes of the endowed fund, Any Cause may use the proceeds of this gift for such purpose or purposes as the Board determines is most closely related to the restricted purpose of the endowed fund.

Example Impact Investment Due Diligence Framework

(Referenced in Chapter 6 and provided by the Walters Art Museum. Used with permission.)

Investment Criteria	Low	Mid	High
Alignment with mission to be a part of the solution for Baltimore	The social impact thesis of the investment is not aligned with the museum's mission.	The social impact thesis of the investment indirectly supports and/or has some direct alignment with the museum's mission.	The primary social impact thesis of the investment is directly aligned with the museum's mission.
Management Expertise	Little management experience generally. No directly related project or strategy experience.	Management has relevant experience and a strong track record. May be developing a new line of business in related field or market. May have strong partnership with experienced organization.	Management is very experienced in relevant industry or verticals and managing capital for repayment. Financial incentives are clearly aligned.
Financial strength of fund manager/ enterprise	Weak. Low level of net worth, experiences liquidity problems or other financial challenges.	Acceptable levels of net worth. May have a financial challenge but working to address it. Satisfactory cash flow position.	Strong financial position as indicated by appropriate levels of leverage, liquidity, and net worth. Portfolio quality is strong and contingent liabilities are negligible. Overall cash flow position is excellent.

Investment Criteria	Low	Mid	High
Financial feasibility of proposed project/ strategy	Financial analysis demonstrates project or strategy is unlikely to return capital.	Financial analysis demonstrates reasonable expectation for the return of capital through revenue and/ or profit generation.	Financial analysis demonstrates high likelihood of financial return.
Geographic focus	Investments targeted nationally or internationally with little focus on Baltimore.	Investments focused on Maryland communities.	Investments focused on Baltimore communities.
Marginal impact of Walters Museum Investment	Walters' involvement has no impact on the success of the project or strategy.	Walters' involvement has a material impact on the success of the project or strategy.	

Bibliography

Afpglobal.org. "Code of Ethical Standards | Association of Fundraising Professionals," 2014. https://afpglobal.org/ethicsmain/code-ethical-standards.

Ali, Aran, and Joyce Ma. "Ranked: The World's Top 50 Endowment Funds." Visual Capitalist, May 16, 2023. https://www.visualcapitalist.com.

Andersson, Fredrik O. "Social Entrepreneurship as Fetish." *Nonprofit Quarterly*, April 11, 2012. https://nonprofitquarterly.org/social-entrepreneurship-as-fetish-2/.

Bearman, Jessica, and Jason Franklin PhD. "Dynamics of Hosting: Giving Circles and Collective Giving Groups." *IUPUI ScholarWorks*. Collective Giving Research Group, November 2018. https://philanthropy.iupui.edu/research/topics/index.html.

"Behavior and Charitable Giving: 2023 Update." *Ideas42*, April 2023. https://www.ideas42.org/publications/giving/.

Birkholz, Joshua M., and Amy S. Lampi. *BeneFactors*. John Wiley & Sons, 2022.

Blackbaud Institute. "The next Generation of American Giving." https://Institute.blackbaud.com/Resources/The-Next-Generation-of-American-Giving-2018, 2018.

Bonnici, François. "Why Social Enterprises Need More Support." World Economic Forum, January 18, 2024. https://www.weforum.org/agenda/2024/01/social-enterprises-financial-policy-support/.

Bristol, JD, Jade. "Can Planned Giving Advance Diversity, Equity and Inclusion?" GivingDocs.com. GivingDocs, 2024. https://www.about.givingdocs.com/post/dei-in-planned-giving-part-3-recommendatons-to-increase-diversity-in-planned-giving.

Bruen, Robert. "*A Brief History of the Lucasian Professorship of Mathematics*." Cambridge University, May 1995. http://www.lucasianchair.org.

The Center for Effective Philanthropy. "Funding Nonprofit Endowments: Foundation Perspectives and Practices," 2024. https://cep.org/report-backpacks/funding-nonprofit-endowments-foundation-perspectives-and-practices/?section=intro.

Comfort, Jeffrey, and Robert Sharpe. "Valuation Standards for Charitable Planned Gifts | NACGP." charitablegiftplanners.org, June 2011. https://charitablegiftplanners.org/standards/valuation-standards-charitable-planned-gifts.

Council on Foundations. "Homepage," n.d. https://cof.org/.

Craver, Roger. *Retention Fundraising: The New Art and Science of Keeping Your Donors for Life*. 2 ed. Civil Sector Press, 2014.

Crimmins, Brian, Nathan Chappell, and Michael Ashley. *The Generosity Crisis*. John Wiley & Sons, 2022.

Crutchfield, Leslie R., and Heather McLeod Grant. *Forces for Good*. Jossey-Bass, 2007.

Dale, PhD, Elizabeth J. "Leaving a Legacy: A New Look at Today's Planned Giving Donors." Giving USA, September 2019. https://store.givingusa.org/products/leaving-a-legacy-a-new-look-at-planned-giving-donors-digital-edition?variant=39331664658511.

Demmert, James E. *The Sustainable Endowment*. New Insights Press, 2019.

"Depreciate." In *Merriam Webster's Collegiate Dictionary, 11th Ed.*, 2020.

Dietz, Nathan. "Social Connectedness and Generosity." University of Maryland School of Public Policy Do Good Institute, January 11, 2021. https://dogood.umd.edu/research-impact/publications/social-connectedness-and-generosity-look-how-associational-life-and.

Dumitru, Oana. "Half of Americans Say They Have Donated Money to Charity in the Past Year | YouGov." today.yougov.com, August 15, 2022. https://today.yougov.com/society/articles/43435-half-americans-donate-money-charity-past-year-poll.

"Endow." In *Merriam-Webster's Collegiate Dictionary, 11th Ed.* Springfield, MA: Merriam-Webster, Inc., 2020.

"Enduring." In *Merriam-Webster's Collegiate Dictionary, 11th Ed.*, 2020.

Fidelity Charitable, and Artemis Research Group. "Entrepreneurs as Philanthropists," 2018. https://www.fidelitycharitable.org/insights/entrepreneurs-as-philanthropists.html.

Frede, Dorothea. "Alexander of Aphrodisias." *Stanford Encyclopedia of Philosophy*, October 13, 2003.

Gallagher, Janne. "Legal Briefs." *Foundation News and Commentary* 44, no. 2 (March 2003).

Giving USA. *Giving USA 2023*. 68th ed. Giving USA, 2023.

GivingTuesday. "GivingTuesday Data Commons." Accessed March 6, 2024. https://www.givingtuesday.org/data-commons/.

Greer, Lisa, and Larissa Kostoff. *Philanthropy Revolution: How to Inspire Donors, Build Relationships and Make a Difference*. HarperCollins, 2020.

HBCU Money. "2022 Top 10 HBCU Endowments." February 21, 2023. https://hbcumoney.com/2023/02/21/hbcu-moneys-2022-top-10-hbcu-endowments.

Independent Sector. "Trust in Civil Society," September 26, 2023. https://independentsector.org/resource/trust-in-civil-society/.

James, JD, PhD, Russell. *Inside the Mind of the Bequest Donor*. CreateSpace, 2013.

———. "Introducing the Epic Fundraiser to the Public: What's Your Job?" *LinkedIn* (blog), August 9, 2022. https://www.linkedin.com/pulse/introducing-epic-fundraiser-public-whats-your-job-russell/.

Justice Funders. "Guiding Values & Principles." Accessed March 5, 2024. https://justicefunders.org/resonance/guiding-values-principles/.

Kaplan, Ann E. "CASE Insights on Voluntary Support of Education." Council for Advancement and Support of Education, 2024. https://www.case.org/research/surveys/voluntary-support-education-survey/findings-and-reports.

Kimball, Bruce. "The Uneasy Convergence of Elite and Mass Fundraising in Higher Ed: The Harvard Endowment Fund Drive, 1915-1925," July 27, 2018. https://histphil.org/2018/07/27/the-uneasy-convergence-of-elite-and-mass-fundraising-in-higher-ed-the-harvard-endowment-fund-drive-1915-1925/.

Klein, Kim. *Fundraising for Social Change*. Hoboken, New Jersey: Wiley, 2016.

"Lady Margaret's 500 Year Legacy." Wayback Machine: University of Cambridge, May 16, 2007.

Lawrence, Tom. "Ohio State Benefactor's Family Seeing Red over Mishandling of $30.3 Million Endowment." Legal Newsline, August 19, 2020. https://legalnewsline.com/stories/548961543-ohio-state-benefactor-s-family-seeing-red-over-mishandling-of-30-3-million-endowment.

Lee, Hali, Urvashi Vaid, and Ashindi Maxton. "Philanthropy Always Sounds Like Someone Else: A Portrait of High Net Worth Donors of Color." Donors of Color Network. Donors of Color Network, 2022. https://www.donorsofcolor.org/resources/philanthropy-always-sounds-like-someone-else-0c68d.

Levy, Barbara, ed. "Case for Support." In *AFP Fundraising Dictionary*, 2017. https://afpglobal.org/fundraising-dictionary.

Lilly Family School of Philanthropy. "Donor Advised Funds: New Insights." Giving USA, September 2021. https://store.givingusa.org/pages/giving-usa-special-report-donor-advised-funds-new-insights.

———."Everyday Donors of Color: Giving Trends by Race and Ethnicity," November 2023. https://philanthropy.indianapolis.iu.edu/research/latest/donors-of-color.html.

Lilly Family School of Philanthropy. "Research." Accessed March 6, 2024. https://philanthropy.indianapolis.iu.edu/institutes/womens-philanthropy-institute/research/index.html.

Lilly Family School of Philanthropy, Indiana University. "The 2023 Bank of America Study of Philanthropy: Charitable Giving by Affluent Households." *IUPUI ScholarWorks*, October 2023. https://scholarworks.iupui.edu/items/31aafdfd-a6a6-486e-978c-35c705409f2c.

Lilly Family School of Philanthropy, and Vanguard Charitable. "Changes to the Giving Landscape," 2019. https://blog.philanthropy.iupui.edu/2019/10/24/changes-to-the-giving-landscape-giving-before-and-after-the-great-recession/.

Lo, Andrew, Egor Matveyev, and Stefan Zeume. "The Risk, Reward, and Asset Allocation of Nonprofit Endowment Funds." In *The Summer Institute of Finance*. Shangai, China, 2021. https://papers.ssrn.com/sol3/papers.cfm?abstract_id=3560240.

MacDonald, Laura. "AI and Nonprofits: Not If or How but When." Forbes.com Nonprofit Council (blog), September 17, 2023. https://www.forbes.com/sites/forbesnonprofitcouncil/2023/09/27/ai-and-nonprofits-not-if-or-when-but-how/?sh=ee5e7eb2bf6a.

McKee, Alia, and Mark Rovner. "The Missing Middle Part Four." Sea Change Strategies and Edge Research, 2024. https://seachangestrategies.com/resources/.

NACUBO, and Commonfund. "2023 NACUBO-Commonfund Study of Endowments." *NACUBO*, February 15, 2024. https://www.nacubo.org/Research/2023/NACUBO-Commonfund-Study-of-Endowments.

Nee, Eric. "Learning from Failure." *Stanford Social Innovation Review*, February 2015.

Nonprofit Finance Fund. "Survey," 2022. https://nff.org/learn/survey#results.

Olsen Thielen. "Your NFP May Want to Consider Licensing Your Name and Brand." Olsen Thielen CPAs & Advisors, October 13, 2020. https://www.otcpas.com/your-nfp-may-want-to-consider-licensing-your-name-and-brand/.

Osili, PhD, Una, Chelsea Clark, PhD, Jon Bergdoll, and Andrea Pactor. "What Americans Think about Philanthropy and Nonprofits." *IUPUI ScholarWorks*, April 2023. chrome-extension://efaidnbmnnnibpcajpcglclefindmkaj/https://scholarworks.iupui.edu/server/api/core/bitstreams/b5904a8a-5081-42cd-bd44-56740b98fb67/content.

Palotta, Dan. "The Way We Think about Charity Is Dead Wrong." TEDTalk. March 2013. https://www.ted.com/talks/dan_pallotta_the_way_we_think_about_charity_is_dead_wrong?language=en.

Philanthropy Together. "About» Philanthropy Together," June 29, 2023. https://philanthropytogether.org/about/.

Propel Nonprofits. "Operating Reserves with Nonprofit Policy Examples," 2024. https://propelnonprofits.org/resources/nonprofit-operating-reserves-policy-examples/.

Pitt, Andrew, Amy Thompson, and Karen Kardos. "Philanthropy and the Global Economy." Citi Group. Citi GPS: Global Perspectives and Solutions, November 2021. https://www.citigroup.com/global/insights/citigps/philanthropy.

Red Wing, Donna. "The Gay and Lesbian Donor." *AFP Advancing Philanthropy*, October 1, 2018.

Saunders, Casey. "Fabulous and Philanthropic." *AFP Advancing Philanthropy*, June 1, 2021.

Schiller, Amy. *The Price of Humanity*. Melville House, 2023.

Sharna Goldseker, and Michael Patrick Moody. *Generation Impact: How Next Gen Donors Are Revolutionizing Giving*. Hoboken: Wiley, 2017.

Smith, Talmon Joseph, and Karl Russell. "The Greatest Wealth Transfer in History Is Here, with Familiar (Rich) Winners." *The New York Times*, May 14, 2023, sec. Business. https://www.nytimes.com/2023/05/14/business/economy/wealth-generations.html.

Uniform Laws Commission. "Prudent Management of Institutional Funds Act - Uniform Law Commission." www.uniformlaws.org, 2006. https://www.uniformlaws.org/committees/community-home?CommunityKey=043b9067-bc2c-46b7-8436-07c9054064a3.

Upstart Co-Lab, Association of Art Museum Directors, and Black Trustee Alliance for Art Museums. "Cultural Capital: The State of Art Museums and Their Investing," June 2022. https://upstartco-lab.org/cultural-capital-the-state-of-museums-and-their-investing/.

Urban Institute. "National Center for Charitable Statistics Data | Urban Institute." www.urban.org. Accessed March 6, 2024. https://www.urban.org/tags/national-center-charitable-statistics-data.

Uri Gneezy, and John List. *Why Axis: Hidden Motives and the Undiscovered Economics of Everyday Life*. New York: Public Affairs, 2016.

US SIF Foundation. "2022: Reflections on Sustainable Investing," December 2022. https://www.ussif.org/.

Women's Giving Institute. "Women Give 2021: How Households Make Giving Decisions." Lilly Family School of Philanthropy, 2021. chrome-extension://efaidnbmnnnibpcajpcglclefindmkaj/https://scholarworks.iupui.edu/server/api/core/bitstreams/717cd2b8-45f9-4133-a3be-f41a2c713329/content.

Wright, Conrad Edwick. "John Harvard." *Harvard Magazine*, January 1, 2000. https://www.harvardmagazine.com/2000/01/john-harvard-html.

www.guidestar.org. Candid. Accessed October 7, 2023. https://www.guidestar.org/profile/61-0445834.

The Donor Bill of Rights

The Donor Bill of Rights was created by the Association of Fundraising Professionals (AFP), the Association for Healthcare Philanthropy (AHP), the Council for Advancement and Support of Education (CASE), and the Giving Institute: Leading Consultants to Non-Profits. It has been endorsed by numerous organizations. Adherence to these tenets is an important step that any organization can take to ensure that efforts to build reserves and endowment are ethical and effective.

The Donor Bill of Rights

Philanthropy is based on voluntary action for the common good. It is a tradition of giving and sharing that is primary to the quality of life. To assure that philanthropy merits the respect and trust of the general public, and that donors and prospective donors can have full confidence in the not-for-profit organizations and causes they are asked to support, we declare that all donors have these rights:

I. To be informed of the organization's mission, of the way the organization intends to use donated resources, and of its capacity to use donations effectively for their intended purposes.

II. To be informed of the identity of those serving on the organization's governing board, and to expect the board to exercise prudent judgment in its stewardship responsibilities.

III. To have access to the organization's most recent financial statements.

IV. To be assured their gifts will be used for the purposes for which they were given.

V. To receive appropriate acknowledgement and recognition.

VI. To be assured that information about their donation is handled with respect and with confidentiality to the extent provided by law.

VII. To expect that all relationships with individuals representing organizations of interest to the donor will be professional in nature.

VIII. To be informed whether those seeking donations are volunteers, employees of the organization or hired solicitors.

IX. To have the opportunity for their names to be deleted from mailing lists that an organization may intend to share.

X. To feel free to ask questions when making a donation and to receive prompt, truthful and forthright answers.

Reprinted with permission from the Association of Fundraising Professionals.

Index

Note: Locators followed by f and t indicates figures and tables.